Notes from a Sealed Room

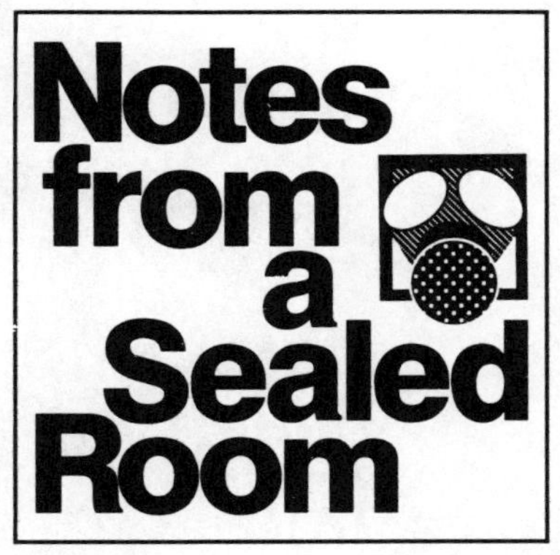

An Israeli View of the Gulf War

Robert Werman

With an Introduction by Gerald M. Phillips

Southern Illinois University Press

Carbondale and Edwardsville

Copyright © 1993 by the Board of Trustees, Southern Illinois University
All rights reserved
Printed in the United States of America
Designed by Mary Rohrer
Production supervised by Natalia Nadraga

96 95 94 93   4 3 2 1

Library of Congress Cataloging-in-Publication Data

Werman, Robert.
    Notes from a sealed room : an Israeli view of the Gulf War /
Robert Werman, with an introduction by Gerald M. Phillips.
      p. cm.
     1. Werman, Robert—Diaries. 2. Jews, American—Israel—Diaries.
3. Persian Gulf War, 1991—Personal narratives, Israeli. I. Title.
DS113.8.A4W47 1993
956.704'3—dc20   92-1319
    ISBN 0-8093-1830-X   CIP

The paper used in this publication meets the minimum requirements
of American National Standard for Information Sciences—Permanence
of Paper for Printed Library Materials, ANSI Z39.48-1984. ∞

. . . Promise was that I
Should Israel from the Philistian yoke deliver;
Ask for this great deliverer now, and find him,
Eyeless in Gaza at the mill with slaves. . . .

. . . .

O dark, dark, dark, amid the blaze of noon,
Irrecoverably dark, total eclipse,
Without all hope of day!
—John Milton, *Samson Agonistes*

Written in Pencil in a Sealed Railway Car
(from the Hebrew)

Here in this shipment
I Eve
With Abel my son
If you see my elder boy
Cain son of Adam
Tell him that I
—Dan Pagis

CONTENTS

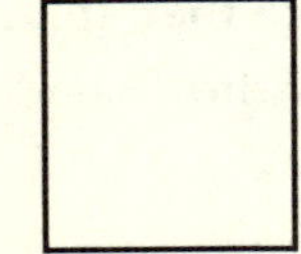

INTRODUCTION

Gerald M. Phillips

Desert Storm was an American epic and an Iraqi debacle. But there were other players: Hafez al Assad seeking respectability; the Saudi royal family seeking stability; European powers confirming themselves as physically powerful. There were the Jordanians and the PLO, picking the losing side and plucking the bitter fruit. There were the Japanese, discredited as loyal allies and losing the lucrative rebuilding contracts, and the Germans, appearing patronizingly righteous and preserving their blood and iron. There were the Kuwaitis, left with a country smoldering and in ruins. And there was Israel.

This book is by Robert Werman, an expatriate American and now an Israeli citizen who lived through the six weeks of Scud attacks, wondering, waiting for explosions, for gas, for air strikes. It is a tale of suspense, although now we know the outcome. It is by and about an interesting man living in an interesting time in an interesting place, and this alone would justify its writing.

It is about living through peril: personal peril, peril to the people you love, peril to your nation. It is about living with misunderstanding, with neighbors who hate you, with your life in jeopardy, with few friends and allies. It is about patriotism and tradition and personal loyalty. It is also about a man past his physical prime faced with the raw peril of personal destruction.

It is autobiographical, a slice of life out of time. It is a testimony to a piece of history, a rendition spoken in the voice of a witness. As such, it comes to us unmediated by the necessity to tell the big story or influence events. And more than that, it is an interpretation of that life made meaningful by the author as Everyman.

JOURNALISM OR ENTERTAINMENT

Israel is a small nation constructed by large nations, a nation built out of guilt without consideration of consequences. The nations of the world that created the State of Israel claimed they were honoring the claims of concentration camp survivors for their own state. What they really did was find a place to dump emaciated and demoralized people whom they did not want to accept on their own shores.

A friend who served as an interpreter at Auschwitz told me that he was required to ask each person released where he or she would like to go. Most chose the United States, Britain, France. A few named South American countries or South Africa. Few said Palestine, despite the fact that the Zionist movement had been active for several decades. They either had not heard of the possibility or knew they would be barred by British policy. Their answers were unacceptable. It was unthinkable for these nations to offer a home to so many Jews. It was also unthinkable to send them back to Germany and Poland. They were the broken remnants, in no condition to be pioneers. They wanted only safety and a modicum of comfort. And they were not wanted in their former homes.

But Palestine was vulnerable. The Mufti of Jerusalem had supported Hitler; furthermore, the West had held suzerainty over much of Arabia for many years. Colonialism was crumbling but it had not yet crumbled, and so a decision was made that would deplete central Europe of its population of Jews. It planted the wretched of the earth in the midst of an Arab population that, at the moment, had no official voice in the council of nations.

But even when the pain-wracked Jews of Europe wanted to come, they were prevented by the British, who did not want to anger the Arab population. And when they did come, the Arabs tried to throw them out.

The rest of the history? There was a war and there was a war and there was another war. There was an invasion of Egypt, there was the demolition of the Jordanian army. There was an exodus of Arabs from the land, told by their brothers to leave so they could return later in triumph. There was the legacy of refugee camps and Arab countries that would not admit their brothers as citizens, only as servants.

But the settlers built a nation, a parliamentary democracy with strong religious overtones, a complex blend of the secular and the religious made up of interacting populations. There were Oriental and African Jews living with expatriate Americans and Europeans, refugees from the concentration camps and those Arabs who elected not to leave. They were all citizens. They had a parliament. In some places they observed the Sabbath by mandate. In other places they did not. There were battles over whether Jerusalem should be an international city, who should administer the Holy Places, who should own the land occupied after the various wars were over. There were United Nations resolutions compounded by more resolutions. There were peacekeeping forces, administrators, assassinations. There was a succession of prime ministers: old scientists, Jewish mothers, former terrorists, military men. There were peace activists and racists, demonstrations and prayers.

In a sense, Israel is a nation on the American model, filled with ferment, jealous of private rights and public freedoms, yet it is paradoxical because of the influence of a state-favored religion. Because Israel has citizens of three major religions, each of which regards it as holy ground, it seems designed to experience every problem a nation could experience.

It is American in the sense of eminent domain as well. Israel has kept the land seized in its various wars. And why not? To the victor belong the spoils. Ask any Native American about this principle of geopolitics. We may shed tears for the Apache on the reservation and the displaced Palestinian in Gaza, but the United States will not return the land to the Native Americans, and Israel appears adamant about not returning the land to its former occupants. Many believe that it would be suicidal to return the land in the face of a war that has never ended with Arab nations that refuse to negotiate.

Empty claims of brotherhood have consigned a generation or two of Arabs to live in squalid camps. Meanwhile, the Jewish homeland has flourished as a bastion of democracy and a beacon of material success in the midst of a hundred million hostile neighbors seeking to destroy it. The Israelis were willing to trade their blood for nationhood.

The Gulf War focused attention on Israel; the issues at stake gained world attention. At the table were Israel, with its powerful, high-tech army and democratic traditions, and the Arab states, hostile to Israel and cold to the needs of their displaced brothers. And the media hyped the issues, as the reporters sought to make their reputations by exploiting the plight of the participants on both sides.

The media played a great game, producing docudramas, not real news. It was the Super Bowl and Miss Universe, *panem et circensis*. And they provided few facts. Retired generals predicted the future, pundits and politicians babbled incessantly. Throughout the Gulf War one could spend twenty-four hours a day hearing the same drone and little news.

We heard no testimony from Iraqis, save what the captive reporters in Baghdad were permitted to transmit to us. The dead Iraqis could not talk, and the live ones did not have access to means of communication. The Werman diary appeared without censorship on an international network. In a sense, it is a tribute to the freedom accorded to citizens of democratic states: there are no truly personal computers in Iraq.

To us in America, the war meant vindication and extinction of the bad memories from Vietnam. Grenada and Panama were trivial encounters, rehearsals for how to handle the press rather than how to fight a war. And the press was tame this time, the briefers relatively open. Who can't afford to be open when the victories are so overwhelming?

As usual, we dehumanized the enemy. Dead men tell no tales. True, one network displayed a dead Iraqi soldier's diary containing poetry for his wife. Iraqi soldiers writing poetry? Unimaginable! We had learned in Vietnam how to dehumanize the enemy, and we would not tolerate seeing human enemies; we preferred watching the faces of our professional volunteer army with its technological know-how and can-do spirit. Young Americans joined the army for the steady pay and the reserves for extra money with which to make house payments. They never bargained to fight, but when they had to, they did, like professionals. Colin Powell and Stormin' Norman became household heroes, living icons, and future political contenders. Our young men and women were the best and the brightest, or a reasonable facsimile thereof. Their training in radar and air traffic control, cooking and shipping, and new technologies of death and destruction made them into personnel insurance for a technological American future. Fortunately, few of them had to die.

There will be movies of the week and comic series coming out of this war. It will be memorialized like World War II and Korea. It will produce comedy and epic but little tragedy, unlike Vietnam, which has yet to spin off a successful series.

THE WAR HITS HOME

But there were people for whom this war was serious business—not a grand super bowl but a matter of survival. This book is by and about one of those people. The author of this book, Robert Werman, is a scientist and a poet, a family man, scholar, and patriot. His existence has been on the line since a massive heart attack fourteen years ago. His life has been under constant challenge ever since his decision in 1967 to leave a comfortable life in America to take up citizenship in a state at war. He has been more than an ordinary citizen in an extraordinary nation. He and his country have faced and continue to face extinction. Thus, his story strikes to the heart of the human condition.

Why would anyone leave America with the world clamoring for the Golden Door to open? Why would anyone open it and then go the other way? It is hard to reconcile patriotism with the bittersweet taste of living as a stranger in the land of milk and honey. Strangers in America differ from generation to generation, but the Jew is always the stranger.

Let's use the dirty word *Jew* now. Robert Werman is a Jew, and according to the Nuremberg Laws, so am I. To the anti-Semites, a Jew is a Jew regardless of belief. The anti-Semites never let you forget. Like it or not, I get a yellow armband.

It is, of course, irrational. I have explored many faiths and ways of thinking. I tried a synagogue or two and focused my research on ancient Jewish law and lore. I tried to believe, tried to belong to something, but a mother completely taken with Anglo-Saxonism had raised me on the mean streets of northside Cleveland as a British country squire, and the cynicism and capacity to doubt acquired on those streets disqualified me from membership in any religious denomination, sect, or cult. For a theology, I adopted the Constitution of the United States, jot for jot, tittle for tittle, the most noble document ever conceived by the human mind: more noble than the Bible, the Koran, and the Bahgavad Gita combined, said I. I had my theology although a legion of persecutors wanted to make me a member of a race that was also a religion. It's hard when blacks see you as white and whites see you as off-color. But Jews soon learn that that is the way it is, like it or not.

Bob Werman faced the same difficulties and chose to leave and take his stand with his "own kind." If you have the name, you might as well have the game. I chose to compete in America, to forget my own origins, such as they were, and ignore the calumnies of the opposition. And so the Orthodox American Jew turned Israeli and met the descendant of a polyglot collection of unbelievers. It was quite an encounter. It generated a fine book . . . among other things.

TWO PEOPLE OF THE BOOK

I saw the first entry in Bob Werman's diary on an electronic bulletin board (more of this later) and felt a resonance I did not understand. I was attracted to the text. I found it strangely compelling. I am, as a conservative old buffalo, opposed to postmodern criticism, but here I sit, declaring that the text spoke to me in a voice different from the way it spoke to others. I found, in fact, that the text was written just for me.

In my initial contacts with the author (I wrote originally to tell him to copyright his work), I found that I could strike up something akin to a friendship. Odd. You do not make friends with electronic pen pals. Is it possible to be friends with a person whose whole identity is embodied in green letters on a black screen?

But as we exchanged notes, quips, jokes, and disclosures, we found a bond—disease! His heart attack and my triple vessel disease enabled us to exchange symptoms, trade drug recommendations, gripe about doctors. Cardi-yakking. Playing organ recitals. And lo and behold, he was a doctor. A genuine doctor, not a Ph.D. He could give me advice. Free! And from overseas, even.

There was more. There was a sense of ethnic compatibility that I do not normally feel. He talked to me as if he knew me, and when he disagreed, he disagreed with what I said, not with who I was.

We found ourselves trusting each other. We all know that there are people we see daily whom we do not trust, with whom we cannot build trust. What were the vibrations? As it unfolded, we discovered that we were kindred spirits: insomniacs; compulsive workers; cardiac cases; husbands and fathers; academics; of a common age and weight and bearing an uncanny physical resemblance; and most of all, sharers of the bond forged by membership in the same outgroup.

Even more remarkable, this strange relationship was carried on through high technology. The chips and circuits heretofore indicted for their lack of feeling were now being used to share feelings. Here we were, strangers, now connected by a miracle form of communication. More intimate than "snail mail" and much cheaper than phone, the asynchronicity of computer network communication allows people to interact at their own pace and on their own time. The idea of a bond forming through such a medium represents a new kind of socialization. So here we sit in our respective places. We have never seen each other but we are friends, now contractually bound on this literary project and others yet to emerge. To date we have exchanged more than two thousand pages of jokes, reminiscences, symptoms, family news. We may never meet. Our health may preclude that, yet our worlds have opened materially through this new form of contact.

SOCIAL AND POLITICAL ISSUES

Let us face the issue squarely. Sociologically speaking, the Jew is still a member of a proscribed outgroup. True, many Jews have assimilated, but only when Bernstein becomes Burns and Goldberg becomes Gilbert do they have a chance at making it. There is nothing necessarily wrong with this. Mastrodeangelos becomes Masters and Papadegeorgopolis becomes George. People ought to have the right to cast their past aside and assume new ways. But the plight of the Jew is somewhat different, for many will not permit them to make the change. In the eyes of Nuremberg Law sympathizers (and they are more numerous than we care to believe), a Jew is a Jew forever.

In 1956 I sought my first job. I was not identified in any fashion religiously and my name is Phillips, a good, old-fashioned, Anglo name. People had come to me in the past, members of the DAR, to ask if we were related. I invariably chuckled and replied, "That depends. What was your name before it was Phillips?"

But I was not prepared for the rejection. When I told the interviewer at one eastern university where I lived, he, apparently knowing the neighborhood, told me that I would not be comfortable at his institution because there were not enough of my people around. I did not know which of "my people" they had in mind. Fat folks? Bald-headed folks?

Another private liberal arts college told me I could "represent my people" for $2,000 a year. I still did not understand. It became clear when I interviewed at North Dakota. "Look," said the department head, "I can pay you only $4,000 a year, but I see you know Hebrew and my friend, the rabbi, is looking for a Hebrew teacher and he can pay you $1,200 for part-time. How about taking two jobs?" You have to eat and you have to practice your profession. I took it.

I also hated both jobs. I did not want to be Jewish because I did not believe. I did not want to be a debate coach on the prairie because I thought it was a waste of time. But as I said, you have to eat and you have to practice your profession.

There were certainly enough people who did not want me in the melting pot, like the folks who introduced me to the Presbyterian Jew in their congregation. I played the role to the hilt. I learned to be a member of a persecuted minority group. It was like the novel (the name of which I have long forgotten) about the assistant professor at Harvard who feared denial of tenure and played on guilt by claiming to be a Communist. I learned how to gain privilege by making people feel guilty. It was easy in North Dakota and eastern Washington because I had the territory pretty much to myself and they could handle one freak. It did not have to become a major political issue as it is today with African Americans.

At no point did universities adopt affirmative action policies in order to get more Jews. They were already gagging on the ones they had. But oddly, people persisted in smothering me with kindness, too. One night my wife and I were invited to the home of a distinguished professor of education. The other guest was an African-American sociologist. The two of us got along like mongoose and cobra, but we colluded that night to spill, to tuck our napkins under our chins, to belch and be crude, all while being indulged because, of course, as minorities we did not know any better.

I have few illusions about the melting pot. I did not melt. I won grudging acceptance by playing the academic game hard and well; in the process I crippled my health. I gained the friendship of a few, grudging acceptance of many, but never full admission to the comradeship of the academy. There were enough people who did not care about my ancestry so I could relate to them as humans. I did not have to deny or even discuss my origins with them, and they accepted my atheistic humanism with either agreement or a minimal grain of salt. I found my place with kindred spirits of all kinds, all fleeing from their ancestry: a British humanist, an Irish agnostic, a few stray nonobservant Protestants, and a backsliding Catholic or two. There were a pair of crazed computer geniuses, the white manager of a black gospel group, an entrepreneur, a gay doctor, a variety of people who lived on the margins. They were all iconoclasts, none members of a country club or a service club or lodge or secret order. A few belonged to churches, but it was their business. It was a group without unity but with strong connections. And we all fitted in.

A joke: once Sam came home and found his wife naked in bed. He opened the closet and found standing there his friend Abe, also naked. "What are you doing here?" Sam demanded. "Everybody has to be someplace," Abe replied. And there is the fundamental sociological principle: everyone has to be someplace.

And there is a reason for going to Israel: to find a someplace. As Bob Werman sent his diary entries to me, I understood more and more that his solution was the counterpart to mine. He wanted to fit where he belonged; I wanted to belong where I fit. I repressed my ancestors (or at least some of them); he honored his. It may be that he is an outgrouper in his own group, but at least it is his own group. I am a member of a group of outgroupers, people who come together out of a sense of not belonging elsewhere.

Political correctness, you see, never reached the Jews. To other outgroups, Jews are the ultimate ingroup. To the real ingroup, Jews are clearly an outgroup (albeit hard to find in an era of assimilation, although they can be easily located if one looks). Jews never had affirmative action or even equal employment opportunity to work for them. Those who made it had to get up earlier, work later, and do it better, and even then it was a grudging tolerance that was granted, quite patronizingly, by the majority. But that was during the 1940s and 1950s. And it was true of African Americans as well. And eventually the sons and daughters of the immigrants intermarried and cast off their ethnic ways and melted into the American society.

The 1940s and 1950s were a time when ethnicity was important. Back in an earlier day, when my Hungarian grandparents came to Ellis Island, the immigrants were fair game. Vaudevillians performed monologues about Abie and Luigi and Pat and Mike. Supposedly comic "blacks" shared the stage with caricatured Jews and Italians and Irish and Hispanics and Poles. Scottish people of impeccable credentials were characterized as tight, Irish as drunk, Jews as avaricious, blacks as oversexed, and so on. Sir Harry Lauder and Willie Howard, Smith and Dale, the Two Black Crows—they made their living selling the conventional wisdom in the form of jokes or shtick.

The real world was not quite as funny. The immigrants peddled the goods, built the railroads, and poured the steel. Their children were schoolteachers, merchants, cops. The third generation down the line had the option to change their names and grow blond hair to facilitate the melting—except, of course, for African Americans, who were fully disqualified, the few Jews who preferred to wear skullcaps, and an occasional ethnic nationalist who grieved for a lost homeland and took appropriate political action. They remained the "unmeltables." And, of course, the unmeltables did not work in banks or brokerage offices; nor did they enter engineering school. The quotas on Jews in medical school were as tight as they had been in Freud's Vienna.

It is odd, though, how now in America members of "ethnic" groups blossom at odd times during the year and hold ethnic parades or food festivals. Now it is considered honorable to have once been something—except, of course, for African Americans, who have to be what they are, and for Jews, who somehow remain what they must be despite what they do.

To be (melted) or not to be (melted)?

An acquaintance of mine married a Mormon girl and converted and is now known as "the Mormon Jew." During my exile in the American Siberia (North Dakota) I met a Presbyterian Jew and a Methodist Jew. They were triumphs for their churches, although a Jesuit acquaintance once told me the profit margin was too low on Jews: they were not desirable converts because they were too hard to get.

Yes, you can melt, but you retain your intrinsic qualities, melted or not, if anyone finds out about them. And some members of the ingroup look. You Jews can run, but you can't hide.

I have a friend who looks every inch the Anglo-Saxon but who bears the papier-mâché cross of a Jewish-sounding surname. In the late forties he got a tenure-track job at a major university. Three decades later and long after he left, a friend of his, also with a Jewish surname, discovered at the university a "Jew file," a fat document in which the issue of hiring the first Jew on tenure track was discussed, in writing, by all and sundry. They cheapen the neighborhood! But that was in the 1940s and 1950s. Could it still be true today? So here I sit, doing my own mini-autobiography, revealing bitternesses long concealed, even from myself, but now awakened by Bob Werman's diary.

So maybe I gave the answer as to why a successful professor would leave the Golden Land. Bob Werman gives his answer in the pages to come.

THE URGENCY TO TELL A STORY

The author of this essay (AE) was once a boy living in Hunkietown (East 105th in Cleveland). He was a deprived youth. Had his father lived today, he would have been "underemployed." Had his mother lived today, her housewife status would have rendered her "unfulfilled." Once upon a time, his mother, in a fit of motherly zeal, went to the local charity authorities and got her son a "scholarship" to summer camp. It was an intriguing kind of summer camp. The paying customers included a lad who later became a major mobster, another who became a great surgeon, another a championship boxer, another a decorated war veteran, and others who became mercantile nonentities. The AE was bewildered by this camp, for the first thing the counselors did was arm the campers with wooden guns and put them on patrol looking for Arab infiltrators on the shores of Lake Erie. The AE understood none of this. He spent his time avoiding religious services, yearning for bacon sandwiches, and digging excessively large latrine pits to cover with leaves and lure the unwary among the campers to walk over to claim a proffered candy bar. The AE also had propitious asthma attacks, mostly when religious services were conducted, and eventually was sent home as "unsocializable." So it went with those whose Jewish connections were tenuous. Even their own didn't want them.

You see, we all want to tell stories. I could go on and write a book without Bob Werman's narrative. We all have stories to tell, but few of us have important stories. I once said I wanted on my headstone the legend "Here lies a man who never was where history was made." Still, I want to tell my story if anyone will listen.

There is a compulsion to tell a story. We all have it, and all our stories are worth telling. They mean something to someone, and they all mean more than an aggregate of demographic statistics, 40 percent this and 50 percent that and the rest undecided. Woe unto the human who has no story to tell. Sorrow for those who live lives where they themselves find nothing to recount.

Studs Terkel may be the living patron saint of storytellers. He told the story of the Depression and the contemporary economy and the great war (World War II) in the voices of ordinary people, urgent to tell their story. Storytelling gives meaning to events and voice to the powerless. We can confess in our stories; we can write novels à la J. T. Farrell or Bernard Malamud or William Faulkner. We can talk of our roots and our yearnings, our hopes and our fears, our good fortune (such as it is) and our catastrophes (which come more often than we like).

"You win some and you lose some, Charlie Brown," said Lucy. "That would be nice," replied Charlie Brown. A bit of Americana by Charles Schulz, the patron saint of the primacy of the American way. We each have our aphorisms, our sayings that sum up our way of life, and they are shards of the way of life around us. We can say that in the 1940s ethnic groups had a hard time integrating into the social stream, but that would mean little. The story of the summer camp, that means a lot both to me, the teller, and to the reader, who might find dimension and meaning and empathy and who might be led to find something in his life on which to ruminate. It is easy to learn demographics for the purpose of taking multiple-choice tests. The demographics are a framework or a skeleton or better yet a shapeless plastic sack, a supermarket receptacle, into which the stories are poured as numbers. The shape of the sack no more defines its content than the poke does. Oh, occasionally a stalk of celery will stick out, and a register slip saying how many stalks of celery and how much they cost will be presented—but the meaning lies in how that stalk of celery got there. The *bracero* who picked it, the warehouser who packed it, the railroader who brought it to market, the clerk who put it on display and sprinkled it with water regularly—all of these people have stories embedded in that celery, just as all humans are composites of the stories told by their grandparents, their countrymen, their neighbors.

Bob Werman has a story to tell. It is an important story of important events, and he is an important man, not because of who he is or what he did, but because of his story and his ability to tell it. There's the rub. Though we all have our stories, few of us tell them well. We must honor good storytellers when we find them, for through them we find meaning in our own stories.

We have always learned from autobiography. We learned of the plague, of life in London, of imperialist Russia, of the French revolution, of the early days in America, of the slums and the ghettos, from autobiography.

These days of deconstruction and postmodern criticism have one sensible bit of fallout: the elevation of autobiography to an important place in research. The typical contemporary comedy club performer does autobiography: problems with mom, the clothes worn by dad, the people in the neighborhood, personal sex problems, disputes, job worries. No more do we have the contrived joke. It is the monologue, an artistic and pungent autobiography at which we laugh and which gives our lives meaning.

Ahhh, the mystic work . . . the allotrion, the meritorious distractions, of the lay preachers who seek an academic life, the justification of leisure and the joys of nurturing the unwashed and semiwashed. Counting beans, mixing chemicals, performing surgery on mice, poring over yellowed papers—all of these are research, but they are mostly objective, done in a detached way by nonpartisans. It is in the story that even we objective and detached academics find ourselves and our audiences. Our footnotes are not alive; they are ornaments on someone else's fabric. Our recollections and interpretations, our experiences, triumphs and tragedies, these are the things that inspire the next generation, and when we can build them into our work, then we become famous, if only for a time and if only to a few. The best that any of us can hope for is an encyclopedia entry: "In 1991 Phillips said . . . but was later proved wrong." The meaning in Phillips's life, however, lies in how he came to say what he said, and how the person who proved him wrong argued it.

The art of the diarist makes events immediate and humanizes them. It reveals the nuances and hidden subtleties in events so horrible and gross as to be unthinkable. Through diaries we can handle what we cannot otherwise confront. We can manage it because we are with someone who was there, who lived through it, who learned from it, and who takes the time and trouble to teach the rest of us. The diarist makes it clear that we are all potential citizens of Hiroshima: what one person has lived, we can all live.

A CONTEMPORARY RHETORIC

Autobiography makes it possible for a person to speak out. There is a kind of arrogance to it, the assumption that your life is more important than that of other people, important enough to warrant killing the trees on which to print the words. It is not only a way to tell a story but a way to state a case. Autobiography is filled with examples and enthymemes, personal arguments now validated by being part of the unfolding narrative. People who write autobiography do not suffer from lack of self-esteem.

The diary or journal is even more important because it is contemporary and personal and thus helps the reader understand without ambiguity. No one worries about being objective when writing a diary. Diarists say what is on their mind, and they assume the reader is sophisticated enough to understand the bias and personal prejudice that shapes the argument. Diaries play the role of denying the austere and neutral statistics (with which one can lie through one's teeth) by declaring beliefs, often passionately. The flaws are there; the errors are there, just as in every human there are flaws and errors.

Thus, the diary is a personal rhetoric, a sophistic exemplar, which can be used to facilitate understanding, to focus commitment, and to forge rebuttal. People who do not read diaries are denied the opportunity to examine their own lives in particularly cogent ways.

This diary is especially cogent because of its afterthought. Originally written in passion, the author treads the ground again, lives the drama again, and comments on it, sometimes bitterly, sometimes sagely, adding details to give dimension to the raw emotion that characterized the first effort. The comments appear at appropriate places in the text, the diary of writing a diary and fulfilling the wish that "I should have said more about that."

There is one more point that must be made. This book would never have happened had there not been a computer network. Through E-mail the human voice in amplified. A person can become an author, an editor. There is a marvelous and versatile interconnection between humans enabling them to communicate in ways heretofore denied.

Frankly, I do not understand the technology. I know Compuserv, one of the private networks for which you pay, and I know BITNET, which is provided for me by my university and for which I do not pay. I use BITNET to teach my classes, to help my students have quick and easy contact with me. I use it to exchange edited manuscripts, comments on term papers. Most of all, I use it to receive and answer students' questions. I am connected with dear friends and collaborators in several states and many countries.

Through BITNET I receive several newsletters. CRTNET, a network for scholars in rhetoric and communication, is edited by a colleague. From a humble beginning of three or four aficionados, the network now runs into the thousands because of his capable editing. The cost is absorbed by the participating institutions, and the individual users are able to work from their own terminals or from locations in campuses and laboratories around the world.

Asynchronicity is the watchword. Participants can write when they want to, read what they want to, keep what they want to, discard what they want to, and print what they want to. All they need is some inexpensive software and mastery of a few simple commands. It is a new medium, a new message, and Bob Werman's diary of the Gulf War represents a brilliant and provocative beginning for it.

BACKGROUND

Although it had simmered for years, the conflict in the Persian Gulf (or the Arabian Gulf, as it is sometimes called) finally came to the world's notice on 2 August 1990, when Iraq invaded Kuwait. Saddam Hussein, the Iraqi dictator, claimed variously that the invasion was a just response to Kuwaiti provocations and that the annexation merely corrected the arbitrary borders that Western imperial powers had forced on the area. Most nations, though, saw the invasion as a simple act of plunder as Iraq attempted to refill the treasuries depleted by its eight-year-long war with Iran.

Saudi Arabia, even more oil rich and poorly defended, feared that it might be the next fruit plucked by Saddam Hussein, and thus its rulers invited the United States to join them in resisting the Iraqi aggression and forcing Iraq to return Kuwait to its former rulers. An odd assortment of nations—most prominently Syria, Egypt, Morocco, France, and Great Britain—also joined the coalition, which received financial backing from yet other nations. After months of UN resolutions, negotiations, threats, and bluster, the coalition forces—following a flat refusal by Iraq to withdraw from Kuwait by the deadline offered—began an air war against Iraq on 16 January 1991; this was the beginning of Desert Storm, the allied assault.

Saddam Hussein's response to the onset of the war was to activate his antiaircraft defenses and make use of his Scuds, mobile, intermediate-range missiles. At the beginning of the war, the destructive power of the Scuds was not clear; only later would we discover that the threat provided by these Russian-developed missiles—now being manufactured in Iraq—was limited. The journalists originally told us that the Scuds were dangerous, nor did the military experts of the West tell us otherwise at the onset. The possibility of the Iraqis using chemical, bacteriological, or nuclear warheads on these missiles was considered great. Later, we discovered that fully effective biological war techniques and almost complete nuclear warfare technology were available in Iraq. Saddam Hussein had already used poison gas against Iranian troops and against civilians in his own country, wiping out an entire Kurdish village of five thousand people with gas dropped from airplanes. Even American military analysts believed that the Iraqis had the capacity to mount chemical warheads on their Scuds, making them even more potent weapons of terror. In this already poisonous atmosphere, all Israeli citizens were provided with gas masks.

The populations of the targeted areas, particularly Israel, were truly frightened. The media made much of Saddam's might, his experienced and heavily armed army, his weaponry. They had not reason then to believe that the threat was nominal or in terror alone. And for all that, the destruction, when it came—to property mostly, rather than to lives—was frightening to behold.

Why Israel, not a member of the allies attacking Iraq, was targeted by Saddam Hussein as early as the second day of the war is clear only in terms of the complex politics of the Middle East. The Scud attacks on Israel lacked military value; they were instead exercises in diplomacy by terror, an attempt to undermine Arab support for the coalition by drawing the hated Israelis into the conflict. Israel, against all its instincts and contradicting its history, did not respond to the Iraqi attacks. The United States had demanded—against all international precedent—that Israel remain passive in the face of the Scud attacks so as not to threaten the fragile allied coalition, which included three Arab states. It was clear that they would not tolerate an Israeli attack on another Arab state, even if that state were an enemy, even if Israel were acting in self-defense. And Israel acceded to the demand.

Saddam Hussein's impotence in the face of the air strikes may have been another reason to indulge in what was seen by many as a gratuitous and cruel exercise in futility: his ground troops had been driven into entrenched and passive defensive positions, and his air force had fled from the better-trained, better-equipped allied air forces.

Israel was the target for half of the Scuds fired. The first Scud fell on Israel on Thursday, 17 January 1991; the second fell at the start of the Sabbath, 18 January. On 19 January, the first entry in Werman's diary appeared on CRTNET, where I saw it, and entries continued to appear until 22 February, when Werman was hospitalized for a heart condition. All of the diary entries are reproduced here, along with Dr. Werman's later comments on them and a prologue and epilogue.

It is, in all, a remarkable record of a human life carried on in the midst of an inhumane war.

Notes from a Sealed Room

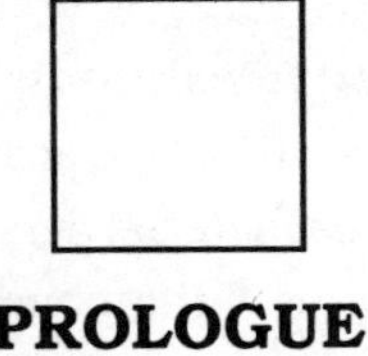

PROLOGUE

My diary of the Gulf War was born in the sealed, poison-gas-proof room in my home where I huddled with my family during the Scud attacks on Israel. We had already weathered two attacks—on 17 and 18 January—in that room: wondering where the missiles would fall, wondering whether the poison gas was even then spreading through the streets. As I sat in the sealed room, a strange feeling overcame me—an intellectual, rather than an emotional, claustrophobia. The sealed room was both a physical and a psychological cage. I felt the need to scream, to tell others what was happening to me. No one could see me; I was cut off from the world. The doors were locked, the windows sealed, the edges taped. We were alone; I was alone.

Those were the emotions that flooded my tired spirit. I wanted to tell others, my friends, what was happening to me, within me. Thus, I began recording the events and my perceptions and posting those reports on the BITNET computer network. Other network users read my reports and immediately began posting them on other computer networks. My diary spread rapidly through various electronic mail bulletin boards. In addition, my pieces were either reprinted or quoted extensively by newspapers in places as remote as Kyoto and Huntsville, Alabama—the home of the Patriot anti-missile missile—and as well known as New York City and Los

Angeles. I followed the spread of my diary entries through those ports where permission to reprint was requested, but some people wrote to tell me about reading my diary on a network or newspaper that I had no idea even existed.

Requests for permission to reprint the diary became so numerous that I had to prepare a form E-mail letter saying I had no objection to reproducing the material in noncommercial vehicles. In fact, I was soon receiving more than one hundred letters a day by E-mail. Most of these letters were complimentary, telling me that my diary filled a void left by the impersonal coverage provided by the media. Of these writers, a majority, but far from all, indicated they were Jewish. Some told me specifically that they were not Jewish but still were attracted to the material I was sending out. I prepared another form letter thanking them, which I called "Plus." Some spoke of difficulties in obtaining the diary entries and asked to be added to my mailing list, which I did. Shortly after beginning the diary, I was engaged in an active correspondence, usually of more than five letters a day, with Gerald Phillips. We found ourselves quite compatible, despite very different backgrounds and fields of interest. We exchanged ideas and together formulated the book that would eventually be published—this book.

Far fewer letters were critical; most of these were argumentative and expected me to engage in a debate with them. I was too busy to oblige. For these I prepared a third form answer, which I called "Minus." A small percentage of the letters were informative, offering information and material that was new to me, some of which I used in subsequent diary entries. Other objections appeared publicly on the nets that published my diaries.

The principal objection to my diaries came from those who were deeply committed to the peace movement. These objectors argued that the war was a war of imperialism, that it was a war for oil, that the government of Kuwait was not worth defending. Some claimed that the U.S. military forces had become an international mercenary army for hire. Others were convinced that the war was a diversionary measure, an attempt to hide the real problems of the United States, mostly domestic and most pressing in the financial sphere. Some agreed with Saddam and his allies that the motivation for the war was imperialistic in nature, a desire to rule the Arab world.

Many American readers were impelled by a deep-seated distrust of the president and the U.S. government, inspired by revisionist historians who find even Truman guilty of a hidden agenda in backing the Korean War, not to speak of Johnson's immorality in Vietnam and Nixon's lying and devious behavior in the Watergate affair. These readers were joined by others who were equally convinced of the nefarious motives of the executive branch of government but who could not specify what the "real" motives were.

Europeans told me that the United States was not to be trusted under any circumstances, that it was responsible for all the major problems in the world. They often stated that all war was bad, that the world had seen enough blood and death, that no cause was worth fighting for.

I attempted to argue that there was a difference between the bad of U.S. presidents and the evil of Saddam Hussein—that the bad could be made to toe the line, to behave well, but the evil could not. I told them that Saddam Hussein provided a threat to the world, that I was no friend of Kuwait, and that Kuwait was certainly no friend of Israel. I tried to tell them that there were times when one had to fight; I reminded them of Nietzsche's dictum that only a slave can find no cause for which he would be willing to lay down his life. I told them that the United States' role as world leader was on the line, that the world was waiting to see if the United States was willing to let naked international aggression go unpunished. I told them that letting Saddam Hussein get away with his unprovoked invasion of Kuwait and subsequent rape and annexation of that country was an invitation to him to continue and to other potential aggressors to join in. I pointed out that the nations of the coalition were not all puppets of the United States; certainly they could see through a devious plot of the U.S. government.

I do not know how convincing I was, but these letters diminished in frequency with time, perhaps in the face of the massive support that President Bush enjoyed. But the letters of criticism did not stop; they changed focus. Now the main thrust of the critical letters was an attack on my politics, on the very use of political thinking in my reports, attacks on the policy of the nets that would publish such material. Most of these letters were or at least pretended to be general, related to the issue of whether or not my sort of material should be included in the nets. Some people felt the topic remote from the main interest of the net. One of the nets decided to make my diary available only to those who specifically requested it. But the overwhelming positive responses sent to the nets—and in the letters sent directly to me—supporting the daily publication of my journal forced the editor of that net to recant and send my daily entry to all members. Other nets rejected the option of removing my daily outpourings.

Another Israeli started sending out her own diary, stating that she was led to this action by her desire to show another side of the Israeli response to the bombings. Other diaries, not apparently related to my work, were also sent out from Israel and appeared on the nets.

Later the letters took on a tone of pro-Palestinian and often vehemently anti-Israeli protests against my views. Someone wrote asking why, even if I hate the Arabs so completely, do I not show some verbal restraint? I answered that I do not hate the Arabs. Did my correspondent believe me?

At all stages and in all forums the positive letters and responses far outnumbered the negative ones. The positive ones were mostly from Jews, by a small majority. Many wrote confessional letters, telling about their confusion in the face of the events of the war. Some told of their hesitant withdrawal from the peace movement, where they had, until recently, found their emotional home.

One of the motives that inspired my continuing to write the diary and to disseminate it was my unhappiness with the view of Israel at war, even though a noncombatant, presented by the media. My hand was strengthened by the large number of letter writers who told me that they, too, were unhappy with the television, radio, and newspaper coverage of the war and that the diary filled a void for them, providing part of the picture that was completely absent from the media. I began to feel that it was me against the media, and particularly television, for—of the foreign press—it was American, British, and French television that I was most exposed to.

Americans in particular seemed to me to be in a dilemma. Many have strong convictions that a free press is an absolute necessity— and for most of them, a free press is one that is completely uninhib- ited, not controlled from within and certainly not from without. At the same time, they were intensely unhappy with the results. Peter Arnett and CNN were only the most obvious examples of lack of responsibility. Other networks, newspapers, and even magazines (*Newsweek*, for example) were likewise irresponsible.

What is our relationship to the media? We depend on journalists for information about those many events, both at home and abroad, that concern us and of which we have so little direct knowledge. When a television anchor (pick your favorite) told us that Iraq's army was formidable, we believed him; when this estimate was confirmed by the testimony of a military expert, retired General X, we believed in Iraq's might even more. We became concerned and frightened: our soldiers' lives were at stake. The few commentators who disagreed, including two former Israeli Army chiefs of staff (on different sides of the political spectrum), were not invited before the television cameras again.

What happened when Iraq's army later turned out to be only a paper tiger? Did the media apologize? Did the expert resign? Not at all. They just carried on, business as usual, and continued to speculate without foundation. Errors of fact did not faze them, nor did their unverified suppositions. This was show business, and the anchor and "expert" went on as if they had no responsibility for what they said. But it counts to us. To the extent that the media ignore our needs, they do not represent us; to the extent that they are willing to engage in activities that they must know deliberately thwart the efforts of the government to save lives—as they did in publishing revealing camera shots, in entering sealed areas, in playing the enemy's game by uncritically reporting whatever they fed to them—they became dangerous and reprehensible.

Why, at the beginning of the war, were the media so unwilling to voice the opinions of those who felt there was no alternative to war? Even Quakers, so active in peace movements, were not uniform in their responses; the press was reluctant to interview those prowar voices, like the Quaker who told me, "War is a horror, but if someone attacked my wife, I fear I would kill him in the most horrible way possible—and maybe my enemies should know that."

The media had an agenda during the war, an agenda revealed by their selection of material, particularly visual material. The agenda was to appeal to the senses and not to the brain, to emotion and not to reason. The object was to attract and hold the audience at all costs. To this end, missiles became aesthetic objects and nothing more: "Let's go up on the roof and photograph the brilliant lights as missiles fly through the night sky." Professional actors who appeared over and over again spoke out in rage—and in good English, too—against the allied bombings that were allegedly hitting only civilian targets. The statements of the Iraqis, known for their cynicism regarding truth, were presented as not less true than those of the allies. When committed pacifists like Ramsey Clark traveled to Baghdad, where they reported that only civilian sites were attacked, no one bothered to voice a contradictory opinion.

The media acted to manipulate the audience into a state of addiction. They wanted an audience for their television coverage, and they wanted an audience that would buy every edition of the newspapers. They would do anything to get that audience. And often did just that: give everything and anything, even when responsibility demanded that they desist.

The networks and the newspapers battled for the listening and reading audiences; they were all showing much the same thing. At times they appeared to work on the principle that it might be dangerous to differ dramatically from their competitors; what was good for the competitor was clearly good for them, too. The newspapers and networks seemed to operate on the single guiding—and totally mercenary—principle that the larger the audience, the larger the advertising revenues. They never showed that they knew or cared that their country was involved in war; they never demonstrated more than passing interest in the fact that they were the press of a country and operating in the framework of its national interests. They were more international in that sense than even the United Nations, for that body had at least condemned Saddam Hussein and Iraq's aggressions. The reporters took their cues from their editors and vied with one another in impressive efforts to further their own careers. "Anything goes" was the operating rule; and indeed it did.

But these are my feelings, and I am prejudiced. I have my own national concerns, which may lead me to see the media through a distorting lens. But even you—did you not also feel that the news media were shallow and vacuous? Fickle and insipid? Particularly when it was apparent that they were engaged in attempts to manipulate your emotions and beliefs? Were you not disgusted that these attempts were usually feeble, ill-conceived, and transparent? When they showed any picture that captured the audience's attention? When they showed an Iraqi boy with old burn wounds and said that it was a civilian bomb shelter and not an Iraqi command center that had been bombed that very day and that this boy was one of the injured in that raid? I know a nurse in Athens, Ohio, who spotted the lie; her husband informed me of it in an E-mail letter. I spotted it, too: I was trained as a physician.

The journalists were not trying to manipulate us to any given position; they were apolitical in a situation that demanded commitment to truth. But they were interested only in presenting the pictures of words that would attract, mesmerize, titillate. When there is no end in mind, no purpose in these attempts to manipulate us, the manipulation became an end in itself and thus pornographic. The pornographer is less interested in the context than in the response. And that is how the media behaved in this case—as pornographers.

PERSONAL BACKGROUND

Diaries are, of course, deeply personal, even when they deal with events of international importance. My reports naturally contained much about me and my family, but many readers—among them Jerry Phillips—wanted to know more about me and how I came to Israel.

I was born in Brooklyn in 1929, received my B.A. and M.D. from New York University, and, after a stint as a doctor in the U.S. Navy, ended up as a research professor at Indiana University. I came to Israel in 1967 and decided to remain there.

Leaving America to emigrate to Israel—it sounds very strange to me even today. It was not something that I consciously planned. Although I was brought up in a traditional home and exposed to a good Hebrew education (which I ignored and forgot almost completely), I had never belonged to any Zionist organization, nor had I ever, before 1961, thought of moving to Israel. I had worked one year alongside an Israeli professor, Felix Bergmann, while he was on a sabbatical in the States. I promised him, not seriously, that I would take a sabbatical in Israel.

While on sabbatical in Cambridge, England, in 1960, I visited Israel with my wife, Golda—a whirlwind visit of two weeks in which I fell in love with the country. Even this visit was a matter of chance. With the Christmas holidays coming, the people at Cambridge had turned off the heat in the old, very cold laboratory where I did my research. Unable to work, I arranged a trip to Israel. We toured the country in the rain mingled with sunshine, smelled the orange groves, traveled by car through the stark desert and giant moonlike craters of the Negev into the subtropical Eilat (104° Fahrenheit in the middle of winter).

I fell in love with the country. I loved the sense of pioneering; after all, I had been brought up in the United States, where pioneer values were still extolled. Perhaps others do not take these values seriously; I do. Israel is a country that is a-building, a country where the excitement of newness and the optimism of naïveté add a rich flavor to life. For me, Israel was a throwback, a chance to relive the golden past of the United States. While the United States was entering the period of student revolution, political nihilism, hippyism, and the trauma of Vietnam, Israel was in the midst of growth and development. I was strongly attracted, fascinated. My wife, with a Zionist background, watched with pleasure and approval the growth of my new passion.

I lectured at the Hebrew University in Jerusalem, where I now teach, and then—with an appointment to a full professorship at Indiana University in my pocket—offered to stay at Hebrew University as a lecturer, an untenured rank roughly equivalent to assistant professor in the States. My offer was turned down. I am a very competitive person, and I now remember—although I promptly forgot it then—saying to myself that this rejection would cost them dearly.

I took the position at Indiana University and moved to the beautiful college town of Bloomington, where I met interesting people and took part in a rich cultural life. It is difficult for city dwellers to understand how rich cultural life in a college town can be, and how much more accessible culture is there than in cities. I taught, did research—achieved some fame, in fact. If not for my children, I could have lived there happily for the rest of my life. I had forgotten my flirtation with Israel.

Jewish life was minimal in Bloomington. The town had only a Hillel, a Jewish student's organization, and some Jewish fraternities. Our introduction to the religious life of this town was our visit to the Hillel and reading the sign on the door, "Tisha B'av [an important minor holiday occurring in the summer, a fast day in memory of the destruction of both temples in Jerusalem] will be delayed one week because of the rabbi's absence." Since Jewish holidays, and this one—known by the date of its celebration—in particular, are fixed by the calendar, we knew that we had entered a world where Jewish life was not what we had experienced or wanted.

Our three children, Michael, Aaron, and Rachel (a fourth, Ariel, would be born in Israel), were the only Jewish children in their classes. When my fifth-grader had to go on a class hike and we tried to explain that he eats only kosher meat, the obliging teacher said that she would have the cook bless the meat. The local newspaper photographed our children lighting the Hanukkah candles and ran it on the front page: Hanukkah was news there. Our contact with the Jewish fraternities was disastrous and consisted of a single night when we chaperoned a dance, bored to death and deafened by the music. We received shipments of meat, packed in dry ice, from a large city eighteen hours away by bus.

Only on the Sabbath were we able to have a *minyan*—the obligatory ten men for ritual prayer. One day a year, I was asked to organize a minyan in my house for the saying of the *Kaddish*—the memorial prayer for the dead—for the father of a rabbi in a neighboring city. This was not an easy task. On one occasion, nine of us were waiting for a tenth to show up so we could begin. A stranger entered wearing a hat, and, assuming that he was Jewish, we proceeded to say the prayers. After we had finished, the stranger introduced himself as the local Methodist minister: he had come to ask me, as the local expert on Judaism, to answer questions about a filmstrip they had received from *Life* magazine, part of a series on the different religions. I obliged, answering questions about why some of the men in the synagogue wore black skullcaps while others wore white ones. On another occasion, a Presbyterian minister attempted to engage me in a debate about a pet theory of his that there was or was not, I do not remember which now, anything Jewish in Paul's writings.

Remember, we loved living in Bloomington. The town was beautiful, and we had good friends. If I was frustrated with my work, and that happens frequently enough, I could go to a free concert, sit and listen and forget. We spent wonderful summers on Cape Cod, where we owned a summer house; I had a laboratory at the Marine Biological Laboratory at Woods Hole, and we could enjoy the nearby beach. It was only the Jewish aspect of life there and concern for the children that detracted from the calm pleasure and richness of our lives.

On one point we were not ready to compromise our Jewishness; that was intermarriage. We believed that our children should marry Jews. Here is the racist backbone in us, if you will. It is so much part of us that we cannot live without it. All of my older Jewish colleagues (there were several dozen of these in a faculty of several thousand) had participated in the marriage of at least one of their children to a non-Jew. Following the Six Day War, when identification with Israel became fashionable, hundreds of Jewish faculty appeared, suddenly rediscovering their origin after they had married off children to non-Jews. This was not an acceptable future for us. Although our oldest child was only twelve, we vowed that this would not happen to us.

The only solution was to move to a large city, where Jewish life is fuller, the chances of meeting other Jews greater. Indeed, I had received a tempting offer to come to a major American university in New York City, but I had already arranged for a sabbatical year in Israel with Felix Bergmann. We were not going to give that up. Moreover, after living in a college town, breathing the fresh air, smelling flowers, bushes, and trees, I was not eager to return to the dirt, smog, and noise of the big city.

We were in New York City, visiting our parents before going on to Jerusalem, when the Six Day War broke out. As a neurologist, I volunteered my services to the Israeli Army. I was originally accepted and prepared to fly there ahead of my family, but the flight was canceled: only orthopedists and anesthetists were required. We continued with the six-week lecture tour through Europe that we had planned, finally sailing for Israel. (Despite having been an officer in the U.S. Navy for two years, I am a terrible sailor and get seasick while still in port. My second son decided to get married on a boat in the East River in New York City a few years ago. I survived the wedding only with the greatest difficulty and with the aid of Dermascope plasters behind my ear.) We arrived in Jerusalem at the end of July 1967.

I spent a year in the glow that flooded Israel after the Six Day War. The victory, so complete, so unexpected, raised everyone's spirits. These were heady times for me, and the work was interesting. My field was poorly represented there, and I could make a singular contribution by introducing the techniques and thinking current in the United States. This was a special feeling, being able to make a singular contribution. There were several hundred people in my field (now there are twenty-thousand) in the States; I was good but I was certainly expendable. In Israel I could partake in the building that was still going on, going on even more now, in 1992. Actually my field is well represented here now. We are now a power in the world in neurophysiology, but it was not my doing—or not my doing alone. When I decided to stay, I was joined by three young Israeli colleagues just back from postdoctoral work in important laboratories in the United States and Britain. We four formed the nucleus of a successful academic endeavor.

To put things in proportion, I must admit that the sense of being able to be part of a pioneer effort was every bit as important to me as the Jewishness of my children. I wanted to contribute; I was brought up with the belief that contribution was the most important goal of life. This was something that I had learned both from my schools and from my religion. And here was the opportunity. It is much easier to contribute in Israel than in the States.

I was asked to stay; I thought the idea attractive, and my wife was enthusiastic. A vice president of the university took me to lunch and told me that there was no chance for me to receive an appointment as a full professor (he himself was an associate professor) as I was too young by twenty years at least. One had to be at least sixty for that exalted rank. I remembered my promise to myself from 1960 and said, "Either professor or nothing." I was offered a full professorship.

I wrote to my dean saying that I was considering staying. In these days he would be happy to have an empty staff line and would give me his blessing and good-byes. But this was in the heady 1960s, when universities were rich. He wrote telling me not to make a hasty decision and offered me an extra half-year sabbatical at full salary (instead of the half-salary usually given).

I finally decided to stay. I returned to the States in January 1969 to sell my home and ship my belongings. I spent three months there, finishing my obligations to two graduate students I had left behind. I then flew back to Israel to live and work in Jerusalem.

I do not regret my decision. There have been wars, and there has been no end of tension. A fourth child, Ariel, was born here, more than ten years after the third. My first three children are married, all to Jews. I have tried living in the States again, on sabbatical. It is very difficult for me, for I do not understand the general concern for career and instant pleasure, and the means to that end—money. I find that other values are more important to me, values more associated with America's past than with its present. I find that living in Israel has ruined me for life elsewhere. I do not regret my decision.

HISTORICAL BACKGROUND

Much of the enmity directed toward Israel by Americans stems from confusion over the history of the nation. In the minds of many Westerners, Americans in particular, the modern State of Israel was simply willed into existence in 1947 by UN action, taken from its rightful inhabitants, and filled with Jewish refugees from Europe. But the history of Israel is much longer and more complex; to understand our perspectives on the Middle East and its many conflicts, you must know something of this history.

The State of Israel has ancient roots, which begin with the biblical settlement of the land by the patriarchs (Abraham, Isaac, and Jacob) and its subsequent capture by Joshua, followed by the Jewish kingdom. The course of this history was not always smooth, and the land suffered capture, exile, and destruction of both the First and the Second Temples, each of which was the spiritual center of Judaism. After more than a thousand years of Jewish rule in the land of Israel, war, destruction of the economy, and forced exile served to thin the population, and finally the Jews were no longer a majority in the country. Even before that happened, a strange anomaly took place as more Jews lived out of Israel than within it. But exiled Jews continued to yearn to return to Zion and recited a prayer for their return at least three times every day. And some did return, usually older people. A community of Jews was always present in Israel. They lived under the Greeks, the Romans, the Byzantines, the Persians, the Arabs, the Crusaders, the Mamluks, the Turks, and the British.

Arabs were never present in the country in great numbers. Some, but probably only few, of those living in Israel and the Administered Territories are descended from the Arab conquest. Arabs ruled the land of Zion for less than 500 years, and their hegemony ended nearly 900 years ago (c.e. 634–1099). Neither then nor later did the Arabs make a concerted effort to develop the land or do more than subsistence farming. During their reign, the Arab rulers referred to the population of the area as backward and of a low intellectual level. Better-educated Christians served as administrators of the country, while talented Arabs fled to neighboring countries where advancement was possible. In the first half of the nineteenth century the population of the area was less than 300,000. Under the British, the Arab-speaking population increased from 600,000 in 1917 to 1.2 million in 1948. The increase resulted from a number of causes, particularly the improvement in health and education and the increase in living standards brought about by the successful Jewish agricultural efforts and the expanded economy that resulted from those efforts. These factors decreased mortality, particularly infant mortality, and increased immigration from neighboring Arab countries.

Starting in the late nineteenth century, Jews began to migrate to the region in significant numbers, hoping to flee persecution in Europe and in Arab countries and to fulfill the dream of reestablishing a Jewish country on this soil, the original home of our people. The thought of return was the glue that had held us together through two thousand years of exile and persecution. When the Jews came, they found the land sparsely settled by small numbers of religious Jews (mainly supported by foreign charity) and nomadic Arabs. The land itself was owned mostly by absentee landlords, effendis, living in Damascus and Beirut. Jews began buying the land from these effendis and rebuilding it, raising oranges groves and drying out the malarial swamps. Despite great hardships, illness (including malignant fevers), starvation, and death—not infrequently at the hand of Arab marauders intent on stealing or murdering—these pioneers succeeded in building a fertile and productive land.

During the early period of Jewish settlement, Palestine (a Roman name derived from the Philistines, a vanished people) was part of the tottering Ottoman Empire. In World War I, however, Turkey sided with Germany, and its holdings in the region were lost to Allied forces, with Israel captured by British and Anzac troops. Anticipating this victory, in 1917 the British government issued the Balfour Declaration, promising the creation of a Jewish homeland in Palestine. In 1920 the League of Nations created the British Mandate in Palestine. In 1921 the area east of the Jordan was settled by Abdullah (son of the Sharif Hussein Ibn Ail of Mecca, who—supported by the British—had been one of the leaders of the Arab revolt in Saudi Arabia against the Turks) and his followers. The British immediately recognized Abdullah as Emir of Transjordan (modern Jordan), effectively removing that country from the promised Jewish homeland. At that time, the Transjordan had a population of about 200,000, mostly Bedouins.

Despite increasing Jewish settlement of the land and the Balfour Declaration, even as late as the 1920s the dream of a Jewish homeland was in peril. Many of the settlers had died of disease and starvation or left in anguish and frustration. As the Jew subsequently began to overcome the difficulties inherent in taming this wild and unfavorable land, filled with desert and malarial swamps and poor in water, their success became visible, and Arabs began to come from neighboring countries to enjoy the prosperity. These Arab immigrants were the ancestors of the majority of the Palestinians, who have thus been residents of the land for only a few decades.

The success of the Jews in settling the country aroused the fears of the Arabs who pressed the British to stop further Jewish immigration. The British chose to favor the Arabs on the issue of Jewish immigration, and they first limited and then completely stopped Jewish immigration in clear contradiction of the Balfour Declaration as well as the mandate they had received from the League of Nations.

Meanwhile, the pressure for Jewish immigration grew during the 1930s because of burgeoning anti-Semitism in Europe and restrictive (and functionally anti-Semitic) immigration laws in the United States and other Western countries. The hostility of American consuls—in whose hands the granting of visas rested—to potential Jewish immigrants was such that in the first four years of Nazi control of Germany (1933–37), fewer than 33,000 Jewish immigrants were allowed into the United States. With the situation becoming desperate, 124,000 were allowed in from 1939 to 1941, but when a German ship, the *St. Louis*, packed with refugees, arrived in New York harbor in 1941, not one was allowed to disembark. The ship returned to Hamburg, and all but three of the almost one thousand passengers were killed by the Nazis. Thus, America was not a valid option for most Jews. The British, in one of many attempts to appease the Arabs—who are still active in attempting to stop the immigration of Jews (in this case, Russian Jews) into Israel—closed the doors of Palestine to Jews. Despite this closure, and largely through illegal immigration, more than 120,000 Jews arrived in Palestine between 1933 and 1943, a number almost double that allowed into Britain itself. Only 811,000 out of 10 million European Jews succeeded in finding refuge in other countries during these ten years. Of these, 190,000 found refuge in France, Belgium, Holland and other European countries soon to be overrun by the Nazis. (In addition, after its creation the new State of Israel absorbed 500,000 Jews from Arab countries, never candidates for U.S. immigration under the quota system built to take in "Nordic" types only: the Nazis did not operate in a vacuum; many of their ideas, if not their methods, were shared by others.) Thus, most Jewish immigrants to Palestine during the period 1933–43 came out of necessity; they had nowhere else to go.

The State of Israel was created by UN action on 29 November 1947; at the same time, the United Nations also sanctioned an Arab state for the major part of the British Mandate in Palestine. The Arabs, who insisted on an all-Arab solution (that is, no Jewish state), refused to set up a state. Instead, holding a small majority of about 700,000 to 600,000, they fought the Jews. Five Arab armies from the neighboring states of Egypt, Jordan, Lebanon, Syria, and Iraq invaded the new country to aid the Arab rebellion.

The local Arab leaders and their allies called for noncombatant Arabs to leave temporarily to clear the way for the "conquering Arab armies." The Jews begged the Arabs to stay, fearing the slaughter that would befall an Arab-free country. Approximately 150,000 Arabs remained behind to become citizens of Israel and to flourish as none of the Arabs in the neighboring countries have; those who left have lived since in the Palestinian refugee camps.

Israel won the war. We could not fail: if we lost, we had no brothers to take us in. The economic condition of Israel's Arabs improved materially after 1948. There are now about 700,000 Arabs within the 1948 borders of Israel. They are all Israeli citizens, as are the Arabs of East Jerusalem and the Golan Heights (about 70,000 became citizens when the Golan Heights was annexed). There are more than 70,000 Christian Arab citizens in Israel and 35,000 Druze; the Druze serve in the army, as do Arab Bedouins.

Currently, about 1.1 million Arabs live in the regions known as the Administered Territories, which were captured by Israel during the 1967 attack by Egypt, Syria, and Jordan. These territories include about 700,000 Arabs in Judea and Samaria (the West Bank of the Jordan) and about 400,000, mostly very poor, in Gaza in the southwestern corner of Israel. They are not citizens of Israel and have a distinctly lower standard of living than do Israeli Arabs. Most live in refugee camps founded in 1948. The camps are a particularly ugly aspect of the Palestinian problem. Before the Six Day War, these camps existed in all the neighboring Arab countries, which had done little to absorb the Palestinian refugees who arrived in 1947– 48. They made no attempt to provide work or better social conditions; rather, they used the refugees as a propaganda weapon against Israel.

Israel inherited the problem of the refugee camps when it occupied the territories. Judea and Samaria (called "Shomron" in Israel) were part of Palestine designated as an Arab state by the 1947 UN decision but rejected by Arabs; Gaza was also designated as part of the state, but it was captured by Egypt in 1948 and held until 1967. (The Egyptians refused to take Gaza back at the Camp David meeting.) The Gaza refugees are stateless and poor. Israel's intention was to return the occupied territories to their original owners, but acceptable peace treaties have not yet been negotiated. The refusal of the Arab countries to deal with Israel has perpetuated the refugee problem; only Egypt has negotiated a treaty with Israel.

Israel also controls the Golan Heights, a sparsely occupied region of Syria. Taking advantage of the region's geographic features, entrenched Syrian army units fired from the Golan Heights at Israeli settlements at will for nineteen years, bringing damage, death, and fear to the kibbutzim of the eastern Galilee, where children slept in bomb shelters for years. The Israeli Army captured the Golan Heights in 1967. The Arab inhabitants fled to Syria, but the Druze remained. Because Syria was unwilling to deal with Israel, even to engage in a cease-fire, Israel annexed this strategic area and settled the territory. Agriculture, absent for the most part from the stark landscape of the Golan Heights, has been developed, and it is now a major wine-growing area. It is possible that a real peace treaty with Syria might produce a consensus to return the Golan Heights.

The territories on the West Bank are also open for negotiation. They can be united with Jordan or become demilitarized with appropriate controls so they do not become staging areas for attacks on Israel. Some border adjustments would be necessary since these territories come within six miles of the Israeli city of Netanya and ten miles of Tel Aviv. In addition, some ninety thousand Israelis live in these regions, and provision would have to be made for them in any peace treaty. Many Israelis insist that the Jordan River, a natural border with Jordan, remain in Israeli hands to prevent attack. Something must be done; there is too much pressure from both the outside and from within to do nothing. Israelis were evenly divided before the Gulf War on returning the territories, but the war may have increased the number opposed to returning anything. The new Russian immigrants are generally against returning territories, and many Israelis fear that the Arabs would use these territories to stage an attack on us.

The problem of the Palestinian refugees extends even to Kuwait, where many Palestinians work, mostly as minor clerks in banks and government offices. They are not allowed to bring their families to join them or to become citizens. Palestinians also supply much of the fruit and produce that is needed to feed the country. It is grown in the Administered Territories and trucked through Jordan to Kuwait.

Israel has not had friendly relations with Kuwait, which has supported anti-Israel activities and is one of the main financial supporters of the PLO. The support of Saddam by the PLO has led to loss of favor in the eyes of the Kuwaiti and even to withdrawal of their support, but it seems unlikely that this will change Kuwaiti policy toward Israel. Indeed, Kuwait is now directing the $30 million monthly budget that formerly went to the PLO to the Palestinian fundamentalist organization Hamas (the name means "zeal"), whose support of Saddam Hussein was rather lukewarm compared to that of the PLO.

So why did we support the Kuwaitis in their struggle? Certainly not from a desire for self-destruction or because we admire their autocratic government. Rather, we are simply against allowing unprovoked aggression to go unchecked. Thus, we found ourselves supporting one of our enemies, while another sent its missiles hurtling toward us.

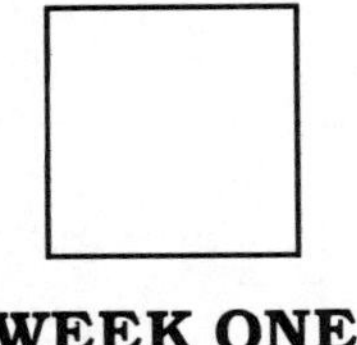

WEEK ONE

SATURDAY, 19 JANUARY: THE THIRD ATTACK

After two nights of air-raid sirens, jumping up to get to a sealed room, putting on gas masks. Two real ones so far; two false alarms. A bit tiring—but relief that the weapons are conventional, and that so few people are seriously hurt.

Schools were closed on Thursday and will remain closed. Since both parents work in Israel, one will have to stay home. Meanwhile, most nonessential industries and stores are closed.

The Patriot missiles that the U.S. is giving us will be too late and too few.

The big question is, Does Saddam have chemical warheads on his missiles? There is little doubt that he will use them if he has.

The elimination of the missile launchers seems a difficult if not impossible task.

Generally, morale seems high. People are told to stay close to home, to have gas masks ready. They, for the most part, listen to instructions.

The peace rallies continue with the thoughtless, fatuous theme "No blood for oil" playing a leading role. Has anybody rallied to protest the attack of Iraq on Israel, the uninvolved? To protest the attacks on civilian concentrations in cities? I doubt it.

■ As I sat in the sealed room, waiting for the missiles to fall, a strong sensation of intellectual claustrophobia overcame me. Although some of my family were with me, I felt isolated from the world, cocooned in fear, cut off by the flimsy tape and plastic that would, we hoped, protect us from poison gas. I felt the need to tell others what was happening to us, to explain to the world how Saddam Hussein was hedging our lives with missiles; and thus I began my record, my ■ notes from a sealed room.

MONDAY, 21 JANUARY: OF BOMB SHELTERS AND GAS MASKS

There is some lack of clarity in the reports about the use of bomb shelters in Israel. As a matter of fact, there are now two rather different kinds of bomb shelters in use in Israel.

The standard bomb shelter is built below ground. For the past twenty-five years it has been a requirement to provide bomb shelters in all buildings erected. Older buildings often do not have such shelters; their residents depend on neighborhood community shelters, which are also found in public areas in the cities. These bomb shelters are (almost) all vented to the outside world.

With the advent of the threat of poison gas attacks, it was decided not to use these shelters (except in rare cases where special ventilation is provided and the shelters can be closed hermetically). The possible damage that can be produced by poison gas, particularly the threat to human life, is far greater than anticipated from a conventional warhead. Since the great majority of the existing shelters cannot be hermetically sealed, and since they are located at ground level or below, where the denser-than-air poison gases concentrate, a new type of improvised shelter was instituted throughout Israel.

The new shelter was a room in a home or apartment, located as high as possible, that could be isolated and sealed, preferably with only one window. These shelters were prepared by putting sponge stripping around the window and door edges, closing the windows and taping all joints and edges, and placing tape on the glass of the windows to prevent splintering in the case of blast. In addition, a thick plastic curtain was pasted over the windows to prevent splintered glass from entering and providing a secondary defense against the entry of gas. The door edges were provided with thick strips of plastic tape to be used to seal them when the doors were closed. Finally, a wet towel was to be placed at the bottom of the closed door.

■   We were told to choose rooms with a minimum of outside walls and as few windows as possible. Air conditioners were not to be in operation and had to be covered with plastic. These considerations were second to choosing as high a room as possible to take advantage of the density of the poison gases. Some saw the choice of rooms as a serious problem; for others, the choice was obvious. One wit said that choosing a room was much like choosing a cemetery
■ plot.

It was estimated that the use of such a room would reduce the risk of morbidity or mortality from poison gas by a factor of ten. This safety factor would be greatly improved by the compulsory use of gas masks (special models for children, incubators for infants) and the presence of such additional measures as automatic atropine injections and anti-liquid-burn powders—all provided to each citizen.

So some eight times already, all of Israel has sat, sealed into their anti-poison-gas rooms, wearing masks and waiting. Some twenty casualties from blast and shrapnel have thus far all been mild. On the other hand, property damage produced by the missiles has, in a number of cases, been extensive. No one resents or regrets the choice of people over property. Several elderly people choked to death by not pulling out the plug on the mask—all on the first day. One Israeli Arab child choked to death when parents forced her to wear the mask. No poison gas has been used—thus far.

Learning to use the masks properly, not fastening the straps too tightly, talking, breathing without hyperventilating—these have been universal experiences. Initially, large numbers of people found themselves sweating unbearably, clouding the glass so as to blind oneself. Others, particularly children, vomited, for the most part after removing the mask. Learning and reuse helped in almost all cases. Radio and TV instructions repeated over and over again helped.

A story: sitting in the antigas room, members of the family try to put on a brave face, make jokes. How we all look like elephants; how an elephant would approach one of us and mistake him/her for his mother. Only the dog, a rather stately collie, sits quietly and does not appear at all excited. We pity the dog, for he is the only one without a mask. But then we remember that—without a mask—he is our canary in the coal mine, the measure of poison gas that has leaked in.

■   We had already begun to react to the threat of poison gas in a way that can never really be understood by those who are not Jews. Even our children, born long after the Nazis were defeated, are educated to respond with hate and loathing to the idea of poison gas.

During the trial of Ivan Demjanjuk—a Ukranian accused, and convicted, of being the infamous "Ivan the Terrible," cruel torturer and murderer in the Treblinka death camp—the interest and attendance of our young people was astounding. The memory of the Nazis lives with us all, never far removed from the center of our existence, never too remote to be recalled without a flood of anger, even hate.

The Nazis sought perfection in an efficient way to kill Jews. They attempted mass shootings; the Jews prepared their own mass graves beforehand. They tried automobile exhaust fumes delivered into the cabins of closed trucks, but that proved too slow and inefficient. They finally hit on the use of Zyklon B, an insecticide that evaporated at room temperature. Jews were herded into sealed "shower" facilities and the gas added. After twenty minutes the bodies were removed, stripped of valuables, and burned in ovens— all this using Jewish labor.

Six million Jews were destroyed, more than one-third by gas. Efficiently, if you will. We do not forget poison gas easily.

Saddam Hussein had not hesitated before to use poison gas on the battlefield against both Iranians and civilians. He destroyed a village of five thousand Kurds in northern Iraq by dropping canisters of poison gas from airplanes. We had little doubt that he would use poison gas on us, sending either airplanes or rockets equipped with poison gas. We have good air defenses, but not good enough to prevent a single plane from getting through to a civilian population center. Who could guarantee that?

I could not understand what kind of blind, unreasoning hate could motivate the use of gas against the Jews of Israel. It was like the hatred that Hitler felt when he used poison gas to murder Jews. Saddam Hussein's willingness to waste bombs on Israel, a noncombatant in this war, was not only an example of blind, unreasoning hate, but it is also a cynical act, meant to enlist the sympathy of others who hate us.

The Kurds have made history by being the first civilian casualties of poison gas warfare. I doubt that this unwilling sacrifice on their part will help them in their fight for independence from Iraqi and Iranian persecution, or from Turkish toleration in the most impoverished conditions. We Jews of Israel have no desire to be second to the Kurds. We will not allow Saddam Hussein to destroy
■ us with poison gas.

TUESDAY, 22 JANUARY: A RESPITE

Another quiet night; all of the Scuds were directed—for the second night—to Saudi Arabia and Bahrain.

The name of the game is sleep. So many people just cannot sleep properly. Fortunately for me, I am one of the lucky ones. A major problem for the sleepless is what to do with the radio. If you leave it on, it disturbs sleep. If you turn it off, you are afraid to sleep. Why shouldn't some of us be neurotic? Wasn't the condition first described by a Jewish doctor in Vienna? Examining Jewish patients? And the other side of the coin is that—if it is not a Jewish disease, i.e., a diaspora disease—why shouldn't we have it? After all, we are now in Israel, our new/old homeland, just like all other nations.

The noise of airplanes drones above us. This is quite unusual as the Jerusalem skies are off-limits to air traffic. We cannot see the planes; they are very high and the sky is very cloudy, with intermittent light rains. The sound—to my unprofessional ear, at least—is that of motors, not jets.

I know that jets are constantly in the air, for weeks now, to avoid being caught on the ground, to be ready to repulse any air attack from Iraq. (We bombed them—a nuclear plant built by the French—in 1981; they can certainly return the favor.) But it still sounds like propeller engines. Perhaps these are the mother ships which will be needed to refuel the jets on their thousand-kilometer trip to Iraq.

Retaliation, national pride, perhaps strange concepts to most readers. You have to understand how we see—the nature of inter-governmental relations (and personal relations, too) in that strange part of the world, the Middle East—retaliation as deterrence. If we do not retaliate, this will be seen by our neighbors as an invitation to attack us; alternatively, if we do retaliate, they will be less inclined to attack us. Thus, retaliation is still very much in the air here. We are praised by the West for our restraint; this very same restraint is perceived by our neighbors as a sign of weakness. And why this cruel word, *retaliation*? It is defending our country. Which we will do.

National pride, the picture of Israelis returning to share our fate, to be here, now, when the pressure is on. My youngest son, after three years of army service as a commando, now relaxing and touring the Far East, calls in the early morning. He tells us that he is returning, cutting his long trip short by months. We try to dissuade him; what will he do here? But nothing helps when he has made up his mind. I fear for his safety but I am proud. He will come back, together with other Israelis, together with immigrants from Russia who continue to come, with immigrants from Ethiopia. I will be happy to see my son.

The news this morning is discouraging. It seems that much of the coalition's successful bombing has been against dummy targets. Most of Iraq's missile launchers are intact, almost all of their planes. The communication facilities are still almost completely intact. It is going to take much longer than we thought.

Life is slowly going back to normal. All are asked to return to work—with gas masks. Schools will be opened tomorrow. Meanwhile some factories are providing nursery services to children of workers in gas-proof rooms. The now ubiquitous gas masks are found on the shelves of the nurseries. Radio instructions include various less likely scenarios. (The Israeli penchant for inventing new words has not gone on strike in the present emergency; the new word for "scenario" is now in universal use—*tarhish*. There was a perfectly good word, *tasrit*. Perhaps the association with movies or plays was perceived as being too frivolous.) What do you do when you hear a siren while in a car? If you are in a built-up area, you turn off the engine, put on your gas mask, and dash for the nearest building, counting on there being a shelter or a good citizen who will take you in. If you are in an open area, stop the car, put on the mask, keep listening to the radio.

Life is going back to normal. Yesterday, my wife and I went to visit a Russian family whom we have adopted, our fourth. They are all wonderful people and each family is different, each with fascinating stories. This is a new family for me; my wife has already met them. We carry our gas masks and presents, a carrot cake my wife has baked and a radio. We decide to walk, we need the fresh air, the exercise. They live twenty minutes away, near the open-air market, Mahne Yehuda, in an old, religious neighborhood. The apartment is large, newly painted but very old under the paint. The man wears a *kippa* (a skullcap), bears a long, brown, curly beard, is short and delicate looking. His wife is short, fat, and has dyed bright-orange hair. They are from Perm, near the Urals. They were both teachers. I look at their sealed room; it is a joke, totally inadequate. I point this out to them, all in a mixture of elementary Yiddish (mine) and elementary Hebrew (theirs), but they are interested only in employment. They have a daughter with three children who came with them and is now living in a *mitzpe* (a small group of families on top of a hill) in the Galil. They are happy to be here; I am happy they are here: more good material for Israel, one less family to suffer degradation in the USSR.

Life is coming back to normal. We walk through the *shuk*, the open-air market. It is already dark, but the lights are brilliant and the *shuk* is teeming with purchasers of the marvelous fresh fruits and vegetables available, and nuts and dried fruit and spices. Some of the stands, only a very few, are empty, closed. Where are the owners? Have they fled? We buy some oranges, some cucumbers and smoked fish.

Back home. Another day in Israel.

■ How can we ask Russian Jews to join us here in a country threatened and under attack? Are they such fools as to come to join us in our time of danger?

Just before the war began, the immigration of Russian Jews peaked, with more than a thousand arriving each day. We know that this immigration will be a financial and social burden for us; nonetheless, we are happy to see them, happy and worried. Their coming justifies our existence; we claimed that Israel was necessary because of the recurring, if not constant, need for a refuge, a place where being a Jew is not a curse or source of embarrassment—a place where Jews may raise their heads high.

Before the Russian immigration began, the demographics were discouraging, to say the least. We were reproducing at a low rate while the Arabs, who are a minority, continued to grow in numbers. This encouraged the Arabs, who dream of outnumbering us, and was a source of concern for us. Now, with at least one and a half million Russian Jews interested in coming here (three hundred thousand have already arrived), the tables have been turned. The Arabs are angry and frustrated as their demographic advantage slips away.

The Russian immigration is motivated by economic hardship and anti-Semitism in Russia. The unwillingness of other countries to absorb large numbers of either Russians or Jews has focused their attention on Israel, whose borders are open to any Jew.

The Russians are seen here as a burden and a gift. They are good workers; it seems that Jews in Russia have to work much harder than non-Jews to achieve any position. Thirty percent of those who have come have university degrees—many of them advanced degrees—as well as rich professional experience. We have unemployment here and a housing shortage. But we are willing to absorb them, have to absorb them, will make every effort to absorb them. They are our brothers and they are our future.

We feel that you have to believe in miracles to live in Israel. Only miracles can explain our history, our continued existence—even flourishing—in the face of unusual and unfavorable odds through all our history. We are at our best when faced with impossible challenges; we surprise ourselves, and we admire ourselves. It is a good feeling to gird up your loins, to have a purpose, national as well as individual.

We know that the Russians are coming here more to escape something bad than to join something good. But once they come here, they seem to want to be here with us. They want to know about their history; most are woefully ignorant of Jewish history and beliefs. They want to believe in something, to be part of something. As Jews they were outsiders in Russia, even when successful. Here they are part of both the problem and the solution. That, we feel, is a wonderful role for anyone.

The Russian Jews do not appear to be frightened by the physical dangers that we face. Those who are capable of articulating their feelings tell me that it is worse to suffer economic and social persecution than it is to face possible death so long as they know they share their fate with others and that intelligence and skill are being exerted to avoid extinction. They are a strong group. Clearly our gain will be Russia's loss.

Is there a special gene for nationalism among Jews? I doubt it; it is a universal quality that expresses itself when the need is felt. Among the Jews, that need is felt often. And strongly.

WEDNESDAY, 23 JANUARY: ON POISON GAS

This is a particularly difficult report to write. I am not ordinarily given to persistent, burning anger, but that is what has happened to me. It is in the air here, and I, too, have been infected. And—just to show the extent of my anger—I feel no guilt about it, I feel that it is the right response, the only possible response.

Last night was not a quiet night; between 8:32 and 8:33 P.M. an alarm was sounded and we rushed to our gas-proof rooms, donned our gas masks (you have to remember to take off your glasses), and turned on the transistor radio. (What if the electricity goes! We have candles and matches ready, too.) Within a minute or two we were told that this was not a false alarm, that there was a missile attack on Israel, and that we were requested to enter our rooms and put on the masks, to wait patiently and to listen to further reports on the radio. Some fifteen minutes later we were told that all people outside the greater Tel Aviv area could take off their masks and leave the room, but to stay at home with our masks handy. About a half-hour later, Tel Aviv residents were also let out of the gas-proof rooms. We were told that a missile attack took place but no details. Later, I hear that the missile struck at 8:37. I calculate four to five minutes advance notice, just enough time to get to the gas-proof room and put on the mask.

We learned the details through a long night's vigil, waiting for news, waiting for another missile: 96 wounded, 4 dead (3 were old folks who suffered heart attacks), 20 multiple-family buildings badly damaged, hundreds homeless. We watched TV, called relatives and friends to ask if they were safe. We could recognize the neighborhood from the TV reports. The Patriots fired missed the Scud, and the illusion of safety disappeared. We watched the rescue crews at work on TV. Wounded, a young man clutching his dog while being put on a stretcher, collapsed walls being raised by heavy equipment to free the trapped. It was terrible.

The eleventh missile, the third attack. All bearing conventional warheads—so far. Should we use the underground shelters? We were told not to, that the threat of poison gas was still real, that gas could do far more damage to human life. We are not sure that Saddam Hussein has chemical warheads for the Scud missiles, but we do know that he has chemical weapons that can be dropped from planes. It is not possible to guarantee that at least one plane with such weapons would not be able to penetrate our air defenses. So, we still will use our gas-proof rooms. Poison gas.

When Jonathan Pollard asked his superiors why the U.S. did not protest at the Soviets and Germany selling poison gas technology to Iraq, he was told that the Jews, since World War II, had become oversensitive to the subject of gas. Oversensitive? These are bad guys, but not evil, just dumb and insensitive, without foresight. The peace demonstrators do not differentiate between bad and evil. They rightly condemn both, but do not see the essential difference. Saddam Hussein is evil. He is accused not of making a fast buck by selling restricted technology but of raping a country, of callously attacking civilian populations in a neutral country. Even if it is true that the U.S. stupidly supported Saddam Hussein in the past, are we to condemn the Americans for coming to their senses? By the way, Pollard got life in prison; Saddam Hussein is not even targeted by the coalition forces. Something seems out of balance.

Poison gas? Yes, we are sensitive to the subject.

Yesterday, we were on our way back to normal life—except for carrying a gas mask. The classical music station came back on the air, final proof that life must go on. Strangely enough, we continue today to act as if life must go on. The schools are still closed but almost everyone is back at work, even in Tel Aviv, except for mothers (in some cases, fathers) who have not been able to make arrangements for watching their children. I meet a young woman on the street who tells me she is going to an aerobics class. With her gas mask in hand. I ask myself, "Is it possible to do aerobics wearing a gas mask?"

The matter of striking back is now in the air; everybody here feels that we should do something to defend ourselves. Anger and frustration at our inactivity are widespread. Our restraint until now has brought us much approbation throughout the Western world. This condition is unusual for us and has even produced a certain sense of pride in us. Approving Israel seems strange to the world as well. A friend tells me that a Los Angeles commentator said, "The American government feels that Israel's restraint should be condemned . . . oh, I mean commended." A new situation, the world approves our action. Or really our inaction. We have briefly enjoyed the approbation of the world; but we now feel the time for inaction has passed. What will that fickle lover, the world, say now?

What sort of an action? It would have to be elegant and pointed, to show that we are not to be dealt with with impunity. We want a response that would involve limited risk in numbers and yet achieve an important and visible goal. The killing of Saddam still seems to be an attractive goal.

It is unlikely that he dares to leave his bunker now. The bunker is reportedly proof against anything less than a nuclear weapon. Could gaseous explosives be introduced into the bunker through the air intakes and detonated? Or poison gas? The latter would have an aesthetic advantage, poetic retribution, as in a Greek tragedy.

Another elegant action suggested in a letter to me would be to free the allied POWs. If the Iraqis do place them—as they have threatened—at military targets, it would be even easier, with no need to penetrate a guarded POW camp or prison, and no need to operate in an urban area.

We are angry, but we are capable of planning while we are angry, and we will defend ourselves. Restraint has its limits. *Retaliation* is not a word that I like, implying as it does returning evil for evil. We will not return evil. We are not evil, we are under attack, unprovoked attack. We will defend ourselves in the only way understood in this part of the world.

THURSDAY, 24 JANUARY: SISMA

Last night another air-raid alarm. Here is how it went, a few minutes of heightened secretion of adrenalin which seemed much longer:

22:10   The radio is interrupted by a sisma, a code name for call-up of an army group, but in this case perhaps the code indicating an attack.

■ We later discovered that this code name—*nahash tzefa*, or "viper"—was the signal to begin the whole response process, beginning with sounding the sirens. ■

22:11   I hear the siren, clearly up and down, the signal for a true attack. (The local joke is that the up-and-down wail of the siren signals our indecision: whether to use the gas-proof room upstairs or the safer blast shelter below.) I help my mother into the poison-gas-proof room and call my wife. I rush to pee (there is no time to waste three syllables on *urinate*) before I enter and we seal the door with tape at all the edges and a wet towel below. We put on our gas masks; my mother always needs help with hers (the instructions are definite about always getting yours on first; if something happens to you, you will not be able to help anyone else), turn on the battery-powered transistor radio. (The electricity might be knocked out or fail.) The radio is reassuring, telling us that as soon as something definite is known we will be told, that the alarm has been given throughout Israel, that we are to go to the gas-proof rooms, put on our masks and listen to the radio. The directions are given several times in Hebrew and then briefly translated into English, Russian, French, Amharic (new Ethiopian Jews are arriving every day), and a Slavic language which I cannot recognize. I notice how much better they have gotten at this, the announcers telling us how much they know and promising to tell us more as soon as they know. Instructions are given to those caught in cars. We are told that the alarm was sounded because of an attack on Israel. We remain tense, make jokes. There are some friends and relatives who have told us they have difficulty in hearing the siren. We have a telephone in the room, their numbers, writ large, nearby. We remembered to call them as soon as we were secured; they had heard, but thank us.

22:17 We are told to remove our masks but to remain in the sealed rooms. We breathe a sigh of relief; it apparently was not a chemical attack.

22:21 We are told that everybody, except those living in the greater Tel Aviv area, can leave the sealed rooms but not to leave home.

22:43 We are informed that a Scud missile was downed by a Patriot antimissile missile in the north. (Later we were told that there were two Patriots and that the north meant over Haifa.) No one hurt. (At 23:00 we heard that many windows were broken and door frames damaged.) What a relief!

And a new source of hope, the Patriots—they really work! Attacks also reported from Saudi Arabia, where the Patriots were again effective. Everyone can leave the sealed rooms.

Sleep is still a problem; everything is, of course, worse in Tel Aviv. I call friends there, listen to their indecisions about whether to stay or leave. I try to help with advice, usually by saying what they want to hear. They wonder: Would leaving be desertion? Just for one night? To get some sleep? On late-night programs I hear psychologists give advice on how to sleep. From a friend in Tel Aviv I learn that one does not shower or use a blower to dry your hair when you are alone—in order not to miss the siren.

Yesterday I went back to work for the first time since last Thursday; most people are there, there is little talk of the war or the bombings. Friends from Tel Aviv call to talk a bit; they are much more in it than we are. Their terror is still real, almost palpable. But they are functioning.

There is a debate on the situation in the Knesset, our Parliament. I miss most of it but get the flavor: almost all of the members feel that we should strike Iraq, but not now as there is nothing we could do that the coalition is not already doing. Two Arab members of Knesset manage to blame us for being bombed by Iraq's missiles. One member says that there is one thing that will never be forgiven Saddam Hussein: that he is responsible for one and a half million children having to wear gas masks.

A Danish military expert claims that the payload of Tuesday night's Scud was too great for it to have come from Iraq. He suggests that Jordan is being used to stage the missile firings. Could King Hussein be so foolish? Is he under such great pressure from the Iraqis? His rule is tenuous enough without inviting us to attack him. What ever could he be thinking? Has he been trapped by the rhetoric of the situation once again, as in 1967?

The Americans announce that they have definitely destroyed the two Iraqi nuclear reactors. It is almost ten years since we took out the French-built Tamuz reactor in Ossirak. We were condemned (a typo: I type "cohndemned") by the world for this action. But we set back the war machine that the West was building in Iraq by ten years. Who will remember to thank us for that? We do not need the thanks, as we, too—not only the troops fighting in Persian Gulf— are the direct beneficiaries of that attack.

We are still looking for a new elegant attack on Iraq. A French engineer who worked for Saddam writes, according to one of my correspondents, that Saddam Hussein's bunker has two weak points: the air intake and the exhaust shaft for a diesel generator. Those two shafts are apparently camouflaged to protect them against bombing. They might be easy to locate from the ground.

Another writer tells me that he is an expert in dust-free environments and that the filters in the underground shelters may be their weak points. He suggests a number of common agents that he has shown can destroy high-grade filters.

Just at the beginning of the attack on Israel, almost a week ago, I found an E-mail address from Cairo on one of the intellectual nets. I thought it might be fun and interesting to correspond with someone so close, and yet so far. He responded favorably and tells me that all is calm in Cairo at the moment, but that "nobody seems to have any information about the war." "Cairenes," he reports, "seem to be very blasé about the whole thing; their attitude is that they've seen it all before." He sounds interesting; I wish I had more time to get know him. After this is all over, I hope.

FRIDAY, 25 JANUARY: FALSE ALARM

Last night, at 22:32, the TV broadcast of the semifinal round European Cup basketball game between Maccabi Tel Aviv and Pop Split, last year's champions—from Yugoslavia—was interrupted early in the second half—Tel Aviv ahead by four—by the flash of a shield in the center of the screen. The strange medallion did not mean anything to me for a second or two, until the message in the center of the shield finally—How could I be so obtuse as not to realize immediately what was going on? Was I not already a veteran of air-raid drills?—began to register—ALERT—written in several languages. I called to my wife and only then did we hear a siren. We hurried into the sealable room upstairs and were all masked and seated, more or less calmly, even my eighty-six-year-old mother—who had to be awakened and did not quite seem to know was going on—listening to the radio tell us that the alarm was for all Israel, when (finally!)—at 22:35—another siren was heard, this time a steady blast. (The alert alarm is an alternately rising and falling wail.) The radio confirmed that there was now an all-clear condition. Did it last only three minutes? It seemed much longer than that; how had we accomplished so much in only three minutes?

After the all-clear was digested by us, understood: yes, we were once again "safe," we could now resume watching the game. How strange it seemed, an Israeli team! (Most have been devastated by the loss of foreign players who left with the onset of Desert Storm, but not our best team, Maccabi, with four African Americans who all stayed and played.) How could they go on playing? But they could not possibly know that there had been an alarm here; after all, they were in Split, in Yugoslavia. Added to our relief after understanding that what we had experienced was only a false alarm—and added to the glow from the effective action of the Patriot, which still is felt— we were treated to a hairsbreadth victory by Tel Aviv. Two points and Split had the ball!

The problems of lack of sleep and increased anxiety are still very much with us, particularly noticeable in children. Teenagers cringe in Tel Aviv, waiting for the sound of the blast that they have already heard so many times. There is more bedwetting, whimpering, and even crying in their sleep among children. We hear psychological advice over and over again on the radio, not only for children. Whole families sleep together, to reassure one another, in a single bed. In other families, a watch is set; one person stays awake to be able to hear the siren. Waiting.

One expert has advised fondling, caressing, and even sex for anxiety. When I ask a friend in Tel Aviv, he says, "You must be made of stronger stuff than me if you can think about sex at a time like this." Truth is, I have not thought about it; I only wondered if sex might be used as proof that you are still alive. On the other hand, fear does remarkable things to your hormones, even producing amen-orrhea. But then again, so do anorexia nervosa and schizophrenia.

Speaking of anorexia nervosa and psychological counseling on the radio, one psychologist advised eating for anxiety. Only in a Jewish country!

Apparently, when I wrote about inviting the American crews to man the Patriots and teaching Israelis how to use them was felt to be a blow to our pride, I forgot to say how thankful we were and are to America for sending the missiles and their trained crews and to the crews themselves. The crews were overwhelmed with home-baked cakes. (A radio announcement pleaded with the public to stop; there were just too many.) When a call was made on the radio for English speakers to entertain the American crews, the response was overwhelming. It is possible to be hurt and thankful at the same time.

■   One U.S. soldier remarked that coming here from Germany, where U.S. flags are being burned, to a country that loves and appreciates the United States is like being transported from night to day. Another said that the United States and Israel were the only two countries he would fight for. He explained that he was a Baptist
■ and therefore loved Israel.

And all this was before the first Patriot was fired. With the success of the Patriots in Haifa on Wednesday night, our gratitude is that much greater. The mayor of Haifa, where the Patriot downed a Scud, brought champagne and a case of whiskey to the American crew which had manned the Patriot launcher. I hope they will not be drunk when we need them again—if we need them again, as most of us are still convinced we shall.

SATURDAY, 26 JANUARY: RAIN

I spoke of the rain as a blessing. Sometimes it is less than that. The electric connections in my neighborhood of old houses are fragile and exposed to the elements; not infrequently there are disturbances of the lines when it rains. Last night we had such a disturbance; result: a total blackout. (Well, almost total: for some reason not clear to me, the heat kept working. My street was totally blacked out, but not the houses across the street.) All this with the threat of missile and plane attacks hanging over us. We had a battery-powered transistor radio going so that we could hear what was happening; the Sabbath candles were lit, and we had light in the sealed room from a lamp that was charged while there was electricity but worked only when the electricity was cut off. But it was still not very comfortable; the lamp worked for less than three hours and that was not enough; it took almost five hours before the electricity was restored. We still had a flashlight after the emergency lamp lost its charge, long after the candles burned out.

■   We are so spoiled, so used to our electricity, so dependent on it. Yes, even in peacetime we do have occasional electrical failures during heavy rains that down transformers and power lines or during periods of exceptionally heavy loads. But it is hardly the same when your life may depend on it.
     Do the warning sirens depend on an intact electrical supply? The radio stations? What happens when the power fails? Are there backup generators for these essential functions? I hope so. I do

know that the rescue vehicles are supplied with powerful lights that allow rescue operations to take place in the absence of external current. That is some reassurance.

And all this was after an attack; we had just sat down to eat our Sabbath meal when the alarm went off. We went up to the sealed, hopefully poison-gas-proof, room, nine of us—including our two grandchildren, aged two and five, and two refugees from Tel Aviv who stayed with us for the Sabbath, to get some rest from the relentless bombardment that had frayed their nerves, slightly. A brother and a sister: she writes a weekly literary column for the second most popular newspaper in the country; he is a TV director.

We managed in the small room; even the incubator for the two-year-old fit in.

The sealed room was based on the principle that plastic sheeting and plastic-backed tape would provide reasonable protection against poison gas attacks. Essentially all connection to the outside world was severed. Window and door frames were lined with spongy material that was compressed when the windows and doors were closed, providing a first seal. The windows were also taped to prevent splintered glass from flying into the room. Finally a layer of thick polyethylene sheeting was placed over the windows and sealed to the walls with plastic-backed tape. (This tape and plastic sheeting became highly desirable items, and their prices soared.) The polyethylene provided another layer of protection against the gas and also a barrier against splintered glass. The door was also sealed with plastic-backed tape, and a wet towel was placed on the floor below the door. All air conditioners were disconnected and covered with polyethylene sheeting.

Although it might have been possible to choose a bathroom as our sealed room, we did not. Nor did anyone else I know make that choice. We never discussed that possibility, but the advantage of having toilet facilities and running water was not enough of a trade-off for the comfort of a larger bedroom with a couch, desk, chairs, and a computer. The use of running water was out in case of a chemical attack. In any case, water in glass bottles, or soda water, was stored in the sealed room together with some nonspoiling food in sealed packages. Toilet facilities consisted of a bucket with a cover; ours was used only once throughout the war, if I remember correctly.

Several correspondents asked me to describe these incubators. They are not called that at all; *incubator* is my name for them. They are more properly called Portable Infant Shields and are used as protection against poison gas for children up to the age of three. Made of heavy, clear polyethylene over a collapsible khaki metal frame, the shields measure 1.2 × 0.8 × 0.8 meters (about 47.2 inches × 31.5 inches × 31.5 inches). The front has two large air filters built into the plastic; below that is the entrance through which the child is placed or crawls. The entrance is closed by rolling plastic over the hole a number of times and snapping it shut. Inside are pockets for bottles and toys as well as a thin mattress. The front also has an arm-shaped sleeve that allows an adult to insert his or her hand to touch or feed the baby while keeping a layer of plastic separating the two. The device does bear a superficial resemblance to a newborn's incubator, but unlike the incubator, it is usually placed on the floor. After the war ended, one of my granddaughters turned three and announced proudly that she would never have to use the incubator again.

One of us, a diabetic, had just taken his insulin injection before the alarm sounded. We worried about him having to eat something, but he held out, wearing the mask for the half-hour before we were freed by the radio instructions. When he removed his mask, we found him some crackers in the box of food prepared for long stays in the room.

The attack was again real, and again relatively far from us, centering in Tel Aviv and Haifa. Seven Scud missiles were fired at these cities, and Patriot missiles apparently damaged some five or six of them. But one or two landed in crowded residential areas again, only in greater Tel Aviv. And the fragments of the missiles—which? the Scuds? the Patriots? both?—are not innocent either and caused property damage and led to injuries. One dead, the first directly attributed to missiles, from the collapse of his house following a missile hit; his wife was also injured. There were sixty-three wounded. And hundreds of homes damaged, some destroyed. One two-story structure, inhabited by three Israelis, was completely destroyed; all three managed to get out, miraculously without injury. Miraculous? We are very prone to use that word these days. More than a thousand more homeless. Well, at least a minor miracle.

Jerusalem was not attacked by the Iraqis. We might think it unlikely that Jerusalem would be a target for the Scuds, since it is home to both Jews and Arabs. But Haifa, a city with a substantial Arab population, was not spared. The historical Jerusalem is the emotional and religious center of three religions. The Arabs have Mecca and Medina, but Jerusalem, or "Al Kuds" as they call it, is a very holy place for all Muslims. Here Muhammed ascended to heaven on his holy charger, a winged creature called *Buraq*. The very stone from which he ascended—marked by the steed's hoofprint—is preserved in the cellar of the Mosque of the Golden Dome in East Jerusalem. Would Saddam Hussein bomb this Muslim shrine?

An El Al plane, bearing *olim*, immigrants from Russia, was ready to land when the attack took place. The plane was instructed to hover until further notice; when the all-clear was sounded, the plane landed, the olim debarked, were handed gas masks. Welcome to Israel! And then they were sent off to temporary lodgings.

The rain goes on; it protects us—but not completely.

I ask the Tel Aviv guests how they have been affected by the bombardment. Neither lives in an area directly struck by a missile or its fragment. But the noise of the missiles approaching is clearly heard and the blast, even when at a distance of miles, is felt, shaking everything in the house. The sister tells me that the worst part is not being able to get on with what interests her; she just cannot concentrate. That is in Tel Aviv; here, in Jerusalem, it seems we concentrate more than we should—on the wrong things.

Have Israelis ignored the instructions not to use the classic bomb shelters? We still go upstairs to the sealed room, accepting the evaluation of the experts that chemical damage is still a greater danger than anything the blasts of conventional weapons can do. I think almost all Israelis are with us in that. We do know one family that has deserted their sealed, gas-proof room for what they perceive as the greater safety of their bomb shelter. The woman of the family is one of those people whose major preoccupation in life seems—to me—to be avoiding being taken advantage of and, as a corollary, beating the system. She would love to survive just because of this asocial action, if for no other reason than to point out to us that, had she been as sheeplike as the rest of us, she would not have survived. Ah, well, I hope she survives, and her family as well.

I understand that sympathy for us has extended to a form of identification; gas masks are selling throughout the world, particularly in the States, like hotcakes, I am told. Someone wrote about one store in Manhattan selling more than 500, another in South Carolina selling 2,400 gas masks, usually an unpopular item. Others report that people are shipping gas masks to friends and relatives in Israel. What would we do with a spare gas mask? The masks, even carried alone, without the rest of the set (pads, antigas burn powder, and an atropine injection), are rather clumsy. They are now a universal sight in the streets. Rich and poor, we carry gas masks now.

Peace demonstrations go on, I am told, although they may be weakening. It is interesting that there were no protests of this dimension when Iraq took over Kuwait and commenced to brutalize the population before annexing the country. Many of the professional peace people are associated with the environmentally sensitive. I wonder if they will respond to Saddam Hussein's newest non sequitur? If the driving of neutral Israel into bomb shelters is not enough to move them against Saddam Hussein, will his wanton dumping of Kuwaiti oil into the Persian Gulf move them? Will they demonstrate against this further manifestation of the destructive nature of this evil and powerful man? The sight of the oil-covered cormorants on TV, barely able to move, their wings inactivated by thick layers of oil, was particularly disturbing. Animals are usually understood better and draw more sympathy in these people than do suffering people.

Is it not strange too that the peace-at-all-costs people are not demonstrating in masses against the Russian oppression of the Baltic states? The fight to rid the world of this evil oppressor, Saddam Hussein, does not move them. What does move them? A desire to stay out of it? To save their skins? Well, that is fair, too. But let them call a spade a spade, and say just that. And that they are willing to sacrifice the dream of Western society to prevent gratuitous international aggression at all costs.

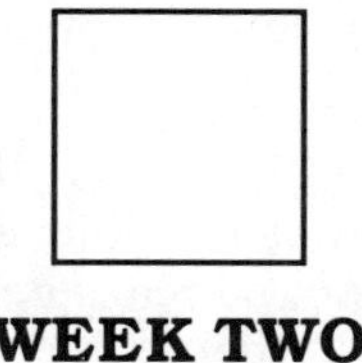

WEEK TWO

Saturday night, the 22:00 news program was interrupted just after the announcer said, "This is the news." A siren replaced his voice, and this was soon followed by a siren heard outside of our house.

We rush into the sealed, gas-proof room, but our movements now seem more practiced. Is it getting to be second nature? Putting on the gas masks, sealing the door, helping one another. And then there are a few numbers to call, friends who asked, saying that they have difficulty hearing the siren. I sound very strange to myself, talking on the phone through a gas mask. The filter keeps banging against the speaker; I have to remember that I cannot bring my mouth close to the speaker.

We are now only five, including our guests from Tel Aviv, who will sleep over Saturday night before returning to their embattled city. The radio keeps reassuring us, giving instructions, very little information, other than telling us that this is a real attack. We are more tense than we should be; there is evidence of a cumulative effect. The night of the first attack—my God, was it only last Thursday night? It seems as if so much more time than that has passed—my wife and I were alone in the sealed room and, wearing our gas masks, we played Boggle, a word game. That now seems so remote, reflecting another degree of calmness, no longer available to us. That was before we saw the pictures of the wounded, of the destruction.

■ We did not have a television in our sealed room; I found the television unsatisfactory. News breaks appeared to come more frequently and earlier on radio than on television. And then there was the period of waiting, when no news was available, a period of tension. Listening to irrelevant songs on the radio was clearly less annoying than watching some singer doing the same in a film clip.

All broadcasting was interrupted by the notices of the alarm; news announcers or Nahman Shai—on television his photo was shown—would speak, and between announcements there were popular songs. One radio station was dedicated to translations of the announcements into a series of foreign languages. The only television broadcast that resumed without break following an alarm was the broadcast of the Macabbi-Split European Cup basketball game from Yugoslavia, which continued after the all-clear as if nothing had happened.

After we were organized in the sealed room, there was little movement. People sat and waited. Occasional comments, sometimes phone calls were made. The telephone lines were overburdened, and older relay stations suffered burnouts. The radio was the center of attraction; both eyes and ears were focused on it. At times ■ we would steal glances at one another, say an encouraging word.

At 22:17, the southern part of the country, including us, in Jerusalem, is freed from the alert. We take off our masks and reassure one another. We are told a Scud was fired at Riyadh and successfully downed by Patriots. And then, before we leave the sealed room, at 22:20, another siren is sounded on the radio, the sound of an attack, not the expected all-clear. The announcer tells us that this is indeed a second attack and that we are all to return to our sealed rooms, to wear masks. This is the first double attack, a one-two punch as it were. Damn it! Why don't they give us more information? This double attack is surely a new tactic. Is it meant to stretch us beyond the limits of our nerve? The radio tells us about Saudi Arabia but not about what is going on here. I start looking at my watch; I am now convinced that we always have five to seven minutes between the warning and the actual missile strike. I have been careful to note the times when these have been given.

At 22:28, confirming my estimate, the southern part of the country is again freed from masks. Now they are checking to see if the attack was conventional or chemical or biological. Biological too? At 22:37, the eastern and far northern regions of the country are told that it is all right to remove their masks; at 22:42, the entire country is told to remove their masks. Only inhabitants of Tel Aviv and Haifa have to remain in their sealed rooms. At 22:46, an all-clear siren is sounded for the entire country. Later, we hear that all missiles were hit and downed by Patriots. (Other sources speak of another missile that landed without exploding, the second dud.) Four missiles, aimed at Haifa and Tel Aviv again, the regions of greatest population concentration, all four downed. We are told that we cannot expect 100 percent protection from Scud hits but that Patriot performance has been improved greatly. Yes, we can see that. Amen.

■ We are the first generation to face high-tech warfare: the war of smart bombs and even smarter missiles and antimissile missiles, heat-guided and laser-guided weapons, missiles that can be launched from distances of hundreds of kilometers and pinpoint individual buildings as targets. We were therefore in a war where distance was no longer relevant, where the cities were just as much the battlefront as were the lines between armies.

The debate about the importance of safe borders has not been solved by the knowledge that damage can be accomplished with great accuracy from long distances. Those who would give up the strategic depth of the Administered Territories in return for peace are more convinced than ever that they are right. Those who insist that a Palestinian state ten kilometers (six miles) from Tel Aviv is intolerable also remain convinced; they argue that these long-distance threats, as terrible as they are, do not threaten the existence of the state.

Israel has known only war and more war in its short existence. During World War II, Italian bombers hit Tel Aviv. Egyptian bombers struck the city again in the War of Independence in 1948. In both cases the attacks were frightening and damage was done, including loss of lives. But the total effect was minor. We do not have that sense of assurance in this war: not with poison gas, bacteriological, and even nuclear warfare as real possibilities.

Most of Israel's wars and battles were fought far from the cities. The small city of Tzfat (Saphed) was the scene of a major battle in the War of Independence. Actions took place in that war in Acco (Acre), Haifa, Jaffa, and Jerusalem. But that was the last time. The cities were not involved in the Sinai Campaign of 1956, the Six Day War of

1967, the War of Attrition in the early 1970s, or the Yom Kippur (October) War of 1973. It has been part of the Israeli Army's strategy to bring the war—as far as possible—into the territory of the attacking countries.

I was in charge of the medical section of a rescue battalion in Jerusalem in that last war (1973); I think we were quite good and would have worked well in dealing with fire, rescue operations from wrecked buildings, and medical emergency treatment. We had only the most rudimentary training in chemical warfare and none at all in bacteriological warfare. Our services were not called on. Israeli rescue teams operated in Armenia following the earthquake there a year ago; this experience was probably useful in the current rescue operations.

World War II was not a high-tech war. There were massive bombings with heavy losses to bombers on both sides. V-1 and V-2 rockets were used at the end of the European war against London; these were crude devices by modern standards, although they did produce death and property damage. The Korean, Vietnamese, and Afghanistan wars were also not high-tech wars, although the devices used did gain more sophistication with the passage of time. The atomic bombs that destroyed Hiroshima and Nagasaki and the fire bombs that destroyed Dresden were indeed horrible weapons of destruction but their delivery was carried out by primitive, vulnerable and inaccurate means. Although some use was made of strategic weapons in the battles for the Falkland Islands, Grenada, and Panama, these were not really wars and the use of the weapons was limited while resistance was nonexistent.

■ This is the first high-tech war. And the cities were declared targets.

We hear that there are no wounded this time and breathe a sigh of relief. Later we hear that for the first time missile fragments have fallen on Arab villages. I have mixed feelings about that, I admit. Haven't the Arabs invited Saddam Hussein to attack us? Are they not still supporting him? When the curfew, imposed on some of the more unruly towns, is relaxed for an hour to allow purchase of food and staples, the Arab youths climb to the roofs, scream "Allah Akbar!" and throw stones. In other villages this has never stopped; the TV crews are busy elsewhere these days, so we do not see it. A new feature, missed by the absent TV cameras, is that the masked Palestinians are now using gas masks; they use them both to hide their faces and to defeat the tear gas which has been used against them.

We hear about attacks on Arabs in the U.S., windows of Arab-owned businesses broken in San Francisco, and even fire-bombing of Arab-owned stores in Detroit; a bombing in Florida of an Indian family mistakenly thought to be Iraqi; a Palestinian man beaten brutally, requiring head surgery. The FBI has been investigating Arab Americans with an eye to reducing the chance of terrorist activities. What a strange world we live in, so subject to change, and yet so inflexible.

But then there are the Israeli Arabs, living in their villages in the northern part of the country, who have invited Jews living in the attacked cities to stay with them. Also Arabs, but ours, caught between their sympathy for the desire of their brothers for an independent Palestinian state and their loyalty to their country, Israel. In this time of danger, they have lined up with us. They can make differential judgments; so, too, for the most part, can we. Why is it so difficult for so many others?

"Are the missile attacks making a serious impact on me?" I ask. I think there is some change. A heightened sensitivity—which I admit was always there, in a milder form—to criticism, yes. Preoccupation with dying? Maybe.

Before the attacks began, my wife insisted on trimming my beard, an avocation of hers which has, I think, a sadistic element— as well as an artistic one. A number of people have commented that I trimmed my beard to get a better seal with the gas mask; large beards are a problem. Mine was never large, certainly not bushy, even before trimming. Now I resent what I see as an implied accusation of cowardice (even though I know that is not what is meant). I also do not want to be caught in a crowd now; the thought of a stampede in the event of an emergency has now become very unpleasant to me. I never loved crowds, but I have never been agoraphobic. I ask myself if I am cowardly. Last night I dreamed of dying, waking from a nightmare. I have never done that before. Preoccupation with dying must be common now.

Big numbers. In greater Tel Aviv 3,400 homes have been damaged. A very large number, indeed. Another number: 13,000 new immigrants thus far this month, from Russia, from Ethiopia. Immigrating into a war zone. They seem united in feeling it is better here, safer even, than in their countries of origin.

Today school began for all tenth- through twelfth-graders, except in the city of Ramat Gan, neighbor to Tel Aviv, where missile damage has been extensive. The mayor of Ramat Gan asked that school opening be delayed one day there to allow for handling of displaced families. All students will study in sealed, gas-proof rooms. They are to bring their anti-poison-gas kits and masks to school. Instructions for what to do if an alarm is sounded on the way to or from school are given. This is as close to normalcy as we can get now.

Our guests from Tel Aviv leave this morning; has it been easier for them here? They get into their car and drive back to the threatened city.

MONDAY, 28 JANUARY: HOPING FOR RAIN

It is bright and sunny today; no sign of rain. Not even a cloud can be seen in the brilliant blue sky of Jerusalem. There was no alarm last night. A relief and a let-down. Not a disappointment. No, not that, but there is the waiting, as if for the second shoe to fall. The waiting takes its toll, too. Irritability is up; this is obvious all over the country.

■ We are interested in rain for a number of reasons. We have had a drought and we need rain; this war will end and we will have to get back to our prewar lives. Without rain we will not export the wonderful fresh fruit, including all the tropical varieties we now grow. And the even more tasty and healthful vegetables depend on the rain. And our cattle need rain to graze. And our gardens—we deserve and need some beauty in this harsh and dry environment— demand rain as well. This arid region has suffered for millennia from lack of rain. Here water is as important as gold—but apparently not quite as important as oil. Saudi Arabia planned on having a fleet of ships tow an iceberg to its shores as a source of water.

Rain dissipates poison gases. Little wonder, then, that we pray for rain with greater fervor these days. The launching of missiles is impeded by rain; the Scud must be fueled with five tons of liquid propellant once it is at the launch site and only after it has been aimed. This takes time and is far more difficult in the rain. We counted on this added difficulty in launching the missiles in the rain.

Later we learned that these calculations were more than offset by the camouflage that rain provided. The rain shielded the launchers from coalition air strikes; in fact, many launchings were made in the rain. But even in that case the rain protected us against our ■ greatest dread, the possibility of being gassed.

We watch the first half of the Super Bowl game, not really paying attention. Why do they keep talking about the Patriots? No, this has nothing to do with our war; I gather it is the New England Patriots, a once-great football team that has fallen on hard days, winning only one out of seventeen games. I hope our Patriots, courtesy of the U.S. government, do better.

■   The American generals who briefed the reporters in Arlington and in Saudi Arabia spoke of the war in terms of American football. But this game is hardly known here; they have only recently tried to explain it, to show how it works, what constitutes a good play. To Israelis, the very word *football* means soccer, the national sport of our country and of most European and many Asian countries. Professional soccer is new to the United States; American football is even newer for us. But to understand strategy in the war, we had to learn the game. That was how the war was explained, by former players, by fans.
■   Football is war, war is football—only a bit more dangerous.

Why have we not had a daytime attack? This is a question that disturbs many of us. So many more people, those who live in the suburbs and those who have fled to avoid the nighttime terror, come into the large cities, Tel Aviv and Haifa, each morning to work. We are so much more vulnerable in the daytime. It is now clear—beyond any doubt at all—that Saddam Hussein's missiles are directed not at military targets but at civilian population centers, both here in Israel and in Riyadh as well. Presumably, the major reason for not sending missiles at us in the daytime is fear of exposing the missile launchers to the coalition air force. But there is an unpredictable element in Saddam Hussein that appears to be a major part of his make-up and makes him a continuous threat to us. We still are not sure that he will not attack during the daytime. Just as we are still not sure that he will not use chemical weapons against us.

So we continue to carry our gas masks, or the whole kit, wherever we go.

■   It became quite a fad to decorate the kits. It probably began in the improvised kindergartens that sprang up and spread so quickly. Certainly the first decorated one I saw (on February 3) belonged to my five-year-old grandson. But the rectangular boxes and the black plastic shoulder straps seemed to invite creative enterprise. Some of the more striking creations included animal boxes with four legs and a tail, imitations of the ice-cream containers carried by young vendors
■   on the beaches, automobiles with wheels, and movie cameras.

The civil defense people announced that appreciable numbers of anti-poison-gas kits are being left in buses and other public places, mostly by young people. They request that we write our names on the kits, and addresses as well.

Striking TV clips now include a hospital obstetrics unit where four women in active labor are seen wearing gas masks during the last attack. So do the doctors and nurses. One of the women in labor is interviewed. It is possible to wear the masks during labor. We learn all the time. The potential mother says that she prefers to wear the mask, that she feels safer in the mask.

One of the regions hit is—in normal times—a well-known staging area for automobile-centered prostitution. One friend asks if the prostitutes are still at work. And if they now do it in gas masks?

Although the tenth- and twelfth-graders are back in school, the great majority of schoolgoers are still out. Local, small kindergartens have sprung up to deal with the youngest group and to free parents for other activities. (A court ruled that both parents could not be excused from work to care for children. The family had to choose: either the mother or the father could stay home.) For the intermediate grades, parents and teachers are organizing one-room school houses, with teachers preparing written assignments. University students are now in their preexamination period. Many report difficulties in concentration.

I heard the chief of staff of the army interviewed on TV. Aluf (General) Dan Shomron left a very strange impression on me. He spoke of a public opinion poll showing that 90 percent of the public here in Israel approved of the policy of restraint. I wondered what a general was doing with popularity polls and why he would be interested in them. I would have thought that popularity polls were the business of politicians, not of the army. If he felt that the best strategy for the defense of the country was something other than restraint, would he be inhibited from recommending that strategy to the government because of the unpopularity of his strategy? Have we all become media people? Is there not something unreal in all this?

■   Have you noticed how generals have changed? The very idea of General Shomron appearing on television to make a speech is strange. He speaks softly and intelligently; he is interested in persuading. I do not recall generals being concerned about persuasion. Certainly not the generals of World War II, not the Eisenhowers or the Montgomerys or even the Marshalls. Hitler, yes. Mussolini, yes. And now Saddam Hussein and King Hussein. But these were generals in name only; they were not professional soldiers. Nasser, Sadat, Mubarak, Qaddafi—even those who began as professional soldiers—became molders of public opinion only as heads of state.

Even more striking are the American generals, the Schwarzkopfs and the Kellys. These are a new breed, technocrats trained in technology as much as in warfare, in communication techniques as much as in strategy.

In this country, generals have already become the politicians of the future. They retire in their mid-forties and enter politics and even the cabinet (e.g., Raful Eitan in the present cabinet) or become prime minister (Yitzhak Rabin, a former commander-in-chief of the army). It is not surprising: they are exposed to public view, and the most successful are clearly good planners and executors.

The United States has had its share of generals who became presidents in the past: Washington, Jackson, Taylor, Grant. The impressive generals of this war may get there yet. If so, they will be a different brand of president. An improvement, I hope.

The inevitability of retaliation grows and grows stronger each day; the blood so casually drawn will be avenged. And the callous perpetrators will be punished. Is it really true that the U.S. will not give our planes their identification codes? Won't this cause them trouble as well? Aren't they interested in avoiding the disaster of a possible clash between Israeli and coalition planes? I understand that these codes can be installed in flight; I imagine that they would be transferred at the last moment, if not before. What can we do? Well, one thing we can do is a better job of bombing the missile launchers in western Iraq, in their staging areas, H2 and H3. How? Coalition bombing is done from great altitude, to avoid antiaircraft barrages. Even though their accuracy is good, even excellent, it can never compare to what can be achieved by low-level bombing. We are less sensitive than the U.S. and other members of the coalition to the possibility of loss, particularly when the threat is real—as it is now—and when the potential gains are great. We are ready to engage in low-level bombing and do things the coalition is not willing to risk. That is one possibility.

MONDAY, 28 JANUARY: AN AFTERTHOUGHT

Jordan remains a problem. I listen to the news from Jordan as we receive their two channels clearly in Jerusalem. I also see the reports from Jordan broadcast by various foreign TV sources. The Jordanians—not just the people in the street but even the intellectuals—believe that the Persian Gulf conflict is a war between Israel and Iraq with the U.S. and their allies fighting for Israel. This kind of distortion of fact is standard for the area, and it is not new to me at all. But in the present circumstances I am afraid that Jordan may be tempted to jump into what they see as a war between Islam and Israel. They would attack us. I am sure we could defeat them, even handily. But it is so unnecessary, so perverse—and will cost lives.

I had not paid any attention to the absence of weather reports. My son pointed this fact out to me, explaining that we did not want to give away valuable information to the enemy, in this case Iraq. My experience with our weather forecasting, and it is not mine alone, is that it is totally unreliable. Even believing the opposite of what is said doesn't work. Someone showed that a better record of prediction of tomorrow's weather than that of the meteorological service is obtained by assuming that tomorrow's weather will be no different from today's. With a record like that, it would seem to me that releasing the weather reports would be a valuable source of disinformation, if the Iraqis were stupid enough to believe the reports. We have given up taking them seriously a long time ago.

Another no-no is mentioning the landing places of the Scud missiles. Supposedly this information would allow the Iraqis to correct their firing and make more accurate hits. All this assumes that there is some way to increase the accuracy of the Scud, which is not too good; the missile has low-tech specifications and a very low reproducibility in targeting, at best one thousand yards. Most of the firings can clearly be seen not to be related to any strategic targets, even by the most wild extrapolation. They want to hit the centers of population concentration; at times they have succeeded, at other times they were way off the mark, missing both strategic targets and population concentrations. And all this was before the Patriots entered the picture, cutting down the Scud effectiveness and success rate greatly. But the strangest part of all is that the TV coverage is clear enough to identify the neighborhoods clearly in most cases. Any self-respecting spy should be—I would think—able to do it. Certainly Israelis abroad identify the hit areas without difficulty; many tell me in their letters. So we are secretive.

Perhaps it is a game. The first person abroad to identify the exact streets hit wins a prize, a fragment of a missile.

On the other hand, this information may be useful to the Iraqis, not so much for correcting their sightings but to evaluate the overall effectiveness of their planning. One correspondent reminds me that during World War II, the Germans used to launch their V-1 rockets during the BBC live concerts so that they could listen to the impacts of their bombs. The location of the BBC studio in London being known, this information could have been useful to assess accuracy.

The same correspondent asks, "But what about other means of communication, and I am particularly thinking about E-mail or electronic bulletin boards? Are they monitored? Is it possible to monitor them (the volume of data being huge)? Are the authorities aware of them?" I am not sure if anybody in the censoring business here is aware of what I and probably many others like me are doing, but they certainly do not seem to be doing anything about it. Perhaps, short of cutting off all these lines, there is nothing that can be done because of the volume, if for no other reason. I myself, despite trying to be careful not to give away information, have been taken to task now and then for "leaking" valuable information.

The foreign TV people are frequently less scrupulous; their concern for human life—which may indeed be on the line as the consequence of broadcasting some information—appears to be less important than getting the desired scoop. A particularly crude example was the "humorous" effort of the local CNN correspondent, Robert Roth, who, in the immediate aftermath of an attack, reported live, "I do not know whether I am allowed to say this. Am I allowed to report that this is a residential neighborhood? I guess I am allowed to report it." (Why are these jokers always Jewish? I ask).

CNN's Peter Arnett, reporting the bombings of Baghdad, has made another, less well known contribution to reporting in general, and to Israel in particular. His Significant Other, left behind, is now broadcasting the news on local TV in English here; her fresh face and pleasant voice are indeed a contribution.

TUESDAY, 29 JANUARY: ARE WE SAFE AFTER AN ATTACK?

Last night, while watching the main news summary of the day on TV (is this repeated timing to be understood as a critical comment on the news broadcasts?), we had, at 21:08, another alarm, with both the screen showing the now familiar medallion bearing the warning in multiple languages and a siren outside. We hurried to the hopefully—we still have not tested its efficacy—gas-proof room, put on our masks, seal the door, turn on the battery-powered transistor radio. The announcer tells us that all Israel is required to go to the sealed rooms, put on gas masks and listen to the radio. At 21:16, Nahman (pronounced "Nachman") Shai, the army spokesman, tells us that we have been fired on, but that the south (not Faful Eiincluding Jerusalem) and the north (not iincluding Haifa and Acre) are now free to remove their masks and leave the sealed rooms. At 21:20 we hear Shai tell us that Jerusalem, Haifa, and Acre are no longer in danger.

Hungry for news, I turn on my terminal, now in the sealed room and, with my modem operating, I connect up to my computer and turn on IRC, a protocol which connects me to the Internet Relay Network, where I can always find one hundred to two hundred more computer freaks from places as far away as Korea, Japan, Australia, Europe, and the States, chatting or waiting for someone to "talk" to them on-line. I quickly ask for a list of current Israeli users and locate one in Ramat Gan (greater Tel Aviv, the object of at least two attacks, with eleven buildings completely destroyed and sixteen hundred apartments damaged) and Haifa and ask each if anything has happened. Nati, from Haifa, writes to me that he has heard a soft boom and that there was some brief disturbance in TV and radio reception there. Ely, from Ramat Gan, says that all is quiet in Ramat Gan.

■ Throughout the war, news interpreters with various backgrounds—reporting, military, diplomatic—flooded the ether. Lack of information never appeared to impede these interpreters. Even worse, they never admitted that yesterday's speculation was wrong; they continued with today's speculation as if all were acceptable in this best of all possible worlds of television interpretation. The Panglossian view that allowed these journalists to report without feeling any responsibility for their words indicates that we are dealing not with what I understand to be reporting, but with entertainment.

Quite a different picture was provided by the generals who briefed reporters in Saudi Arabia and Arlington, particularly Schwarzkopf and Kelly. Schwarzkopf, allegedly a lover of ballet and opera with an

IQ of 180, blunt and bearlike, spoke with an authority that came with complete knowledge of the situation and allowed only information that he wanted to be released. His control was complete, his secrecy obvious, but he did not produce resentment in the listener. We appreciated him as a reliable source who would not lead us astray but was forced, for the safety of his mission and the troops under his command, to withhold some information. His authority was unimpeachable, as was the sense of intelligence and control that he radiated. General Kelly at the Pentagon was a different matter. Avuncular and benign in appearance, he led the reporters—schoolchildren at his feet, assiduously taking notes—down the garden path at will. He is one of the great foxes of our time, telling what he wanted told, promising to bring back information but also not hesitating to say that he would not respond to certain questions. Watching Kelly in action, one had the sense of true professionalism. Had he studied communication techniques? He could certainly teach the subject.

Two former chiefs of staff of the Israeli Army, Raful Eitan and Motta Gur, both now members of the Knesset but on different sides of the political spectrum, were exceptional. They both said that Iraq's army was a paper tiger and would not put up a good fight against trained, equipped troops. Those who interviewed them as well as those who watched these interviews did not want to hear that. Eitan and Gur were not invited again as experts, and their testimony—accurate in the end—was ignored.

Not only were the newsmen at the mercy of those who briefed them, but they were clearly constrained by, even the prisoners of, the producers of the news "shows," who selected for viewing those portions of the reports that coincided with their own programmatic interests. Reporters can easily get the message, "Give me what I want and I will show your footage; don't give me what I want and you will not be exposed to the viewers." These are performers; can you imagine how performers would react to such a message?

What do I want from reporters? First of all, I want to know the constraints in their reporting. I would like to know what they are not allowed to show. It is not enough to tell me that they are showing damage to civilian facilities unless they also tell that they are not allowed to view, let alone show, damage to adjacent military targets.

In the case of interpreters, I want to know what their batting averages are; they should be posted in the corner of the screen while they are speculating. I would like them to assess the likelihood of their speculation. I would not object to reasonable explanations for their failures; they would help me understand what is going on.

At 21:39, inhabitants of greater Tel Aviv are instructed to remove their gas masks but to remain in their rooms. Seconds later a general all-clear is announced. At 22:02, we hear that the attack consisted only of conventional weapons. Much later, we are told that the single missile fired at us landed; no Patriots were fired, it seems. Why? Because the missile descended too far from the coast, where the Patriots are, landing very close to the Green Line, the pre-1967 border separating Israel and Jordan and now separating Israel from the Administered Territories. The missile produced damage to property in Arab villages on both sides of the line; luckily, nobody was hurt.

A popular sport among the Arabs of the Administered Territories these past two weeks has been to stand on the roofs of their homes and cheer and wave, encouraging passing missiles headed toward the centers of Jewish settlement. I would suspect that this activity will now stop, with the Palestinian Arabs joining us in sealed rooms. When Saddam Hussein was interviewed before the war and questioned about the possibility of hitting Arabs if he were to attack Israel, he replied that he would not have time to sort out the pebbles among the dried lentils. We again see that he meant what he said. Now the Palestinian Arabs who have supported him so enthusiastically can also see that.

■　　Israeli Arabs are under great pressure, living in a situation where loyalty to one side—Israel, their country—means disloyalty to the other—the Palestinians, their brothers in origin and religion. These 700,000 Arabs—as distinct from the 1 million Palestinian Arabs occupying the Administered Territories—are citizens of Israel. Many resent having to prove their loyalty to the country over and over again. They resent the transfer policies advocated by the right-wing political parties. They also resent the conditions of their villages, which they feel are not as well treated as are Jewish ones. But some are not so loyal, as in the case of the group of Israeli Arabs uncovered during the war who were spying for Iraq.

Israeli Arabs feel a close identification with the Palestinian Arabs and helped supply them with food during the period of curfews imposed by the army in response to unrest in many Palestinian settlements during the war. This unrest expressed itself as dancing and cheering on the roofs of their houses during missile alerts, burning truck tires, placing stones on highways to block traffic, stoning cars—many driven by Israeli Arabs—bearing Israeli license plates, stoning army units, and generalized rioting.

Just as the Israeli Arabs are ambivalent about their loyalties, Jewish attitudes toward Israeli Arabs are split and often contradictory. Some Israelis look down on all Arabs; one of the correspondents reporting from Israel during the war spoke of his "tame

Arab." Those Jews originating in Arab countries—they were until the beginning of the Russian immigration a majority in the country—bear great distrust of and resentment to Arabs based on their experiences with them in their countries of origin.

Generalizing from isolated acts of disloyalty among Israeli Arabs has led to ideas such as transfer, the moving of all Arabs out of Israel. However, a chance for peace in the region has to be seen as an extension of the coexistence of Jews and Arabs in Israel since the founding of the country. Coexistence with tension, yes, but peaceful coexistence nonetheless.

A pattern to the attacks has emerged and we act—with reservations—as if these patterns are real and can be counted on. One pattern is that there are no attacks in the daytime; so we act more freely and with less care in the daytime. Another that is now clear is that there is only one attack each night. Even the one double attack that came was characterized by the firing of two groups of missiles separated by only twenty minutes, for our purposes not really different from a single attack. Why is the validity of this pattern of such importance? Because it relates to the problem of sleep that has become so prevalent; even the most hardened citizens of the Tel Aviv and Haifa areas report difficulties in sleeping. Not only does this sleep disorder reflect the relatively high level of anxiety prevalent, it also, at least partly, is related to a real fear of missing the alarm when it is sounded.

It has therefore become important to discuss this pattern, to see if others believe it. Can one trust it? Are we really safe after an attack? Will the Iraqis remember that they have had their one attack this night? These questions are now central to our thoughts, and the answers we adopt will help determine the success of our getting a good night's sleep, which seems so important to us now, or at least to getting even a fair night's sleep.

We are now given instructions on recognizing poison gas attacks from the symptoms produced. These are (1) generalized production of watery secretions on the skin or mucous membranes, tears; (2) strange movements or no movement at all; (3) difficulties with breathing.

Some of these symptoms are clearly symptoms that can be seen in hysteria or with severe anxiety. But it is better to be safe than smart at times like these. We are told that the medications available against poison gas work very well and that it is imperative to bring individuals stricken with any of these symptoms to a hospital immediately. We are reassured that stories of a new poison gas that penetrates gas masks is pure fiction; that the combination of a gas mask and a sealed room provides 100 percent protection.

■ We had seen the film clips of the destruction that Saddam Hussein had wrought on a Kurdish village in northern Iraq by dropping canisters of poison gas from airplanes. The Kurds wanted independence and were a thorn in Saddam Hussein's side; he put them out of action by showing what he was prepared to do to suppress revolt. He killed all five thousand citizens of the village with gas—men, women, and children. He also used poison gas in repelling Iranian attacks in the eight-year war with that country. Again we saw film clips of the horrible skin burns suffered by the Iranian soldiers who survived.

From Jonathan Pollard we learned that Iraq had factories producing poison gas in large quantities; we also learned from him where these were located. The U.S. Defense Department did not want to share this information with us; they felt that they could afford to violate a treaty that specified exchange of such information with us. After all, Israel had destroyed an Iraqi nuclear warfare plant in Ossirak in 1981; we might be tempted to destroy chemical warfare plants as well—and Iraq, fighting the enemy, Iran, was an ally. Pollard thought we should get the information. We got the information; Pollard was sentenced to life in prison.

We knew that our air force was superior to Iraq's; any attempt at bombing us would cost the Iraqis heavily. But could we stop every single airplane in a concerted attack? We did not have that assurance. We also knew that Saddam Hussein had long-range missiles that could reach Israel. Did he have the technology to fit a chemical warhead to one of these missiles? We did not know. We knew that Soviet, German, and French scientists were helping him develop that capability; the best that money could buy in technology was Iraq's aim, and its oil revenues bought the best that money could buy.

One gas attack in a major population center would produce death and injury beyond anything we were willing to tolerate, or even imagine. And this is without talking about the very bad associations that the term *poison gas* has for us as Jews.

We have faith in our army intelligence and in our scientists. We do not think they are idiots; we do not believe that they would bring this up to frighten us. We do not think that they are engaged in some cover-up plot, trying to conceal inefficiency or crimes. When they told us that it was their reasoned judgment that chemical attack was a real possibility, that the best protection was the sealed room and gas masks, that the damage that could be done by poison

gas outweighed that possible from conventional weapons—we believed them. And we followed their instructions.

Turkey has also been threatened by Saddam Hussein, and the threat of poison gas attacks is being taken very seriously in southern Turkey, which borders on Iraq, partly at least because of the largely Kurdistani population there. Kurds will not easily forget how a village of five thousand Kurds in northern Iraq was wiped out by Saddam Hussein's poison gas. Although gas masks are not available there, they have produced sealed, gas-proof rooms. The TV pictures are not reassuring; the suddenly very high price of plastic curtaining has forced families to use substitutes which cannot possibly be effective, such as blankets, to shield their windows and doors. Some depressing effects of this activity are also reported: families dying of suffocation after sealing the room but leaving an oven burning within.

My wife is an inveterate and indefatigable matchmaker; for her, the sight of an unmarried man—marriage is still the most common mode here—is like a red flag to a bull. Well, there is a certain young man, bright and sensitive and—above all—unmarried. She has finally found the perfect girl for him, bright and good looking. And they both agreed to meet. So far so good.

My wife finally got a report on the meeting; they were sitting in a popular Jerusalem cafe, having onion soup, when the alarm went off. They spent the next hour huddled against the wall in the cafe's sealed room, together with the other customers and the employees of the cafe, including some Arabs working in the kitchen. A new form of social activity.

Oh? What happened? They seem to like one another. (I later received E-mail letters asking that my wife act as a matchmaker for cousins and friends.)

Brigadier General Nahman Shai, the new army spokesman, is now a national hero, the subject of long reports in all of the papers last Friday—the weekend here; there are no newspapers on Saturday. He came to our general attention on that memorable Thursday night of the first attack, almost two weeks ago. The initial radio instructions were characterized by lack of clarity, a slight sense of panic, and no sense of authority and knowledge—until Shai came on the air. His soft voice registered concern and knowledge, and that impression has persisted.

The news reporters have improved immensely, are now models of calm and clarity, but the whole country waits for our Nahman. When he tells us not to force masks on children if they are panicky, he speaks of his own five-year-old.

Usually, at least in the early stages of an alarm, he offers no hard information other than telling us it is a real attack and not a false alarm—there have been any number of these, usually local and reflecting both nervous and inept fingers as well as technical problems—and that we are to enter the sealed rooms and don our masks. But we know that the information that he will eventually give us will be accurate—if sparse—and meanwhile all Israel continues to love Nahman.

A thin, bespectacled, young man—younger looking than his forty-four years—in an army uniform, he speaks with a soft voice that radiates certainty—or certainty to come—and confidence. He bears some superficial resemblance to Pete Williams, the Pentagon spokesman, but makes a much softer impression; he is both less incisive and less quick in his responses. Nonetheless, Nahman Shai continues to radiate believability and remains our hero, at least for the time being.

In response to my questioning Aluf (General) Shomron's appearance on TV to publicly announce a 90 percent level of support for the policy of restraint, one of my readers reasonably points out that he might have been saying something like "We are doing what we have to do, and thank you (or at least most of you) for agreeing."

I stand corrected; but it would have been better—if that was his intention—that he had said it explicitly.

WEDNESDAY, T'U BI-SHEVAT, 30 JANUARY: AFTER THE WAR

We had no alarm last night; at 3:00 A.M. I finally—in a state of exhaustion—went to sleep; I slept three hours. Waiting for the siren.

■ The tension produced insomnia; insomnia lowered my threshold to disturbance and thus increased my sensitivity to tension—a truly vicious cycle that ate away at my nerves. Which was more important? To be calm so as to be able to sleep? Or to be able to sleep ■ so as to have my wits about me, to be in control?

Waiting for the other shoe to drop, waiting for the Scuds to reach us from Iraq, has become a national sport. You finally get to sleep at some hour early in the morning, with the second army radio channel, the one that is silent at night *unless* there is an alarm, set at high volume, so that you will not miss the siren. At 6:00 A.M., the radio starts blaring the regular morning broadcast and you are shocked into the semiawake state that will last all day. These are not, however, normal times and 6:00 A.M. is just too early.

■   The silent radio station became an important issue. We worried that we would not find it since it was silent. What if we mistuned the station? If we tuned the radio to the silent station early enough, when it was still broadcasting, we effectively put that radio out of action until an alarm sounded. Sometimes I felt that the silent station produced more problems than it solved.

Religious debate arose over which was a worse violation of the prohibition against work on the Sabbath: continuing to broadcast throughout the Sabbath or going from inactive silence to an active alarm. One famous rabbi, a neighbor of mine, a saintly looking man who looks much older than his seventy years, favored leaving the radio tuned to a station that broadcast continuously since turning on the alarm on the silent station constituted a new activity, new work. The chief Sephardic rabbi agreed, but visited the radio station, asked many questions of the technicians, and reversed his decision.

I suddenly realized that I had not taken the possibility of a power failure into account. I had plugged the silent radio into the house current. Surely I should have used the battery-powered radio.

After we began to stock our sealed rooms, batteries became hot sellers. Batteries for the prescribed flashlights, batteries for the battery-powered radio, batteries in case of power failure.

Some of the gas masks, especially models for children and bearded men, used active filters powered by batteries. Although the government promised to replace these in time, there was a rush on these unusual and rare lithium cells. The government indeed replaced the batteries, starting in Tel Aviv, whose inhabitants had spent the
■ most time in gas masks, and going on to Haifa, next in use time.

Today is T'u bi-shevat, the New Year for trees; we used to plant trees today. We also have parties where we drink white and red wines and eat dried fruit. Usually; not this year. Our minds and hearts are elsewhere. These are not normal times.

Someone writes to suggest a fitting "punishment" for those strange Jews—Edward Alexander calls them "Arafat's Jews"—who are so active in movements that oppose every action of Israel, those who are sure that Israel is so intrinsically bad that any action, even seemingly good, of Israel's must be condemned. These same perverse Jews seem also to be convinced that any action of the PLO, even the most heinous, should be excused because of the suffering the Palestinian Arabs have undergone (even that which is not our fault at all). The "punishment" is to plant a tree in Israel in their name and to mail them a certificate of the "gift." A truly mild punishment, so gentle, perhaps much too gentle. He only regrets, he continues, that he would not be able to see their faces when they read the certificates.

■   It is painful to realize that some Jews subscribe to the calumny widespread among anti-Semites and held by most Arabs that Israel's existence is itself an act of aggression. These Jews are proud to be among the leaders of the movement to disestablish Israel; everything that Israel does and stands for they see and report only in the most pejorative terms.

Since establishment of a Palestinian state is the most realistic approach to destruction of Israel, these haters of Israel are in the forefront of those who support the PLO, the self-designated sole representative of all Palestinians. There are PLO support groups made up exclusively of Jews, with attractive names such as the Jewish Peace Lobby, the Jewish Committee on the Middle East, and the New Jewish Agenda. The PLO has pledged—and never refuted, rejected, or modified that pledge—to destroy Israel. Their Jewish supporters cannot find fault with any action of the PLO, not even murder of innocent civilians, not even murder without trial of their fellow Palestinians who do not agree that the PLO is the only organization representing Palestinians.

We understand the Palestinians, who are frustrated by losing their chance for a state in 1948, when they rejected the state offered them by the United Nations. Encouraged by their Arab neighbors who promised to destroy Israel, they gambled on an all-or-nothing solution—all of Palestine or none of it. Palestine, instead of being divided among the Israelis and Palestinians as originally planned, was divided among Israel, Jordan, and Egypt. The Arab countries did nothing to compensate the Palestinians for their failure; most were placed in primitive refugee camps without opportunity for work and without the possibility of citizenship.

The motivations of Jews who support the PLO so enthusiastically are clear; they want to see an end to Israel. But why Israel should be such a bone in their throats is not at all clear, except in rare cases. I know of anti-Israel Jews who have offered their services to Israel at some time in the past and interpret what they see as a lack of enthusiasm on our part as rejection. It is beyond the scope of this discussion to list the activities of these people; a detailed study of a number of them appears in Edward Alexander's book *Arafat's Jews* (1992).

It is not surprising that these Jews were leaders in promulgating Saddam Hussein's idea of "linkage," in claiming that Kuwait had provoked Iraq into invading, in suggesting that Kuwait's disappearance would not be a loss to the world. If ravaged Kuwait was expendable, what fate did they have in mind for Israel, the true "cause" of all the trouble, according to them?

In their distorted view, all problems in the Middle East can be traced to the existence of Israel. Just as there would not have been a problem between Iraq and Kuwait without Israel's "poisonous" presence, all problems in the Middle East can be traced back to the destabilizing influence of Israel. They would have us believe that without Israel there would be no Christian-Muslim conflict in Lebanon, no problem with Kurdish ambitions for independence, no temporary resolution of that problem by Saddam Hussein's gassing of the Kurds, no slaughter of Arabs by Arabs in Syria, Jordan, or Saudi Arabia.

In their zeal to justify all actions of anti-Israeli Arabs, they wrote that Saddam Hussein's attacks on Tel Aviv and Haifa were not attempts to hit Jewish population centers but attacks on military installations—actually military complexes established by the British during their control of the country—deliberately placed by Israelis in the heart of these cities. (It is interesting how they took Saddam Hussein's use of hostages to protect military targets and turned it into Israeli use of civilians to protect military targets.)

I am pleased to note that a majority of Jewish pro-PLO Israelis responded to the Scud attacks with revulsion against Saddam Hussein and his actions and cold withdrawal from positions of support for the PLO, now an obvious ally of Saddam Hussein. It was clear to them, unlike their American counterparts, that the proposed Palestinian state that they had advocated so strongly would have placed Iraqi artillery, and its poison gas, less than ten miles from Tel Aviv.

I recall the wanton destruction by fire of eight thousand trees in the Carmel forest last year. I presume the Arabs who lit the fire considered the trees to be Jewish trees.

The flight of one hundred of the best Iraqi aircraft to Iran is particularly disturbing. These aircraft will be spared the bombings of the coalition and this frightens us, now that we know that we are indeed high on the Iraqi agenda; that more Scuds—by one—have been fired at us than at Saudi Arabia, where the coalition forces are mainly based. The obvious collusion of Iran in this flight for preservation of the Iraqi aircraft adds another element of uncertainty. We speculate on the meaning of this flight; none of the scenarios is encouraging from the Israeli point of view.

The coalition views the picture differently; from their point of view, the straightforward, pragmatic conclusion is operative: these planes have been removed from the war scene, guaranteeing coalition air supremacy. This difference in viewpoint indicates that Israel and the coalition may have very different goals in the present conflict and raises the issue of what, exactly, are the minimal goals for the coalition. Since Israel is neutral, except in the eyes of Saddam Hussein and his supporters, both in Iraq and elsewhere, it is not strange that our goals should be somewhat different from those of the U.S. and its coalition partners in this conflict.

There is little doubt that the death of Saddam Hussein, the destruction of the Iraqi military machine, and even stripping the ruling minority party, the Ba'ath Party, of power would please President Bush, and perhaps his partners as well, even Arabs—President Mubarak of Egypt, for one. But these do not appear to be goals that must be obtained in order to satisfy the coalition, always worried about the ephemeral nature of home support for so distant a war, particularly if the price in casualties is too high and if the war continues beyond the brief attention span that characterizes mass opinion. The added burden in real cost must also be taken into account; Britain, already burdened by a recession, is now anxiously debating the cost of the war and where the money to pay for it will come from.

What, then, are the minimal goals that the U.S. and its coalition powers accept? There is good reason to believe that if necessary—read: in case of wavering home support—Iraqi withdrawal from Kuwait and paying some sort of fine will be sufficient. It is clear that the damage to the country's resources, supply lines, heavy equipment, and armament will prevent Iraq from entering into another similar adventure for some reasonably long time. This worst-case goal, however, cannot be acceptable to Israel, which of course has no say in the matter.

Israel's goal—of necessity—includes destruction of both Iraq's long-range missiles and their launchers and the air force, the sources of Iraq's capability of attacking Israel. In addition, Israel cannot rest until Saddam Hussein is eliminated; we remember too well the reemergence of Nasser after his dramatic resignation speech in the aftermath of Egypt's defeat by Israel in the Six Day War.

The scenario that sends chills down our spines is one that begins after the war, with Saddam Hussein and his air force—more than seven hundred planes—intact. A call by a postwar Iraq, with Saddam Hussein at its head, for a holy war of all Muslim nations, including Iran—a long-time leader in the Islamic campaign to destroy Israel—as well as the Arab states in the region, led by Syria and financed by Saudi Arabia and the oil-rich Emirates, is a reasonable possibility. The blow to Arab pride that will follow any suit for peace by Saddam Hussein, even with Arabic nations represented in the coalition, is predictable; Muslim right-wing elements, in Iran and even among the Arab nations in the coalition, continue to undermine cooperation with the Western powers in the fight against Iraq. Syrian, Jordanian, and Lebanese newspapers do not hesitate to suggest that the war is really between Israel and Islam, with America and its partners fighting for Israel.

A combined Arab air assault on Israel, with the participation of an almost intact Iraqi air force, may or may not be repulsed by Israel; but there is little reason to doubt that the cost in lives and property damage will provide—even in the best case—cause for Jewish tears for generations to come. Coalition forces will probably be far from the scene by that time; even if not, why would they interfere?

Are these nightmares unwarranted?

Can we rely on Israel's new popularity to galvanize worldwide support to prevent such an attack by the Muslim air forces?

As a Jew, and as an Israeli, I am suspicious of our newly gained popularity. As pleasant as it is to be the sudden recipient of such welcome warmth and approval—after so long a time in the cold, after so much disapproval—from the nations of the world, something is wrong. In view of our recent history all the expressions of admiration for our restraint do not quite ring true.

Even the Pope himself has joined in the chorus of praise, although his court, the Vatican, still does not recognize Israel's existence.

Why is our popularity dependent on our suffering loss? Is this the requirement for winning the approval of other nations? Or are other nations judged by different rules, by their actions and inactions alone? When the Israeli Air force attacked and destroyed Tamuz, the Iraqi nuclear reactor at Ossirak—the French nuclear engineers now freely admit that it was built for military purposes alone—we were condemned by all. Were we better off, some ask, with the disfavor of the world weighing heavily on us, with confidence in our being in the right and our ability to defend ourselves? Better off than today, with our dead, our wounded, our homeless, with the status of an obedient client state and the favor of the world?

Is our blood, we ask in Israel, worth the favor of the world? And how ephemeral is this favor? Will it continue when we stop bleeding? Will it continue if we finally act to defend ourselves?

And even if we behave, bleed silently, show restraint, we ask, how long will the favor we have found last? The very same politicians and governments that praise us so fulsomely now were those that condemned us, placed economic sanctions on us, when was it?

Why, only yesterday. Why are we to trust them now?

■ The end of the war with Saddam Hussein alive, in power but most of his military machine destroyed, has not yet been digested here. It is a good end for us, but clearly not the best end we might have imagined. We want to forget the Scuds, get back to our lives, our work, our interests. But we will have to face the future.

We have moved to the top of the agenda. The world, and the U.S. State Department with it, is tired of the Israeli-Palestinian conflict; they insist on resolution of the problem. The PLO has lost some of its almost universal support as a result of Arafat's and his chieftains' outspoken support of Saddam Hussein. As I predicted, Kuwait has renounced any possibility of normalizing relations with us that their representatives hinted at during the war. Israel will not deal with the PLO, and it is unlikely that any Arab nation will sit down and negotiate a cessation of hostilities, let alone peace, with us. Recent events, including so-called Peace Conferences in Madrid and Washington, have not been encouraging. After the initial excitement—the representatives of the Arab states and the Palestinians had actually met the Israelis, shook hands, and survived—a deafening silence was heard. Now there is even less hope. I suspect that any solution in the Middle East will be patchwork at best. Another war is not out of the question. I hope that it will come later
■ rather than sooner.

Today, in a rush to appease the Arab nations, to prevent premature dissolution of the coalition, just as our restraint is meant to do, the U.S. and Russia announced—without consulting us—that they will lead a conference to settle the Middle East problems immediately after the successful resolution of the Persian Gulf crisis. What do they mean by this? I do not know. But the Muslim states in this region will understand it as a promise to create a Palestinian state, all our objections notwithstanding. And they will not allow any other interpretation.

Did our restraint earn us the right to consultation before making so untimely—for us—a decision and announcement? No, not even that.

No linkage, we were promised. The Iraqi conquest of Kuwait is not linked to the Palestinian problem, we were told. Has Saddam Hussein already won one victory, so early in the war?

So to what end do we toil? The PLO, despite its commitment to and support of Saddam Hussein, is to be punished by having its dream realized. And Israel, after behaving "well," showing restraint, absorbing loss to life and property quietly, will be rewarded by being forced to swallow the poison we fear most. Is there any question that we have a right to be skeptical?

Moreover, the position we find ourselves in, characterized by complete dependence on the U.S.—only some of the military information obtained by satellites shared, refusal to give Israel aircraft identification codes to prevent clashes with coalition aircraft—and restraint where we would usually punish attacks on us, is both unnatural and perhaps dangerous as well. We have invested heavily over the years, since the founding of our state, in the development and strengthening of our ability to defend ourselves. Our environment is hostile; all the surrounding nations—both those in the coalition and those opposed to it—have signed a compact to root us out of the Middle East, to destroy us.

It appears that our good behavior has brought us one step closer to realization of the Arab/Muslim goal to rid themselves of us.

This is too heavy a price; we will not remain passive.

I have been asked if this is a good war. I do not think that there is such a thing as a good war. War is bad. Killing can be justified only to prevent wanton murder. (By the way, the seventh commandment—in the original Hebrew—does not read "Thou shalt not kill," as it is usually rendered, but "Thou shalt not murder.") That is the case with this war; it is a justifiable war, born out of necessity. Out of the need to prevent wanton murder.

Maurice Samuel once pointed out that war is horrible and if you are in it, do anything you can to win it and do not apologize.

THURSDAY, 31 JANUARY: CAUTIOUS RETURN TO NORMALCY

It has rained and the winds continue to howl as winter finally comes to us. For the second night we have had no attack. Those of us who succeeded, myself among them, slept well. I managed a solid seven hours. It helps. The rain has been plentiful and it has again snowed on Mount Hermon, all needed to replenish our waning water supply. And there have been loud thunderstorms as well.

In Tel Aviv, many were frightened by the thunder and thought that they were under attack, with bombing quite close. The radio kept broadcasting reassurances. This morning, life in Tel Aviv is beginning to return to normal. Cafeterias at places of work, empty until now, were filled. Appetites had returned. It is wonderful what two days of quiet can do to frayed nerves.

Women tell me that they have undergone a change in their sense of time. Women who used to feel that there never was enough time now find themselves sitting down to watch TV early in the afternoon. If—as they had formerly believed—twenty-four hours is not enough time to do all they had to, how is it now possible for them to waste time? Men feel the same, but do not admit it.

People speculate on the effect of our exposure on world TV. Will we now be more acceptable, less strange? Even more attractive in their eyes? We think that we did not do too badly on CNN. Does this mean that—once this is all over—more tourists will come, that more people will want to meet us, face to face?

But life is still not normal. Yes, we can see joggers once again, a few; we had not seen them for two weeks. A few brave people in Tel Aviv have returned to the abandoned swimming pools. What a place to be caught in a raid! In a bathing suit!

We are—with some embarrassment—a bit proud of ourselves. All Tel Avivians thought of leaving the city at one point or another. Only relatively few actually did so. We have survived! It is as if we went through the Blitz. We have faced the unknown and survived—and that is a very good feeling. But there still is uncertainty as to tonight, and tomorrow. We do not talk about that. People actually look better. You can see it. Less haggard, less worried.

■   Israel is too small a country for any part of it to be truly safe; probably all parts of the country are within missile range of Iraq. Is there an Israeli equivalent of Atom Haven, Montana, founded in 1950 as the safest place in the United States in the event of a nuclear attack? Not really: our country is too small, only the size of New Jersey. The radiation effects of "dirty" nuclear weapons and all but the most sophisticated "clean" weapons used against us would be felt throughout the country.

But Eilat, at our southern tip, is separated by an appreciable distance—the mostly barren Negev—from other population centers. It is also separated by a subtropical climate and coral reefs, not shared by the rest of the country, which make it an international winter tourist center.

In the last stages of the war, missiles were directed at the southeastern portion of the country, alleged to be the site of Israel's legendary—never proven, never denied—nuclear weapon facility. The distance between Haifa, a site of early attacks, and this region is more than 50 percent of the longest straight line that can be drawn through Israel.

Modern intermediate-range missiles should be targetable to a single building from up to 1,500 kilometers (900 miles). The relatively primitive Scud is alleged to be accurate to within 1,000 yards from half that distance, roughly the distance traversed by the Scuds in this war. There were a number of gross misses of Scud firings, far from any target (in most cases civilian population concentrations); these were probably the result of technical failures in the missiles and the time pressure at firing produced by the threat of coalition air attack.

With these factors taken into account, where should one go in Israel to avoid an attack? If the civilian population factor is the most compelling one in your considerations, there are a number of sparsely settled regions, particularly the southern Negev and the northern Galilee. (Kiryat Shmona, a northern border town, was the site of more than ten years of heavy, unceasing Katyusha rocket attacks from Lebanon, until Israel's invasion of that country. It was rare to find anyone from Tel Aviv who was willing, in those days, to visit Kiryat Shmona. Now the situation was reversed; a good number of Tel Aviv citizens, fleeing the Scuds, chose Kiryat Shmona as a haven.) For political reasons, some considered Jerusalem safe, and Jerusalem's hotels were crowded with refugees from greater Tel Aviv. Finally, Eilat was chosen by a good number as refuge because of its remoteness and because the Negev Desert separates it from the rest
■ of the country.

No, it is not yet over. But we have had a breathing spell, a much-needed breathing spell. And we are stronger now. That is good to know, important to know.

People go home earlier than they used to. As early as 14:30 the major roads in the cities begin to fill up; trips that took only fifteen minutes in normal times now take an hour—the congestion.

Sex? Even that. We have begun to talk about it; that must be a first step.

At this time jokes were not in the air, but some funny things did happen. An Israeli sexologist, when asked whether sex in the sealed room was all right, disapproved: "You never know who will come first, you or the Scud."

An unpredictable increase in the purchase of training suits has taken place here. People do not want to be caught in their pajamas, nightgowns, underwear, or without clothes at all if an alarm is sounded at night. The training suit is the solution to that problem.

Tomorrow, my son returns from the Far East. We had worried about his wandering alone in such strange places, but when the war began, my wife and I, his sister, and his brothers all agreed that he was much safer there than he would be here. When he called and said that he wanted to cut short his trip—it has been "only" four and a half months—we tried to talk him out of it. We were proud that he felt he had to return; after all, he had been a severe critic of Israeli policy, what he saw as intransigence. But we were worried about his safety. "There is nothing for you to do here," I said. But he was adamant and is now about to return. We still are proud of him—but wish that he had stayed.

Palestinian Arabs in Lebanon have been bombarding us with rockets for the last three days. Most of these rockets have landed in the security zone in the south of that country, where a local militia of Lebanese, aided by us, has become a buffer between the warring factions in that unsettled country and us. The motivation of the militia is not to aid us but to keep out these guerrillas, who do not hesitate to kill local citizens, steal, and occupy villages. We share interests with the militia, which is strongly supported by the local population, a very workable relationship. Luckily the rockets have caused insignificant damage.

West of the security belt is another, less effective buffer zone, policed by troops of various countries, under UN auspices. In the past day and a half, three Palestinian guerrillas, attempting to reach northern settlements in Israel, have been killed. The mission of these Palestinian Arabs was to attack settlements, kill settlers, and prove Palestinian identification with Saddam Hussein. Thus far, they have not succeeded. We retaliated by bombing staging centers for these guerrilla attacks.

What was the UN response? Why, naturally, it was to reduce the number of soldiers under UN supervision in the area. Just as the United Nations did in 1967, in Sinai, when Nasser threatened Israel. Is it not yet understandable to the rest of the world why we are so loath to rely on the promises of external agencies or countries when it comes to our safety?

Meanwhile, Peter Arnett's staged interview with Saddam Hussein has been released. We can understand the Palestinian drive to actively identify with Saddam more easily when he says that he "sees through the plot; he knows that it is Israel who is fighting with Iraq" and the U.S. and its coalition partners are only doing Israel's work.

Saddam Hussein did not forget to thank the peace demonstrators, whom he characterizes as agreeing with him that Iraq is fighting a war against coalition aggression.

I have suggested that Israel might be more effective than the coalition forces in eliminating certain strategic targets—especially the Scud missile launchers—because of Israeli willingness to engage in low-level bombing and our expertise in that form of bombing.

There is good reason to believe that U.S. satellites can, at the time of firing, pick up the launch heat flare and thereby locate launchers. The U.S.—we believe—will not take full advantage of this knowledge because of a policy not to engage in low-level bombing runs, a hesitancy bred by an attempt to minimize U.S. casualties. There is reason to believe—as part of U.S. desire to keep Israel out of the conflict, at least as an active participant—that the U.S. is not sharing knowledge of these launcher sightings with Israel.

Twelve U.S. Marines dead. Sad. War is a process which increases the chance of dying. "Will the U.S. stand fast?" we ask.

The F-117 videos that have been shown are indeed impressive, showing pinpoint accuracy during night flights. Most bombing, however, is carried out from high altitudes, where U.S. smart bombs are reported to have a 60 percent accuracy rate, meaning that 60 percent of the bombs land within ten feet of their target. Misses are usually the result of failure of sophisticated aiming devices; for example, if the bomb is unable to follow the laser beam into its target—as the result of malfunctions or weather disturbances—it may land as much as five miles from the target. The American decision not to engage in too much low-level bombing has been reinforced by the excessive losses suffered by the British Tornadoes, which specialized in low-level attacks on airfields.

Moshe Arens, the Israeli minister of defense, in a TV interview seemed to indicate that Israel was being inhibited by U.S. refusal to share the identification codes used in their aircraft. Israeli jets, like the coalition aircraft, carry the IFF (Identify Friend or Foe) transponder. This device, when used by the coalition, allows allied planes and even Patriot missiles to determine whether to attack or not. Modern planes can shoot down enemy jets which the pilot cannot even see; moreover, if we are talking about night bombing, the pilot must depend completely on his instruments. Thus, any plane not broadcasting the proper IFF codes might be shot at. The Patriot missile was originally designed to shoot down planes, and it still can; it too looks for the IFF signals. Even though Israeli planes are different from Iraqi planes, if the Israelis launched an attack, the U.S. planes would have to intercept the Israeli planes and confirm that they were indeed friendly.

Moreover, it is likely that Israeli planes, not equipped with IFF codes, would not be able to differentiate between French and Iraqi Mirage aircraft. Thus, the likelihood of someone beginning to fire, with everybody joining in, is real. Furthermore, coalition interceptors would be diverted from their other missions in order to check out the Israeli planes, whose presence would be unexpected (both to surprise the Iraqis and to circumvent American calls for restraint).

It rains. We have had two quiet nights. Another night closes in on us. What will it bring?

THURSDAY, 31 JANUARY: SHOULD WE RESPOND?

The second night of quiet has passed. No missiles here; they all seem to be directed at Saudi Arabia now. It is as if Saddam Hussein tried to involve us in the war but has given up the effort as a bad job. Or will he come back to us? His pet peeve, it seems.

The southern part of the country is now back to normal life; other than carrying gas masks with them, it is back to work for the citizens of Ashdod, Beersheva, Eilat, and surrounding regions. Schools will probably reopen there tomorrow. Some universities are cautiously reopening, although the end of the first semester was advanced a week. The universities are now in intersemester and exams are to be given. All trains—only a minor form of transportation here—are now running on full schedules.

For the exhausted citizens of Israel, this was a chance to catch up on sleep. I was one of the lucky ones who could. Others—a great minority, it seems—could not; their nerves frazzled, they sleep only fitfully.

A fair number of Tel Aviv citizens have chosen to leave the city. They are camping with relatives and friends in what they perceive to be safer parts of the country. Kibbutzim are crowded with guests, and hotels in Jerusalem, Eilat, and Tiberius are enjoying a small boom.

How do citizens of Israel feel about the government's decision not to react to Iraq's attacks by retaliating? A great majority appear to think that this decision was correct; the Left, of course, totally surprised by Shamir's "mature" decision, are enamored of Shamir now. Government critic, MK (Member of Knesset) Dedi Zucker of the Citizen's Rights Party spoke of wanting to embrace Shamir and would have done so, he said, but for Zucker's self-confessed embarrassment. The hard line Moledet (Homeland) Party insists on retaliation, now.

Most Israelis are for retaliation in some form. National pride demands it. How can we passively accept an attack, gratuitous as it was, by a foreign nation? The problems with retaliation are both distance and a proper target. The choices seem to be between a massive attack or an elegant one. There is reason to believe that the air force is capable of a massive attack even at the distances involved, which will require refueling in midair. But can we compete with the coalition? What can we do that they can't? The possibility of an elegant retaliation seems more attractive; it would involve limited risk—in numbers—and achieve an important and visible goal. The killing of Saddam Hussein comes to mind as a possibility. Is this feasible?

Meanwhile, the threat of attack on us still exists. The missile launchers have not been taken out of action. The Iraqi Air Force is still intact, its performance capabilities a question mark. Anxiety here is controlled, people are going back to work.

Another blow to Israeli pride has been the arrival of U.S. Army personnel to operate the Patriot missiles. Israel has always prided herself on never before using foreign troops to fight for her. There is some consolation in the training of Israeli crews by the U.S. teams and the knowledge that the Americans are not here for long.

What we can be proud of is the performance of the civil defense, the hospitals, the army, the air force—airplanes are flying all the time so as to be ready and not attackable on the ground—the radio and TV and the general population, who have behaved—almost entirely—in an intelligent, praiseworthy fashion.

■ Israel is a small country of 4 million Jews surrounded by hostile Arab nations with a total population of 100 million. Within Israel itself there are now more than 1 million Arabs, a gigantic potential fifth column. The destruction of Israel is an official position of all these countries. Though Egypt has signed a peace treaty with us, it must still control a large number of intransigent Israel haters. Can so vulnerable a country as Israel afford even to consider the bellicose position that retaliating against Iraq would entail? Strange as it may seem, not retaliating could make Israel even more vulnerable.

The U.S. request that Israel show restraint must be understood in these terms. Israelis did not see the request for restraint as a relief, as a lessening of responsibility. It was a request to invite the Arabs to both immediate and long-term aggression. It was a request to allow our neighbors to see us in terms of disgust and contempt, a ■ view that can only cost us lives and security.

There is little doubt that there is much about which one ought to be disgusted in the background of this war. The West cynically supported Iraq, against the advice of, among others, Israel. Many think that this support of Saddam Hussein was engendered by an exclusive interest in oil. I am less convinced that this was the chief motivation for the support he received. I think that, in the case of the U.S., a major motivation was to support an enemy of Iran; the U.S. was deeply committed to support of the Shah (perhaps oil was a major motivation, then), and later its national pride was deeply wounded by the ill-treatment of the American hostages and the embarrassing failure of the ill-fated rescue mission. Thus, support for an enemy of Iran was perceived as an extremely inviting method of "getting back."

Other nations were in it for money, as simple as that—just plain greed, the denials of France notwithstanding and the confessions of Germany confirming. The Soviets, who need no oil at all, were in the game for power, in their attempt to gain influence in the Middle East (and perhaps, at least partially, to compromise Western oil sources).

■ Stupidity is another factor that must not be overlooked: the U.S. Department of Commerce was blithely issuing export licenses because they saw their action—a remarkable example of tunnel vi-
■ sion!—as a way to full employment in the United States.

For these reasons alone, the slogan "No blood for oil" is at the very least simple-minded.

The protest against the war may be likened to the statement "Yes, you seem to be behaving with adequate motivation now, but we know how corrupt your motivation was in the past; therefore we do not trust you and we will not support you." The possibility for rehabilitation is ruled out by a cynicism that seems to imply that nations never behave well. Isn't that a great oversimplification? Even if there is reason to accept this cynical approach—which would, by the way, rule out all meaningful international action—is it not possible that out of the most selfish motivation imaginable that a nation may act properly? Is there not sufficient reason to examine the action in the light of its intrinsic correctness? Taking into account motivation, of course.

■ Americans have a great fear of government corruption and cover-up that is not completely understandable to an outsider. Certainly there have been examples of corruption and attempts to cover it up, both in the United States and elsewhere. This is one of the givens in the concentration of power that accompanies centralized government. But an alert press and public make these less real, less dangerous than they might otherwise be. After all, one does choose the government in a democracy. You choose the people you can most trust and keep an eye on them. but you do not paralyze them and prevent them from acting.

James Joyce asked if it were possible—if angry undirected action had accidentally produced a thing of beauty—to call the product art. That problem is not settled; but he had no difficulty in admitting that the object might be beautiful (or worthwhile, or correct). That is what is asked of the peace demonstrators, at the most fundamental level.

The Western nations have been bad; but Saddam Hussein is evil, satanic. (Saddam Hussein, in a fit of self-insight and projection worthy of the devil himself, has co-opted the language of religion, calling his opponents "satanic.") He has invaded, captured, raped, and annexed a nation, Kuwait, without provocation. He has bombed civilian concentrations in neutral and distant Israel without cause or provocation. He was given a reasonable chance to withdraw from Kuwait; he not only refused, he laughed at the presumption of the West and taunted them. He attempted to make hostages of foreigners in his country and use them to "protect" military targets (and has repeated the threat with captured soldiers, forced to testify on television in his behalf). He invented unauthenticated scapegoats, a plot by Israel and another by Kuwait against Iraq. He could produce substantiation for neither.

Yes, Saddam Hussein is evil. While there is reason to believe that the West has been bad, there is a fundamental difference between bad and evil. Unlike the evil, those who are bad can and indeed do behave both properly and well. Those who cannot see that difference, I fear, are trapped in a one-dimensional world where neither action nor choice is possible.

FRIDAY, 1 FEBRUARY: WE LOOK FOR PATTERNS

Someone here said that there is nothing as old as yesterday's danger. Now I think that I have found something just as outdated, and much more useless: yesterday's sense of security.

Last night we were again attacked. For the first time, I was not at home. It was at 18:00, already dark for a half-hour outside, and I was still at work. I actually did not know where the sealed room was;

but a colleague quickly directed me to the comfortable, spacious students' laboratory that had been sealed for just such times. At this late hour (suddenly 6:00 P.M. has become late), only a dozen of us were there; I was among the first to arrive, but others wandered in over the next ten minutes. Most of us—I among them—had their masks and donned them; someone had remembered to bring a radio (not a battery-powered model, but luckily there was no problem with the electricity).

■   It is amazing that there were no power failures during any of the attacks, although we did have some between attacks. How much worse it would have been during an attack if we had had to sit in pitch darkness; see the entry of 26 January for a description of a power failure soon after an attack. Tel Avivians, more sensitive to the threats than anyone else, always carried battery-powered radios ■ with them wherever they went.

We now know that a direct link from the U.S. spy satellite hovering above Iraq has been set up—to Israel and to the Patriot antimissile missile batteries. This should increase the warning time from one and one-half to five minutes. (Before, the data was sent to Australia first, and then, after decoding, forwarded to the United States, and only then to us.) Everyone seems much calmer than I feel; but two of us, a man and a young woman, have repeated difficulties with their masks—they take them off and put them on, readjusting the straps.

Another two of the dozen—I recognized one face but did not know who he was; he looked Russian to me—had no mask. No one remarked on this. I did not feel secure; I wondered where other members of my family were.

I do not think that I have mentioned that you have to take off your eyeglasses before putting on the masks; it was clear that a number of the people in the room were effectively blind. Attempts to put the glasses on over the mask are foiled because the arms of the glasses are about one inch short; furthermore, the extra distance from the lens of the eye puts the image a bit out of focus; I tried it, I know. I wear glasses, but manage well enough without them to read the time on my wristwatch, to keep notes.

On the radio we hear translations of the alarm notice—all Israel is requested to enter sealed rooms and put on the anti-poison-gas masks—in Russian, English, French, and Amharic. Only later, with the arrival of the appropriate translators, did we hear Arabic and Yiddish translations of the announcements.

There is no computer terminal in the sealed room.

18:08 A confirmed attack is announced: "A missile (or missiles) has been fired at Israel from Western Iraq."

18:11 The whole country is still required to sit in sealed rooms, wearing masks.

18:13 Inhabitants of the north—including Haifa, unusually early for that city—and the south were allowed to take off masks and leave the sealed rooms. Is it greater Tel Aviv again? How many missiles? What damage have they done? Were the Patriots effective? What kind of warhead did the missiles bear?

18:15 All of Israel other than the east central region is now freed, including Tel Aviv. It seems to be the other side of the Green Line again. Mostly Palestinian Arabs with some Jewish settlements as well. We take off our masks. I am told that I have been tightening the straps of mine too much; my face is slightly purplish, it seems. Some attempts at joking. We wander back to our offices. Some rush, to telephone, to be reassured, to reassure. My wife—at her latest adopted Russian immigrant family's apartment—is safe and calls me; she actually remembered, and had her gas mask with her.

18:42 We hear that there have been no injuries, no damage. Good. No Patriots were fired. What does that mean? This is the second time in a row that no Patriot was fired. Is it for the same reasons?

18:47 A small part of the country is still confined to sealed rooms, wearing gas masks. It appears that there is difficulty finding the missile, determining its nature. It must have landed in the hills. (In the morning we learn that it fell in the western part of the Shomron [Samaria] between two Arab villages.) A number of false alarms are sounded in various cities; nervous fingers, it seems. I am glad that it has not happened here, in Jerusalem.

19:00   As suspected, the missile has not been located.

19:23   Only now is a general all-clear announced.

This is the second attack, one after another, in which a single Scud is fired and the missile falls far short of its mark. It is hard to believe that the missiles were fired at the Arab population, both because they are not Saddam Hussein's professed enemies—a title he has bestowed on us—and because the effectiveness of the missile is so much greater in areas of larger population concentrations. There are certainly no significant military installations in the regions of these missile landings. Indeed, we later find out that during the attack Radio Baghdad announced (Iraqi General Staff Communiqué number 33): "At 19:00 [Baghdad time, which is one hour ahead of us] our units fired Al Husseini [an improved, long-range version of the Scud] missiles [*sic*] at Tel Aviv, which rained Arab, Islamic, and Iraqi anger on the heads of the Zionists."

There are several possibilities to explain these misfirings. It is possible that there was insufficient time to fully fuel the missiles; they are fueled only after being placed in position. Coalition bombing limits the time that is available for preparation of the missiles for firing, a process that normally takes as much as six hours. (Later we learned that fueling can be accomplished in as little as ninety minutes.) Mechanical failure is another possibility and may in part result from firing the missiles from makeshift launchers, improvised in the face of coalition bombings that have destroyed many of the original launchers.

Why have the Patriots not been fired? We have all become armchair generals, working with limited information. Is it because the Scuds can be seen by Patriot radar not to be threats? Is it because the missiles fall when they are still out of the range (seven miles) of the Patriots? Is it because there is a problem with the Patriots? The absence of information frustrates us, worries us. Bleak scenarios are not difficult to find.

We continue to seek patterns. The pattern of no firings during the daytime is still intact. We are not the only ones who have noticed this; schools are being reopened at a much quicker rate than we thought would be possible a few days ago. Yesterday, all junior high school classes—except in Tel Aviv and Haifa, which will begin to offer these classes on Sunday—have reopened. Teachers who worked furiously to prepare lessons for home study, only to find that these efforts were wasted, are angry and frustrated, not knowing what to expect next. It is a strange situation when it is the government, that ponderous and slow-moving mastodon, that is able to show the greatest flexibility, to change plans with ease, sensitive to the winds of changing circumstance.

It is now planned to reopen classes in elementary schools, first through sixth grades on Sunday as well. Again all over the country except for Tel Aviv and Haifa, which will follow in one or two days.

Daytime movie houses are also open; no move has been made to reopen them to evening and nighttime showings. Nobody whose work does not require it is out of their houses after 19:00. Supermarkets, all-night pharmacies, and other businesses close at that time—or earlier.

Now we try out among ourselves the possibility of other patterns. Twice we have had exactly two consecutive nights without attack. Is that pattern to be relied on? Or is it but a random association? We don't have enough information for a statistical evaluation.

Another pattern is that the firings seem to be undertaken on the hour. As this attack was at 18:00, there was also one at 02:00, and so on. Can it be that the Iraqi Army command says, "Shoot off a Scud at Israel at X o'clock, where X is always a whole number, from 1 to 24?" Or, would it be from 18:00 (our time) to 03:00, the hours of darkness, if that pattern is correct as well?

And so it goes. Black magic? Perhaps. But we do not have anything better.

We have survived our eighth attack now, thirty Scuds.

It rains hard now, it is cold outside, the wind is strong, fog covers us. The world is gray. Yes, gray, but still livable.

■   Throughout the war, few voices were heard from Arabic or Muslim countries—Turkey was a notable exception—on the E-mail networks. There are E-mail nodes in Egypt and Saudi Arabia; I have communicated with network users there. The Arab universities here, in Israel, do not seem to have any E-mail connections. Arab users of my central computer are not infrequent. I see their names on the board—Ibrahim, Muhammad, and so on—and Arabic surnames as well, but they do not contribute to the E-mail nets. Are they intimidated? There is no censorship of the E-mail.

Much of the difference reflects the level of technological development in Israel as compared to the surrounding countries. Israel is far ahead of all these countries. We have developed sophisticated technology, particularly military and medical, but also in desalination and solar energy, that can compete with any in the world. Only in military technology do our Arab neighbors rival us, and even in this arena they rely heavily on the support of advisers from America, France, Germany, and Russia.

How much of the absence of indignation, anger, fear, hatred, pride, helplessness that one might expect to come out of the Arab states is a reflection of a general inhibition of expression? These countries are all, to a greater or lesser extent, repressive; free speech is often dangerous there, often a luxury. Unpopular ideas are expressed only by the very brave or the foolhardy. One must be trained and encouraged to express oneself. It may seem natural to some; if so, they have not properly appreciated the nurturing atmosphere in which they were raised. This training and encouragement for self-expression is absent in the repressive regimes around us.

As much as Israel may be disliked by Westerners—for its policies, for its unwillingness to grant the Palestinians their country, for its strength—it is still the only legitimate democracy in the region. The unpopular policies of Israel are the result of a national consensus, of our perception of the needs of the country and the threats that we face. Unpopular, yes. Undemocratic, no.

For those who are willing to sacrifice Israel, I have a simple question: Is democracy so common that it can be wasted? Perhaps it is easier to perceive the value of democracy in the political desert of the Arabian subcontinent.

SATURDAY, 2 FEBRUARY: SO MUCH FOR PATTERNS

Friday was uneventful; we waited for the attack which we knew would come, but it did not. Although we were relieved to be free of the drill—ascent to the sealed room, closing it, putting on the masks, turning on the radio, and waiting, waiting—I felt a distinct disappointment. We had undergone nighttime attacks on the two previous Fridays—the only ones in the war until yesterday, despite Friday being the Islamic Sabbath. No attack on this third consecutive Friday meant no pattern. I did not realize until now how important to me was seeing patterns in the attacks.

Why did I not feel more empathy for the Iraqi civilians? I tried. I shared their fear of bombing, of death, and yet I found myself strangely cold, indifferent. I was not happy to see the news footage of bombed shelters, of the dead and wounded, particularly the children. My natural tendency is to feel a special sympathy for women, too. Feminists, I know, disallow this: they insist on not being the object of special, sexually based sympathy.

I felt sympathy for the peoples of Afghanistan, Africa, Cambodia, Vietnam; even for Poles and Ukrainians, whose countries have such long histories of anti-Semitism. But I could not find in myself more than the most general feeling of discomfort and malaise at the position of the Iraqis.

As a physician, I was horrified at the twisted and burned Iraqi bodies shown on television. My tendency as a physician is to want to help. I would help if I were there, and I would do a competent job, but my work would be accompanied, I know, by an undercurrent of coldness and distaste.

I even find it easier to sympathize with the Palestinians who want my land, my house, my life, than with the Iraqis. The Palestinians have been deprived of a chance of life in their own country, betrayed by their leaders and their allies, time and time again. They have a legitimate quarrel with me; they think it is I who stole their land. Their leaders tell them this rather than admit their own perfidy.

But why do the Iraqis hate me?

Some of the victims of the bombings were anti-Saddam; we know that there is an underground, ineffective because of Hussein's ruthless repression, but real nonetheless. These Iraqis also hate me. A call to destroy Israel is the only thing that can unite all Iraqis. Even the Shiites, a majority in Iraq and oppressed by Hussein, want the destruction of Israel more than his downfall.

It is impossible to understand why this hatred of my people and my country is more important than freedom to the Iraqis. It is difficult to forgive these people their gratuitous hatred of me, of my land.

And when I saw the Iraqi use of hospital scenes, of dead bodies, for cold, calculated propaganda, I asked myself, What sort of people are these? Have they no respect for their own dead, for their wounded? Is life and limb so meaningless to them? If they think so little of their own citizens, if they are so willing to make cynical use of them for propaganda purposes, even to use professional actors as they did to protest the abuses of the coalition bombings — with what wantonness would they threaten my children and grandchildren?

I do not like these people who hate me so thoroughly. A good Christian might be able to forgive the Iraqis their excesses. They seem able to forgive the Germans theirs. I am a Jew, not a Christian. ■ I find it more difficult, even impossible, to forgive them.

I was trying to make order out of the chaos of war; by seeking patterns, I hoped to find rules and laws. Rules and laws that would counter this disturbing and unsettling feeling of uncertainty that was now almost as bad as the thought of being injured or killed. This attempt on my part was doomed to failure, I now see—but it was comforting while the illusion lasted.

Writing the previous paragraph reminds me of my daughter-in-law's annoyance with me; she had looked at some of my reports, and when she came with her family to dinner on Friday night, she told me that I was picturing our situation as if we were objects of pity. She resented that, was convinced it was not true; but she had been born here in Israel, had only spent a few years in the States. This was normal for her; not the actual Scud attacks and the procedures we follow with each attack—they were new. But the idea of being under attack, of having to defend herself—that was part of the turf for her.

Of course she is right. It is just that my background is so very different; I have spent more than half my life abroad, in the bosom of decency and democracy. (Not that I do not feel that I now live in a decent society where democracy prevails; indeed they do, but their geographic limits are so very narrow. Size really makes a difference, in terms not only of political security but also of psychological security.)

I even left the States before the cities became dangerous at night. (Except for Scuds, the cities are still quite safe at night here.) I don't feel that I am one of the downtrodden of the world, and I do not want to give that impression. It is just that as an American (originally, and it seems irrevocably) I am always surprised by evil. My initial response is to deny it; to say it is just not there. I need time to regain my equilibrium in the face of evil. I lived through two and a half wars as an American and this is my fifth here in Israel. I have had enough experience of the world to have learned; but as an American, I fear, there are some things I can never really learn.

For Americans, the distinction between degrees of bad is a very difficult one to make. One bad is perceived as just as bad as any other bad. That appears to be a consequence of the ultimate optimism of the American. The American can and still does believe in a perfect or perfectible world. (To that extent, I am no longer an American.) It was to the Americans that Santayana spoke when he said that one who does not learn from history is doomed to repeat the same mistakes.

When I speak to Americans about evil, they do not understand;

they think that bad is the same as evil. Until they learn—will they ever? can they ever?—they will be trapped by this confusion. Bush, some of them tell me, is bad. I say to them, "Maybe or even yes. But Saddam Hussein is evil." And they do not understand me.

There is a world out here that has different guiding principles. You have to listen; some people are not sportsmen and do not play by the rules.

Only a few months ago I was in China. There a distinguished savant, a member of the Academica Sinica who has traveled extensively in the West—and is a nice guy, too—told me in deadly seriousness that he knows that the U.S. is preparing to invade mainland China with a force of ten million soldiers. Does this sound wild to you?

This was not a joke; nothing I could say to this Chinese intellectual would convince him that there was no basis for this wild belief. He showed me his relaxed attitude to this anticipated disaster; he joked grimly, telling me that China would make good use of the dead American soldiers that would result from such an invasion as fertilizer.

Well, Saddam Hussein's claim that this is a war between Israel and Islam with the U.S. and its coalition partners doing the fighting for Israel is just as wild. And Saddam Hussein has succeeded in convincing many Muslims, including intellectuals, that he is telling the truth. And some Americans as well, I am afraid to report.

My son sent me a newspaper clipping from India that said, as if everyone knew it as truth, that the U.S. jumped through hoops whenever Israel called the tune. This is India, not an enemy of the U.S. This is not cynical lying, not the work of another Goebbels, but something much worse. They believe it. Even at the top.

I am just enough not an American to see the difference. And the threat. And to fear the death of people in the name of lies. And the picture I see is sad. But I am enough an American and enough an Israeli—and perhaps enough a Jew, as well—to believe that there can be better. Better, yes; not perfection, but better. And better is good. And I see that it is sometimes worth fighting for a life of truth and meaning in a world that will always partially confuse me. Particularly when I think I have achieved a life of truth and meaning and someone is trying to take it away from me. (Nietzsche said that a slave is someone who cannot find anything worth fighting or dying for.)

War is bad, but it is sometimes necessary. *Discrimination* is an out word these days. (The out word of my youth was *rationalization*.) I understand the reasons for the disfavor that has fallen on use of this word, but it is still a pity to lose so fine a word. After all, discrimination (like rationalization) is a higher function of the brain. And it takes discrimination to tell the difference between a bad person and an evil person. Just as it does to tell the difference between just any war and a necessary and justifiable one, as this one is.

So I apologize to my daughter-in-law. But not to Saddam Hussein.

But I was talking about losing faith in patterns. As I am beginning to now.

On Saturday night, after beginning this report, we had another alarm. And at 20:27! Another pattern, ever so tenuous, down the drain. In this case the pattern of attacks on the hour is the victim of fact destroying Werman's feeble efforts at finding patterns.

20:27   This time, I heard the siren outside, or rather my wife did. I ran to the TV, saw the familiar medallion announcing—in various languages—the alarm. I took my mother and ascended the stairs, where we were joined by my wife in the sealed room. Closing the room, adjusting the tape on the door, placing the wet towel at the foot of the door, donning our masks, turning on the radio, checking my mother's mask—all this is now pretty much routine. No different than brushing your teeth. And busy with the routine, I have no time for fright or pessimistic thought or even serious worry. Translations in English and Amharic. Later there will also be Russian, French, and Yiddish.

20:33   We learn from the radio that this is a real attack and that all Israel is asked to don masks in sealed rooms. Nahman Shai tells us that we do now have more warning time than previously. I once again attempt to get onto the IRC net through my computer to find out what is happening in other cities, but the IRC server in Israel is down. I try

20:40 to connect up through an IRC server in the States—this will allow me to find out who is on-line in other cities in Israel and "talk" to them almost instantaneously—but without success.

20:40 Instructions about how to handle heating up of the incubators that all three-year-olds and younger enter during these attacks. If you have a fan in the room, blow it at the filter of the incubator; if not, put cold, wet rags on the incubator without covering the filter. Check the infant to see if he/she is pale or having difficulties breathing. If yes, check that the door is properly sealed and—only then—take the infant out for one or two minutes, until he or she seems better, and then replace the infant in the incubator.

20:43 Just as in the last two attacks, all of Israel is released from masks and sealed rooms except for Shomron (Samaria), in the occupied territories.

20:45 We are told that a single missile was fired from western Iraq and that it had fallen in the region where people were still in masks and sealed rooms.

20:57 The southern half of that region is also released.

20:59 We hear that there are no known casualties or damage to property.

21:03 An all-clear announcement is given on the radio; we are told that the all-clear siren will not be blown. Why? Could it be that too many people mistake it for another attack?

I am tired and subjects I wanted to write about will have to wait until tomorrow. If nothing happens to push them further away.

■　The Sabbath (*Shabbat* in Hebrew, *Shabbos* in Yiddish) is Saturday, the Seventh Day; the name is derived from the Hebrew verb *shavat*, "to rest" or "to stop." Observing the Sabbath is a biblical injunction and central to Jewish observance. It is also central to Moses' covenant with God, where it appears as the Fourth Commandment, or *word* in Hebrew.

The Sabbath begins with the lighting of at least two candles by the woman of the house to recall the double nature of the commandment: to remember the Sabbath (Exodus 20:8) and to observe the Sabbath (Deuteronomy 5:12). For each meal (two, to recall the double portion of manna available only for the Sabbath), whole loaves of bread, called *hallot* (singular, *halla*), are covered with a cloth. The parents bless the children before the *Kiddush*, a blessing on wine, is recited. (A Baptist neighbor in the Midwest argued that Jesus, as a good Baptist, would never have drunk the four cups of wine at the Last Supper, a Passover meal.)

Special prayers are recited in the Synagogue in honor of the Sabbath, and a weekly Torah (the five books of Moses) reading is done. At the end of the Sabbath the *Havdalla* blessing is recited over wine, spices (to make up for the loss of the beautiful Sabbath), and a lit candle (which cannot be lit or blessed on the Sabbath). All told, the Sabbath lasts twenty-five hours: we add an extra hour to make sure that we do not miss even a moment of the sweetness that is the Sabbath.

Work cannot be carried out on the Sabbath, including cooking, but *cholent*—food, usually beans, flour patties, and meat—can be placed in a pot in an oven before the Sabbath and eaten on the Sabbath. One can walk only within one's town and an additional two thousand cubits (a cubit is about twenty inches). Traveling in vehicles and the use of money, radio, and television are similarly prohibited. There are many other prohibitions, but all can be and should be broken to save a life; saving a life takes precedence over all prohibitions in all cases. Those who follow these rules are called Orthodox Jews, although right-wing conservative Jews are also known to adhere to the rules.

Some believe that the introduction of the Sabbath, a weekly day of rest, is the greatest contribution of the Jews to civilization. A lovely *aggada* (legend) tells that God created the world in six days and rested on the seventh day to give man a chance to join in the process of creation. All week long man toils; on the Sabbath he is free of work, is king of his household, and is free to think, study, and speculate.

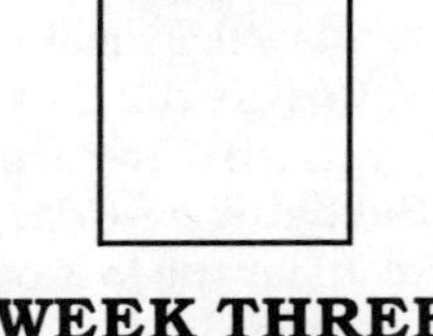

WEEK THREE

I was sending off yesterday's report to various friends and to nets where they are reprinted and to those who have written and told me that they had difficulty in obtaining the material but wanted it. It was actually after 1:00 A.M. this morning when I began to send out the copies. My tardiness resulted from a number of factors; these included the fact that I am an observant Jew and do not write or use a computer terminal between sundown Friday and sundown Saturday, in fact do no work at all in that twenty-five hours. (When I tried to explain this prohibition to my hosts during my recent trip to China, they obligingly decided to lock me in my room for that period. I explained to them that this tactic was not necessary, that I could walk around within the city. Reasoning logically, they argued that I should be able to ride in a car, for after all riding in a car is even less work than walking. A number of other interesting confusions arose from their never having had to deal with Jewish mores and religion.) Thus, I was delayed by the wait for the exit of the Sabbath and then, later, there was the attack that I have already reported. That had to be survived and recorded and added to the report. As I said, it was after 1:00 A.M. and then we had another attack, the second this night.

1:37   I hear the radio broadcast interrupted by the sisma (the code that indicates that a certain group has to go into action). All of Israel now recognizes this sisma, which clearly is a signal to the operators of the local sirens to turn on their sirens. It may also activate other groups, but that is not obvious to us. (Did the sisma activate Patriots? Not likely. They seemed to have, just as the general staff did, direct access to the sightings reported by the U.S. spy satellite over Iraq.) In fact, some thirty seconds later, the siren is heard clearly.

I note that this and the last attack both took place on or about the half-hour. But I must avoid this silly game of looking for patterns, looking for meaning. A friend (Jerry Phillips) writes that my search for patterns is a product of a Western outlook; to understand Saddam Hussein better, I should study chaos, of which Saddam is a prime example.

My wife, mother, and I are joined in the sealed room by our son, who arrived from the Far East on Friday afternoon, and his girlfriend, who is visiting. His second attack; and he has been here less than twelve hours.

1:43   Nahman Shai tells us that this is a real attack and not a false alarm; all Israelis are requested to enter their poison-gas-proof rooms and don their masks.

1:45   Shai tells us that one Scud has been fired and landed in Israel, that the situation is similar to the last attack, five hours earlier.

1:53   We are all released from the sealed rooms except those living in the Shomron (Samaria) and in greater Tel Aviv.

1:57   Those living in Tel Aviv are also released.

1:58   Only those in the northern part of Samaria have to remain in their rooms. The same pattern as in the earlier attack.

My son's girlfriend has to call her mother to tell her that she is safe; other calls. Some confusion. I forget to note when the general all-clear is given—on the radio, again no siren is used. Once again this compulsion to record, to tell takes hold of me; I do not go to sleep until after 3:30 A.M.

The last four Scuds have fallen short of the coastal population centers which have been the targets of Iraq's missile attacks. The missiles have all landed in the Shomron, or Samaria, in the occupied territories, where mostly Palestinian Arabs live as well as far fewer Jewish settlers. The Palestinian Arabs are bewildered by these events. A short-lived sport popular in the first week, climbing to the roofs of houses and cheering encouragement to the missiles passing to the west, on their way to the Jewish population centers, is no longer so common. The Palestinian Arabs have made a great emotional investment in Saddam Hussein, whom they see as a possible savior, the only effective Arab leader on the scene sympathetic to them as well as strong enough to make the hated and—in their eyes—treacherous West back down. They find both reasonable explanations for the rain of missiles on their territories—either it is deliberate or the Iraqis are screwing up—unacceptable.

The Palestinian Arabs note that the Patriot antimissile missiles have not been used against these last four Scuds and feel that this is the result of a deliberate decision on the part of the Jews, whom they perceive as wanting to exterminate them. (They were not impressed by the arguments that the Patriots have an effective range against missiles of only about five miles [estimates of the range kept falling] and that the concentration of Patriot batteries near the large cities did not allow interception of these Scuds, which fell out of range.)

Some Palestinian Arabs even claim that the missiles are actually fired by the Israelis and aimed at them, the Palestinians. Good heroes are hard to find, and apparently even harder to give up.

As in most modern countries, the literary establishment in Israel is one of the strongholds of the non-Communist Left. So complete is their control of the literary magazines, the media—in this book-hungry country, all the newspapers, even those directed at the least serious reader, have serious literary supplements in every Friday (weekend) issue and expanded literary editions for the holidays—and the formation of the literary taste and opinion in this country that when David Shahar, a novelist associated with the Right politically, won a major literary prize for the best novel translated into French several years ago, the almost universal response was "David who?"

Shahar, who had already published three novels as well as collections of short stories, was a virtual unknown here as a result of his systematic exclusion from the eyes of readers. (It is quite common here for the better-known novelists to publish chapters or smaller parts of works in progress in the literary journals and in the holiday editions of newspaper literary sections.) Shahar was forced to publish through Hadar, a small, little-known press also run by a right-winger, a former operations officer of one of the separatist, right-wing groups (Etzel, Lehi, the Stern Gang) that operated during the waning days of the British Mandate in Palestine. Nor was he reviewed: as a right-winger, he simply did not exist.

I am pleased to say that Shahar, following continued and repeated success in France—and a split with his right-wing publisher (Shahar is still politically on the Right)—is now published by the largest publisher in the country, Am Oved, the organ of the Histadrut—the overall labor organization, closely identified with the Labor Party. Shahar's long series of novels tracing a group of interesting and colorful characters in Jerusalem from the 1930s on has continued to have great success in France and moderate success here. As far as I know, only one of his novels, *His Majesty's Agent*, has been translated into English. This novel—not part of the series—is a romping, pornographic roman à clef that is probably not too meaningful for American readers, except for a broad, cruel parody at the beginning, a portrait of a famous American Jewish literary figure who allegedly attempted, unsuccessfully, to prevent publication of the translation. In my opinion, the third novel of the series, *The Day of the Countess*, is the finest novel written in Hebrew in the past fifty years and is world-class.

Two successful novelists—both deserving of their reputations—in the camp of the Left, Amos Oz and A. B. Yehoshua, have been outspoken in their support, both here and abroad, of dealing directly with the PLO. (There are subtle differences in their political postures, but these are not relevant to the present discussion.) They are both clearly embarrassed by the PLO's support of Saddam Hussein and have backed off, to different degrees, in their support of that terrorist organization (my words, their implied criticism). I do not think that either rejects—even after all this—the option of dealing with the PLO and even entering formal negotiations with them, on the basis that there is no alternative. But the latest difficulty they find themselves in is their inability to make common cause with their leftist brothers, especially in Europe, from whom they formerly drew support and sympathy. They see their European leftist friends leading the peace demonstrations against the war in the Persian Gulf and happily marching in the first rows—and feel confused and disappointed, isolated and betrayed.

It appears that Oz and Yehoshua are shocked by the inability of their former colleagues to distinguish between war and war. They no longer can understand how anyone can be against all wars, no matter how evil the nature of the war. For Jews, even on the Left, and for Israelis especially—we have the questionable fortune of being reminded, time after time—Hitler's war is too close, its purpose too unbelievable. But Hitler's war gives us a criterion with which to measure other wars. Panama, Nicaragua, the Falklands, and Grenada fail that criterion. Saddam Hussein, who is willing to rape Kuwait and cynically blame Israel, to fire missiles on civilian populations who are not at war with him, to murder five thousand Kurds with poison gas—this Saddam Hussein passes that criterion. This— for all right-thinking people—must be a war worth fighting.

The Israeli left is in a very difficult position. They find they are no longer supported by their counterparts elsewhere who cannot see the different nature of this war. Moreover, their willingness to sacrifice so much—to give the Palestinians the state they want—is at least partially meant to find favor in the eyes of their leftist fellows. Perhaps the realization that their leftist fellows are willing to see them and their families die—in the name of "justice"—is just too much for them.

■ Jews do have this inability to fit in on the Left as well as on the Right. Trotsky had his Soviet anti-Semites. The *Commentary* right-wing Jews (neoconservatives) are embarrassed by the company of William Buckley and much more so by Pat Buchanan.

Jerry Phillips tells me that "the hatred of Jews in the United States is insidious, subtle, and unrelenting. In that sense, Israel is purifying. In Israel the enemy is identified, as are the friends, like ■ them or not."

One of my correspondents points out to me that the Hadassah-Hebrew University Hospital in Jerusalem—generally thought to be the best hospital in the Middle East—has been designated as a "first stop" for allied casualties from the Gulf War. Until now, a U.S. Army hospital in Wiesbaden, Germany, was the "first stop." It would be interesting to see if any of the Arab members of the coalition allow their wounded to be taken to Israel. Probably the designation of Hadassah is for Westerners only.

Another correspondent forwards to me the following "interesting piece of trivia." The name Patriot is in fact, an acronym:

> P hased
> A rray
> T racking
> R adar
> I ntercept
> O n
> T arget

And I can add that the H2 and H3 staging areas for Scud missiles in western Iraq were originally the Haifa 2 and Haifa 3 pumping stations of the Iraq Petroleum Company, which was British-owned until 1948. These stations served to pump oil from the Kirkuk oil fields in Iraq to the refineries in Haifa.

MONDAY, 4 FEBRUARY: BACK TO SCHOOL; CENSORS

We had no alarm last night. The relief from attack was appreciated (should I thank Saddam Hussein?) and relaxing. I did not quite believe, even at the moment of falling asleep.

Waiting for the other shoe to fall.

Schools continue to reopen. The ninth grade is now open in Tel Aviv and Haifa; elsewhere, the first to twelfth grades are open. But in Tel Aviv many of the classes are still only half-filled—at least in the more affluent neighborhoods. There has been a conspicuous flight from Tel Aviv; hotels and guest houses in other cities such as Jerusalem and Eilat and more remote places such as the kibbutzim are filled with Tel Aviv escapees. Even those without money who have friends or family elsewhere take advantage of this and leave the threatened city. The number of commuters who drive into Tel Aviv every morning has increased greatly, another sign of flight from the city. Interesting consequences of the flight include a marked increase (20–25 percent) in the number of births in Siroka Hospital in Beer Sheva; Jerusalem hospitals also report obvious increases in birthrate.

■ Many of my readers were confused by this comment: they thought that the increased birthrate was the result of premature labor. The increase was, of course, caused by women seeking safer areas to
■ give birth.

The mayor of Tel Aviv, a former army general of obvious charm and popularity, Shlomo "Chich" Lahat, responded to the flight of Tel Aviv strongly and called the refugees "deserters." This strong reaction has produced much comment, both positive and negative. The City of Tel Aviv produced a car sticker saying, "I Stayed in Tel Aviv," which also has been a source of controversy. When a Tel Aviv car carrying such a sticker is seen in Jerusalem—perhaps on business—it elicits snickers. A number of Tel Avivians, in an effort to show that they have remained in the city, have hung Israeli flags from the windows of their apartments and houses. To spare feelings, maternity patients in Siroka Hospital—in thus-far safe Beer Sheva—are no longer asked where they come from. In fact, escapees who now commute to Tel Aviv daily and sleep out of the city (all attacks have been after dark) are called, with gentle humor, outpatients.

The movement away from Tel Aviv is now—slowly—reversing itself, and families are returning to the city. Both the cost of living away from home and the failure of Scuds to land in the city this past week contribute to the reurbanization of the city.

The psychological effects of the attacks still occupy us and are subjects of radio discussions among psychologists, psychiatrists, social workers, and lay people as well as features of personal conversations. A friend tells me that his neighbor's four-year-old son reported, "My *bulbul* [the most common children's word here for penis] is a Patriot missile with a chemical warhead."

My remarks about censorship appear to have incensed—or at least worried—some of my readers. In fact we were treated here yesterday to an American TV program devoted to the "sins" of Israeli censorship of the media. One broadcaster was actually required—not to stay alive or avoid banishment, but to maintain his press card—to announce that he had broken censorship rules—as the result of ignorance of the rules, he added—and to apologize.

I know—and have seen—the censorship rules prepared by the office of the army spokesman (Nahman Shai). They are clear and are distributed with every press card. But the playing of games, including that of the innocent, is standard practice for newsmen. (I am from the pre-"newspeople" generation; by "newsmen" I mean both sexes and even Kantian nonpeople, a term that I sometimes apply to certain journalists—particularly those who have made a full-time vocation of Israel bashing.) The CNN correspondent whom I described as tricking the Israeli Army censor by revealing—while asking in a live broadcast if he was allowed to mention—that the area bombed by Scuds that night was a residential district did so with pride at his own resourcefulness. The possibility that—by revealing this information—he was endangering lives was of no interest or of only secondary interest to him. These are acts of malicious and selfish self-aggrandizement, under the hypocritical guise of "free speech." All this took place under censorship; what limits could we, should we, expect in its absence? None?

I am aware that there is responsible journalism and have even witnessed it in action. But these are rare and remarkable activities that are more anecdotal than frequent. And as praiseworthy as responsible journalism is, the more frequent lack of responsibility shown by reporters is reprehensible and may even be the direct cause of deaths of innocents.

Israel is chided and castigated for imposing censorship on reporters. We say that we are not willing to risk lives for the titillation of TV audiences. Do you really think that your vicarious involvement in our suffering is an expression of the value of free speech? So it sounds—at least from this vantage point in space and history.

What of censorship in Iraq? Why is that not the subject of a TV exposé? Peter Arnett's cooked, strained, and digested interview of Saddam Hussein is shown throughout the world as if this were unrestricted reporting. And he is pretty much the only reporter there. No reporting at all and what there is completely staged. But that is Iraq, we are told, and you are Israel. We are—or should be—used to being judged by a double standard, a much higher one for us, a much lower one for our opponents. But it still gets under our skins.

Americans are convinced that freedom of speech is an unlimited virtue. They are cynical about their government and do not believe it is as innocent or idealistic as it claims to be. They believe that the truth, as exposed by motivated and glory-hunting reporters, is an unequivocal virtue. Perhaps. But free speech has its limits. First of all, free speech may also allow the spread and acceptance of lies, defamation, and character assassination. But there is a free marketplace for ideas—this from the very same people who are against any other form of free market, by the way—and the good ideas will rise and the bad ones sink. But is there really a free marketplace for ideas and for "truth?" If the reporter who apologized had—by his report—been responsible for the death of innocent citizens of Israel, what good would his apology have done them?

The limits of free speech are not obvious, but they should be understood. First of all, they exist. No person should be allowed to cause death or damage by such speech. Libel law is now a joke; no one can possibly win a libel case these days. But the public is aware of this and the caveat is—or should be—obvious to anyone who enters public life. But what if someone in a crowded place starts screaming "Fire!" and causes a stampede, resulting in wounded and even dead? Is that, too, to be allowed? Of course not. And that situation is quite similar to some of the reporting I have seen from here. It places lives in jeopardy and cannot be either excused or allowed.

Another form of free speech that must be curbed and denied is that which incites to overthrow governments which advocate free speech. Such speech is dangerous in that it wishes to eliminate free speech. Arnett's broadcast of Saddam could—without stretching the point too finely—be included in that category. Once again, we cannot say that Arnett or the networks were unaware of the dangers. Did not Ted Koppel go the same route with Saddam Hussein? And later apologize for being duped and used? That was before the war. Apologies of that sort in the time of war are less than pathetic; they tend to ridicule the value of human life.

Censorship has a long and not completely dishonorable history, even in the U.S. The *Ulysses* court case—the decision is reprinted in editions of the novel—would not have been of interest in the absence of censorship. And American history did not begin in 1933. It was possible to free the slaves at a time when censorship was accepted as a norm. True, Americans now have *Penthouse* and hard-porn movies. I don't; I am not sure that the quality of life—another interesting and perhaps dangerous new Americanism—I experience is inferior to that of those who enjoy them.

Finally, war is not a normal situation. And this is war. Standards of behavior that are unacceptable in normal times are everyday events in war, not the least killing people and destroying property. Our priorities are different, a state of emergency exists and everything else—or at least most other things—must take a temporary back seat to the priority of preserving our country, our way of life, and the lives and properties of our citizens. Even reporters. The threat of a poison gas attack is still upon us; it seems very real to us. We know that there are at least ten to twelve Scud missile launchers still functioning. Saddam Hussein may be becoming desperate. We do not know. Nerve gas was released in the bombing of a chemical works in Iraq. We are not quiet.

TUESDAY, 5 FEBRUARY: WAITING

Another night without an attack. We are waiting. Last night was the second night in a row without an attack. Since the onset of the war, we have not had more than two consecutive nights without an attack. Does this mean that there will be one tonight? We do not know. The attacks this past week have been ineffective, with Scuds landing short of their marks, in uninhabited regions. Is this a reflection of reduced capacity of the Iraqis to fire missiles in the wake of the one-per-minute sorties of the coalition? Or bad weather, too? Today it is sunny and cold here; is that a reason to be concerned? We live in a vacuum, an information void that renders us impotent when our overwhelming desire is to know, to understand—a desire that grows from day to day.

There clearly has been general relaxation here; it is now quite obvious. As I walk through the streets of Jerusalem, carrying my gas mask with me, I am clearly in a minority. Relatively few people are now carrying masks; only a few days ago almost everyone carried his mask with him.

Two motifs can be clearly identified in the Israeli character to explain the relaxation. One is the macho impulse, to be a *gever*, a real man (or woman; the masculine word serves both sexes in modern Hebrew). The other is not to be a *fryer*, a sucker. (I think the word, not Hebrew in origin, is derived from the German *frei*, or "free." How did *free* degenerate to a pejorative? It seems that the term referred to a person so free as not to think as the crowd did; it still does refer to someone who is not a member of the herd, but what was originally intended as a compliment has come to mean, by an interesting but not unnatural transition, a state of being to be avoided.)

I have spoken of the psychological impact of wearing gas masks, especially on children. I would like to report on the responses of my three oldest grandchildren, eight, five and a half, and five. Adi, the oldest, was least affected. She refused to leave her home until school began again for her grade and now seems unaffected. Anat, five and a half years old, still will not go back to school, is much more restrained and quiet than usual. When asked why she did not want to go back to school, Anat answered, "Because I do not want to die."

Yochai, five, needs the proximity of his gas mask and his own sealed room. He appeared completely normal when my wife took him home from his improvised kindergarten (no more than five children, per instructions)—until she saw that they had forgotten to take his gas mask. When he understood this, and on the way back to get the mask, he became uncontrollably disturbed, his behavior bordering on hysteria, until the mask was retrieved. He will no longer eat in my house although he loves my wife's cooking; he insists on being near his own sealed room; ours will not do. He makes a papier-mâché model of a child with a gas mask.

None of these children live in a city that has been attacked yet.

I am not so much afraid as I am angry.

An educational spin-off of the present emergency: Elementary school teachers were asked to prepare worksheets for pupil use and to meet, one hour to each group, the next day with small groups—no more than five in a group—of pupils to go over the work. This approach, a solution to an emergency situation, has not only proven successful but is seen by many educators as an improvement over the classroom-centered activities practiced until now. (A cousin, Samuel "Tami" Baskin, formerly of Antioch College, years ago introduced a similar method of instruction for college and university students, called—I think—Office Universities, where students were given office space, access to reading materials, and long-term assignments with occasional consultation with teachers. He would be interested to hear that it works for children as well. He has a son now living in Jerusalem, working in Tel Aviv.)

The problems of the deaf and the blind are particularly apparent in the time of alarms. The deaf cannot hear the siren or radio and TV announcements; and the blind are subject to the stress of having to find their way and seal their poison-gas-proof rooms, and then there is their dependence on seeing-eye dogs. Some thought has been given to these problems, with sensitivity to the added strain placed on relatives and neighbors of these disabled people. The deaf have now been provided with buzzers whose vibrations indicate the beginning and end of an alarm. There are plans, not yet implemented, to add words to the TV screen announcements that report the progress of the alert, important to all of us, or to use signers to spell out the announcements. The blind now have muzzle masks for their dogs, a benefit to all owners of large dogs.

Terrorist attacks, promised by both Saddam Hussein and the PLO, have begun here. It is interesting that even here, in the land of Israel, the common enemy, the attacks are directed not against us, Israel, but against members of the coalition. The British Airways office in East (mostly Arab) Jerusalem was trashed last night; windows broken, gasoline poured inside and ignited. No injuries. Just property damage. The phenomenon has been reported elsewhere. It will increase.

Some more on censorship. Is an interview with Saddam Hussein just distasteful? Or broadcasting to the world scenes orchestrated by Iraqi propagandists of the problems with a children's hospital whose electrical supply has been compromised by the coalition bombings? I am not sure that it is not much worse than that.

Why is it necessary to broadcast these things? Does it add to our insight into the conflict or just pluck on untuned emotional strings in us? What cynicism dictates the production of these film clips?

Do not the Iraqis share responsibility for the plight of the infants by their unprovoked invasion, rape, and annexation of Kuwait? (Share? In fact they are primarily responsible.) Why does no one ask if the incubators shown—out of use because electric power supply is unreliable following coalition bombings—are the very same incubators stolen from Kuwaiti hospitals? After throwing out the babies in them? What motivates the TV producers to show them? Is it really concern for justice or fair play? Pardon me if I doubt that.

My impulse is to say, "Shame, shame," to the TV producer who showed that clip.

"Peter Arnett's reports from Baghdad," writes a correspondent, "as well as all reports from Saudi Arabia, Israel, and the Pentagon, are clearly labeled 'cleared by Iraqi/Israeli/U.S. military/whatever censors.'" But is there no difference between these? Do you think that everybody understands the difference?

I am told that I missed seeing a BBC "Newsnight" program that examined censorship in Iraq a week ago. This program pointed out that scenes of damage to civilian population areas were cuts of previous footage. It also showed a Japanese crew in Iraq interviewing what purported to be an ordinary civilian complaining about bomb damage; he was being prompted by a military person standing off-camera.

Am I the only one who missed seeing that program? I doubt it, just as I doubt that the TV producers who play this faked footage missed the BBC exposé. But, in the name of Freedom of the Press, they continue to play the released material with the very same (fair?) censorship disclosure used for Israeli/allied film clips.

There is a difference.

It is also possible not to broadcast "cooked" news.

I am sometimes amused by the rows of distinguished reporters listening to Pete Williams' briefings in the Pentagon. (Wolf Blitzer, who sits in the front row, left, used to be a *Jerusalem Post* reporter and is the author of a rather unsympathetic book on Jonathan Pollard. His "authoritative" reports on CNN have gained him some fame in this war. Does he really have news to report, other than the managed news passed along to him?) This scene is repeated in Saudi Arabia, where the daily military report is given out, just so much and no more. The reporters take notes assiduously, aware of their own role as players in this TV drama. They ask questions. When Pete Williams or Captain Harrington do not want to answer, they say so or say that they will get the information and come back with it. They don't, as a rule. They only let out what they want. This is not censored, but it certainly is managed—and TV producers have the effrontery to show this management itself as news. Ah, well.

■ The military is supposed to win in any conflict it enters; that is what it is trained for. Sometimes the enemy uses unconventional weapons; sometimes it is well disguised. The military appears to be heavy, even ponderous, as it tries to overrun the opponent, although it can move gracefully, swivel-hipped, outflanking its opponents.

But a good army has to win if it wants to be taken seriously. And it does want to be taken seriously, and it does win, as it eventually did against Senator McCarthy, using the then brand-new television and the venerable breed of New England lawyers as their weapons. And it did once again, defeating the reporters in the Gulf War.

Do most spectators appreciate that another war was fought by the military during this conflict, a war between the military and the press? I am sure that the military is celebrating its victory—and a smashing victory it was—over the press with as much joy and pleasure as it did in celebrating the elegant crushing of Saddam Hussein. *Elegant* is the operative word here, too; the victory over the press was accomplished without anyone understanding what happened. The press knows that they were had, but I think that they still have not fathomed how.

The press had become a self-indulgent, swaggering bully feeding on everything around it. You are interviewed and assumed a criminal until proven otherwise—a prerogative of the press, granted to them by whom? By the Constitution? Not at all. It is an award they have given themselves in a maneuver that would embarrass even Joe McCarthy; this prerogative is not granted even to the courts. I find it a bitter potion to realize that the same press—which, led by the Fred Friendlys and the Ed Murrows of an earlier time, took on and defeated McCarthy, is now guilty of the same excesses that he was. The press can go anywhere, ask any question, express any opinion; responsibility is not required.

Until now.

Now the military has taken on the press, reduced them to minor players in the major drama of the decade. The military outsmarted the press in the press's home court. They turned the interview into a game where they had all the good lines, where the members of the fourth estate were bit players at best. The television producers and editors needed the coverage and were willing to sacrifice their stars to these bit roles; they did not revolt, did not attempt to black out the military. It was the other way around; the General Kellys and the Admiral Neals called the tune.

Bravo to the military. (I can hardly imagine my saying that.) The ■ press needed a lesson in humility. They got it.

I gather that my remarks about increased birthrates in hospitals outside of Tel Aviv were unclear and misunderstood. This increase does not reflect an increase in premature births but rather tells us about expectant mothers in Tel Aviv who have decided to give birth away from their threatened city.

An advertisement in the newspaper yesterday:

> Black-Brown Yorkshire Terrier Lost
> Answers to the name "Bonnie"
> On Jabotinsky Street, Tel Aviv
> The honest finder will be rewarded

Has the smart dog joined others who decided that Tel Aviv is not the most safe place these days? Not even for dogs.

WEDNESDAY, 6 FEBRUARY: AFTER THREE QUIET NIGHTS

It is sunny and warmer than yesterday; it was pleasant to walk through the renewed-by-the-rains grass on the campus of the university. There was something springlike in the heavy, lethargic feeling that accompanied me in my walk. But something is wrong.

It is not spring, not here, not anywhere, not even in the southern hemisphere where everything, including the direction that flushing water swirls, is backwards. You can't even get oriented from the stars in the night sky there. And here we have gone through a third night without an alarm, three in a row. We feel this both as a blessing and as a threat. What does this chaotic mind, this Saddam Hussein, have in store for us?

Until now we have not had three consecutive quiet nights since the Scud attacks started. Does it mean that Saddam Hussein's missile launchers have really been effectively inactivated by the massive coalition bombings? Or have these same bombings so distracted him that we are no longer (or at least not for the time being) on his agenda? Perhaps he has killed all the officers responsible for sending missiles at us for their failures—the last five falling short of their marks, landing impotently in uninhabited areas? He is capable of killing his officers; his past record shows that. It was Saddam Hussein who, when urged by one of his cabinet members during the Iraq-Iran conflict to abdicate—as a ruse only—and once the conflict was settled to resume power, walked up to that devious but unfortunate minister and executed him (for his deviousness? for his disloyalty?) by shooting him through the head. Saddam

Hussein does not use decapitation as his neighbor, Saudi Arabia, still does, but dead is dead.

Or, as we fear, is he saving up something for us, even possibly waiting for us to let down our guard? For Saddam Hussein has a long unsettled account with us, ever since we bombed and destroyed his nuclear weapon capability in the June 1981 raid on the French-built Tamuz reactor in Ossirak. Well, destroyed the reactor if not his capability, but at least we set him back ten years. He has never paid us back for that and we know that he has neither forgotten nor forgiven us for that slap in his face. His impotence against our attack and his inability to pay us back in like coin has strengthened his hatred for us, his enmity to us—a hatred and enmity which can only have grown over the years, for our demonstrating as we have his weakness and vulnerability—not the most desirable qualities for a self-announced savior of Arab pride, for a new Saladin.

Saddam Hussein is still motivated by his need to galvanize Arab and Muslim support to his cause. Motivated to hit us hard. Although his efforts to date with the Scuds have not been as successful as he may have wished, he has had some success. Popular support for his cause, perceived as an Arab or Muslim fighting the imperialistic West intent on turning the Arab world and its resources to its needs, has spread through the Arab/Muslim world, even among members of the coalition. Three hundred thousand supporters parading for Saddam Hussein in Morocco join similar but smaller rallies in Egypt and Jordan. Volunteers for his army are being recruited in Pakistan and Indonesia. Iraq is perceived as suffering only for its being Arab and standing in the way of Western aggression and imperialism.

We understand the phenomenon here in Israel. We have watched the PLO turn the Israel-Palestine story upside down. The unsuccessful Arab attempts to oust us from our country are said to be and then understood as and finally remembered as Israel's stealing the country from the Palestinians. Just so, Saddam Hussein's unprovoked invasion of Kuwait, its subsequent rape and annexation, are now forgotten, and only the U.S.-led invasion of the Arab subcontinent is seen, understood, and remembered as proof of imperialistic Western designs on Arab hegemony and oil.

Israel is still a crucial element for Saddam Hussein in galvanizing Arab/Muslim support and forcing Arab nations to withdraw from the coalition, where only the U.S. and Britain appear to be fully committed. Even the threatened Saudis feel the pressure of groundswell support for Saddam Hussein. He who ravages Israel, the symbol of Western intrusion into the Arab subcontinent, has the best chance to rally this support and thus to pull apart the coalition.

We know that Saddam Hussein has poison gas; his own citizens have been poisoned by it. He has already used it to kill five thousand helpless Kurds and in battle against the Iranians. There is good reason to believe that he also has the armamentarium of biological warfare at his disposal. He hints that he has nuclear weapons, but all we know is that Iraq had functioning reactors; he has never tested such a weapon. These are the three threats that most concern us. And we wait. And wonder. And question. And speculate. And try to return to normal routines—as much as possible.

The need for information is compelling. Those remote from the battles need it and spur the media on to provide it, at almost any cost. We who are closer need information even more; we hunger for it, we thirst for it. We watch TV while keeping the radio on in the background and a third ear peeled to the possible sound of a siren. And we buy more newspapers than ever before—and we are a newspaper-buying country even in peaceful times. Not a few people read as many as three or four different newspapers each day. And many more join them in buying the Friday (weekend) editions.

■ We do not always believe our government. We know that we are not told things; we frequently read about them first in the foreign press. But we do not think that our government is hostile to us; we know that they are on our side. They are trying; sometimes they make mistakes, but the ultimate goal is always the same—the survival of our way of life.

We also know that the government can be very stupid. Stupidity is a characteristic of governments. But we can choose between different forms of stupidity; that is the nature of democracy. If we do not like what the government says or does, we protest, loudly. We try to defeat them in the next election.

But when war comes, we are all on the same side—the side of
■ survival.

During an alarm, this need becomes acute. The Israeli wife of one of the foreign ambassadors tells that during an attack her husband insists that she translate every word broadcast. We can understand that. Most wives and children of diplomats were evacuated. A notable exception is the wife of the Egyptian ambassador, neither Israeli nor Jewish. She insists on remaining in Tel Aviv during the attacks, sharing our fortune and misfortunes. The example of Mrs. Bassioni is reassuring; it suggests to us that peace with the Arab world is possible.

Dr. Ruth Westheimer, sexologist and American TV personality, is visiting us. She is a Holocaust survivor and lived here for some time. Her Hebrew is still quite good and she explains her visit as both professional—to study conditions under stress—and personal. "In 1945, the only country that would agree to accept me was Palestine/Israel. My family was killed in Auschwitz; now I must be here."

She expresses her views about sex problems during a war. If there are problems, the added stress will only make them worse. On the other hand, she admits, the problems may be dwarfed by the real danger.

In a TV interview, she said that it was better if sex were deferred until after the conflict. The interviewer interjected, "I have a friend . . . ," his point being that the need was great and sex could be relaxing and reassuring. Dr. Ruth, as she is called, said that in such a case the sealed room with its negative connotations should never be used. In fact, it was advisable not to have sex at night. "Do it in the daytime, send your children to the neighbors—Israelis are so cooperative and helpful, especially in emergencies."

We cannot, as a modern Western society, function without opinion polls. And so the latest poll shows that 60 percent of us believe that the war will be prolonged; 80 percent of us are for the government's policy of restraint, but 83 percent feel that Israel must respond immediately if unconventional war measures (chemical, biological, or nuclear) are used against us; 57 percent of us complain of feeling "down"; 7 percent are actually elated.

For 19 percent of us—the most common response—the hardest part of the current situation is worry about members of the family. For another 18 percent, a close second, it is the uncertainty that bothers most. Other responses were much less common; 8 percent were not bothered at all.

As to leaving home in face of the threat, 35 percent of residents of

Tel Aviv and 16 percent of Haifa residents had already left or were ready to leave home for safer parts if the attacks continue.

Jerusalem's cafes are again filling up, at least during the daytime. These popular refuges are doing a good business, with their *café hafuch* (cappuccino; that name is reserved here for espresso coffee served with whipped cream and cinnamon) and rich cakes. I overheard the following conversation at the next table:

> He: You are a nonreactor.
> She: Yes, a nuclear nonreactor.

THURSDAY, 7 FEBRUARY: A NEW ORDER

It is raining hard again, thundering as well. Last night was another night without missiles, but the sensitized Tel Avivians were startled and even frightened at midnight by the thunder, thinking it was yet another attack. Here in Jerusalem, we can afford the luxury of first checking the source of the noise, for we don't really believe—but we are not sure—that the sudden boom signals an attack. There is no attack. This was the fourth night in a row without attack.

For several days now, Jordan's Crown Prince Hassan, the brother of King Hussein, has been giving TV interviews condemning the U.S. and coalition indifference to Jordan's plight. The signs were clear, the signal given to the West to bail out Jordan, but there was no response.

Jordan was already in desperate financial straits before the onset of the Persian Gulf crisis; the two waves of refugees that have swarmed across the border from Iraq—the first with the capture and ravaging of Kuwait in the late summer, the second now with the bombing of Iraq—have placed a tremendous additional economic burden on Jordan. In addition, two-thirds of Jordan's oil supply came from Iraq, and oil shortages present in Iraq following the coalition bombings are also apparent in Jordan.

Moreover, Jordan has been dealing with Iraq despite the sanctions and boycott of that country for the past five months, providing produce. (And even Israeli farm products, as West Bank farmers— whose trucks change their license plates as soon as they cross the

Adam Bridge from Israel to Jordan—drove their produce to Iraq, as they formerly did to Kuwait.) Indeed, the Jordanian port of Aqaba has served during the period of the sanctions as Iraq's only outlet to the sea; trucks carrying containers from steamers arriving in Aqaba—none ever searched by U.S. and coalition vessels patrolling the Red Sea—left Aqaba before the war at the rate of one every five minutes.

■ The bridges over the Jordan River, the Allenby and particularly the Adam bridges, are the only direct routes between Israel and Jordan. Only Arabs can go from Israel to Jordan. Non-Arabs, non-Jews are not allowed to enter Jordan from Israel: they carry passports with an Israeli stamp, and admitting them would be tantamount to admitting that we exist. They usually carry Israeli, Jordanian, and Kuwaiti license plates, changing them at each border. Palestinian Arabs who carry produce grown on the West Bank have free access to both sides of the bridges; they truck their wares to the east and south, before the war primarily to Kuwait. Iraq, rich in water with the Tigris and Euphrates rivers, grows most of its own produce.

Non-Jewish tourists can pass from Jordan to Israel without any problem, unless they are Arab. Palestinians with residence permits and Arabs with relatives on the West Bank are allowed into the West Bank after being searched by army authorities for concealed weapons.

Both sides of the bridges are monitored by soldiers, Israeli on the west, Jordanian on the east. The heaviest traffic is seen during the *Hadj* (related to the word *hegira*), the annual pilgrimage to Mecca, an obligation for Muslims. At this time busloads of pilgrims cross
■ the bridges on their way to and from Mecca.

More than half of Jordan's residents are Palestinians, many still living in refugee camps set up in 1948. These, like their fellow Palestinians elsewhere, see Saddam Hussein as a possible savior, as a Saladin who will lead the Arabs to a victory over the West, and particularly to the dismantling of Israel. It is no surprise that they support Saddam Hussein overwhelmingly; they see the present war exactly as Saddam Hussein has tried to sell it to the Arab/Muslim world, as a battle between the good Arabs and the evil Israelis (their placards add "Israelis = Jews," so there will be no doubt), with the U.S. and its allies doing the fighting for Israel.

Scud missiles fly over Jordan on their way from Iraq to Israel. It has been rumored that some of these may actually have been fired from mobile launchers driven to Jordan. Now a new rumor has it that the last missile fired at Israel actually fell in Jordanian territory. Jordan knows that any Israeli retaliation on Iraq will involve Israel aircraft flying through Jordanian airspace; the Jordanians are pretty much helpless to prevent this: their air force and anti-aircraft defenses are just not up to stopping the Israeli planes.

■ After the war we learned of an Israeli plan to fly through Saudi Arabia, with U.S./Saudi permission. This clever possibility was less
■ obvious as it involved much greater distances.

Thus, it was not a great surprise to me that King Hussein, in a dramatic speech yesterday, allied himself with the Iraqis in a war of the Arab nations to keep the imperialistic forces of the West out of the Arab subcontinent, where their purpose is—says King Hussein—to subjugate and humiliate the Arabs and thereby control Arab resources and propagate Western influence.

Jordan was caught in a pincer with little room to maneuver; its dependence on Iraq, its largely pro-Saddam population, and the lack of desperately needed economic aid from the West together tipped the scales in favor of a pro-Iraqi stance.

■ I suspect that Jordan will not suffer greatly—just as their partners in support of Saddam Hussein, the Palestinians, will not suffer too much—for King Hussein's decision. After the war, the Americans will again see Jordan as one of the moderate and more stable states in the region, and therefore worthy of support. This has happened before. How can you learn that crime does not pay if it
■ does?

The Americans have already announced that they will be responsible for rebuilding Iraq after the war is over. Shades of *The Mouse That Roared*. Just as Germany and Japan were helped—with U.S. aid—to regain their pre-World War II status and to achieve even greater economic power than they ever had. And now they are allowed to enjoy the envious status of reluctant economic supporters—without participating in the military actions or casualties—of the coalition efforts. This is, of course, particularly disturbing in the case of Germany, which supplied encouragement funds to German firms that aided in the building of the Iraqi war machine and supplied the technical know-how that may now be responsible for the deaths of U.S. and coalition soldiers as well as Israeli citizens.

With the possibility of being "rebuilt" by the U.S. after the war now a tangible option, perhaps there is every reason in the world for the Jordanians to side against the U.S. and its allies.

King Hassan of Morocco, a member of the coalition, has also joined in the general Arab/Muslim support of Saddam Hussein, calling him a modern Saladin who will restore vanished glories of the Arab nation. The three hundred thousand participants in the pro-Saddam rally in Fez this week probably helped convince him of the wisdom of this action. This is indeed strange, with a U.S. ally extolling the allies' chief enemy and villain.

Continuing the line of topsy-turvy results that might be expected after an allied victory is the announcement by Secretary of State Baker that after the war is over the Middle East will have to undergo changes to guarantee its stability and to undo injustice.

Is this announcement meant to bring hope to the Kurds dispersed and persecuted in Iraq and Iran and barely tolerated in southern Turkey? Not at all: it is another reference to pushing a Palestinian State down Israel's already gagging throat. For clearly—by *Mouse That Roared* logic—the PLO, which sides with Saddam Hussein, is to be rewarded, while Israel, which has been a good little nation, showing "admirable" restraint at U.S. urging, is to be punished.

Is that clear now?

In the discussion of a general Middle East settlement after the war, the phrase "A New Order" (in the Middle East) has been articulated. Use of this expression must reflect the height of insensitivity, worthy of some special award. It is not enough that Israel is again being threatened with poison gas attacks while the Nazi use of Zyklon B to exterminate the Jews is still fresh in our memory, but now we are treated to a rebirth of another Nazi relic, "The New Order." And directed at us—again.

Mayor Dinkins of New York City has joined the new pilgrimage to the Patriot launchers. Carrying the obligatory gas mask—I wish that Israelis were as conscientious about carrying theirs as our visitors are—he is interviewed at one of the launcher sites in the Tel Aviv area. He praises us, our restraint, calmness, fortitude. (Will he tell that to Farrakhan? To Jesse Jackson?) He proves his political astuteness by asking one of the American soldiers in the Patriot crew if it is true that they deliberately withheld fire from Scuds that appeared destined to land in areas populated by Arabs. The GI breaks into a broad smile and says, "Hell, no!"

They are all coming now, German, Italian, Czech parliamentarians, American sexologists, African-American congressmen who tell us that the Black Caucus's record is 100 percent behind bills supporting Israel. They all visit the Patriots—our new tourist attraction. Israelis are not allowed near the batteries; fathers take their sons to see them from afar, explain their purpose, that they are now "ours."

I wonder if the African-American visitors have seen our Ethiopian immigrants, who—on the average—are much darker than the visitors. At any rate, they have nothing to say about them. I gather that the limited support that they give us—and we welcome even that in the face of widespread African-American anti-Jewish feeling—cannot be compromised by excess, by admitting that we are also black, and that being black does not seem to be an issue here.

■ An Israeli correspondent informs me that Dinkins did indeed get himself photographed kissing an Ethiopian Jewish baby. He is a ■ more polished politician than I imagined.

There is another group of Black Hebrews—that is what they call themselves—here, mostly living in the town of Dimona, better known for other things. They are here as converts to a new religion/new-old people with their own prophet. Originating in Chicago, they have come on tourist visas and stayed on. They claim that they are the true Hebrews and that we, the Jewish Israelis, are usurpers who will be thrown out one day. There were some attempts years back to deport them; they are here illegally and are generally a financial burden where they live. But the fear of negative responses among African Americans and other black nationalists stopped that.

This has not stopped the Farrakhans of America from inciting blacks to anti-Semitism, nor the Bishop Tutus and Nelson Mandelas from siding with the PLO against us.

We still tell jokes. Here is a recent one: They are selling building lots in H2 now. They are only seven minutes—by missile—from Tel Aviv.

FRIDAY, 8 FEBRUARY: READY FOR THE GROUND BATTLE

For the fifth night we had no attack; at 02:00 we heard that a Scud was fired at Saudi Arabia and that two Patriots were fired to intercept it. We do not know if any damage was done. We are both worried and relieved. We act as if there is no longer any threat; we are convinced that a chemical attack is in the winds.

Movies are to open tonight for the first time—there are already daytime showings. But only 50 percent occupancy of each movie theater will be allowed. (We continue to worry about crowds, about the danger of mass casualties, of stampedes produced by panic.)

All schools will return to normal schedules. Government scandals and investigations which occupied our interest before the war are finding their way back into the newspapers. The price of electricity is lower; it was raised with the booming oil prices that first characterized the Persian Gulf crisis. Everything is normal, except for the sight of people carrying gas masks, in Tel Aviv more than in Jerusalem.

But we also hear of new weapons in Saddam Hussein's armamentarium, weapons that he has been saving, weapons that threaten us, that can kill us. We know that he would like nothing better than to make a successful strike in the heart of the "settlers." (*Settlers* is a term used by the PLO for Jews who have moved beyond the Green Line, into territory captured by Jordan and held by them until 1967, when their attempt to share in the spoils of an Arab war against Israel was rewarded by a loss of these territories. But it is clear that Radio Baghdad means something else when they talk about "settlers": they are talking about the "settlers" of Haifa and the "settlers" of Tel Aviv; they mean all Jews in Israel.)

Saddam Hussein has thrown down the gauntlet: it is all Arabs and Muslims, with himself at their head, against Jews; he has invited all Arabs and Muslims to join him; a groundswell of Arab public opinion in his favor threatens the cohesiveness of the coalition. (Hussein even made strong overtures to his one-time irrevocable enemy, Iran, to join in the "holy" objective.) Will the Arab nations in the coalition—particularly Morocco, Egypt, and Syria—be able to withstand the pro-Saddam surge of support in the streets of these countries?

Although the bombing of Iraqi military targets as well as supply and communication lines in Iraq and Kuwait has been very successful, it would appear that there is yet more to bomb, more to soften up. This form of warfare has the advantage—with coalition airplanes the only ones in the sky—of involving relatively few coalition casualties. But the threat of dissolution of the coalition appears to be sufficiently worrying to advance the timing of the ground battle. Secretary of Defense Cheney and Chief of Staff General Powell are in the Gulf to obtain an up-to-date evaluation of the situation before beginning the ground phase of the war—earlier than might be best from a purely military viewpoint.

If beginning the ground war has become an urgent matter for the U.S., so, too, has galvanizing Arab/Muslim support become to Saddam Hussein. With the name "Israel" a red flag in front of the bull for Arabs/Muslims, what better way is there for him to achieve this support than to show that he is capable of hurting—or even more—Israel? We know this and wait; we have already prepared as best we can. We have interceptor airplanes in the skies at all times; Patriot antimissile missiles are in position. We have distributed antipoison masks and related equipment; we have prepared sealed rooms—we know how to use them.

We hear that Saddam Hussein has other weapons that threaten us, weapons that he has not yet used. Russian SS-12 missiles were supposed to have been destroyed in 1988, following a disarmament agreement with the U.S. But now we hear that some were distributed before that among Russia's allies, including Iraq, before the public destruction of these weapons; these missiles were not destroyed. The SS-12 is a missile of much higher accuracy and longer range than the relatively crude Scuds which have been used to date. The SS-12 range of 950 kilometers (about 570 miles) is more than enough to reach Israel.

Another weapon that we might have to worry about is the giant cannon. This device was brought to the attention of the world when Israeli pressure forced various European nations to seize "pipes" of enormous size that were actually components—parts of the barrel— of the cannon. Now we hear that three such cannon, with a range of 750 kilometers (450 miles), far enough to reach Israel's cities, did reach Iraq.

Even the best air defense cannot guarantee that not a single plane will get through. We fear an air attack as even one plane reaching Tel Aviv or Haifa with a chemical weapon would be disastrous to us.

We go on as if life is returning to normal. But we know better.

A military pilot suggested — after examining the pictures of damaged Baghdad shown on TV — that a large portion of the damage is the result of Iraqi antiaircraft (AA) activity and not the aftermath of allied attacks at all. He pointed out that in the video footage shown of Baghdad at night coalition aircraft are all but unseen — mostly flying at high altitude — while streams of Iraqi tracer bullets and rockets fill the sky, apparently hitting nothing. On the principle that everything that goes up must come back down, much of the damage is probably caused by Iraqi antiaircraft installations themselves, concentrated as they are throughout the city of Baghdad, in the most densely populated regions. Many of the major military targets are indeed near the center of Baghdad. With the breakdown of communications that has resulted from the heavy coalition bombings, the AA generally do not have the benefit of coordinating radar — most large radar units have already been knocked out — while the radars of individual guided antiaircraft missiles are misled by coalition jamming and incoming fire. These added sources of inaccuracy contribute to the number of returned "friendly" missiles.

Even visible guidance of the AA fire is difficult; the only visible parts of the attacking aircraft at night are the aircraft engines, which are not easy to identify in a sky full of tracer bullets and AA missile rocket engines.

Coalition planes are equipped with sophisticated evasion mechanisms which are programmed to neutralize the local radars or heat sensors of the AA missiles. (According to legend, good pilots can still escape missiles by sudden evasive action, again resulting in wasted missiles falling to earth.) When the planes come in low, the AA guns fire up, hoping to produce some damage by luck alone. On low runs, the AA missile radars frequently do not have time to lock on to the planes or to arm properly. This was already proven in the American raid on Libya, where the Libyan gunners fired many AA missiles that either had no radar lock-on or passed the attacking aircraft before the warheads had armed themselves. These missiles fell back to earth in Tripoli, producing considerable damage.

AA missile warheads generally detonate only when they are quite close to a plane—or another sizable target such as an Iraqi building.

A correspondent sees an unexpected—and encouraging if true—phenomenon taking place in the U.S. as everyone senses that the ground war is approaching; he calls it "a great healing." He perceives the Unites States now acting as a united nation, even as an angry—righteously angry—nation, for the first time in twenty years. As an example he cites a congressman's response to Secretary of State Baker's comments about rebuilding Iraq after the war; Baker was told that this would not occur "in this lifetime"!

He attributes this unity and determination, at least partly, to accumulated hate for the Arabs that has grown in the U.S. since the Iranians—who are perceived as Arabs—held the Americans hostage in 1979. The humiliating failure of the rescue attempt added to the wounded pride of American withdrawal from Vietnam (which is a source of very mixed feelings in America: all negative on the Left and in the media—witness the rash of negative movies—negative only in the area of wounded pride for an ignominious involvement and withdrawal on the side of the Right and the silent majority). According to this view, Saddam Hussein just turned out to be a convenient focus for the smoldering hate and frustration already present. Of course it was important that he be evil, opposed to the U.S., and Arab. But he was "just unlucky enough to be in the gunsights when we lost our collective temper."

A number of congressmen have called for the use of hard-radiation nuclear missiles on Iraq prior to beginning the ground battle.

King Hussein of Jordan has come down squarely on the side of Saddam Hussein. In his speech declaring his commitment to the Arab cause, the king denounced each Arab nation in the coalition, one by one. Except for one. He failed to denounce Syria. Since Iraqi oil—which provided two-thirds of the source for Jordan before the war—is no longer available, Syria has become the only supplier of oil to Jordan. Syria, a member of the coalition, but no lover of Israel, finds nothing wrong in supplying Jordan—the ally of Syria's declared enemy—with oil. Business as usual. And, what's more, Syria may yet change its mind, with President Assad coming down on the side of Saddam Hussein.

The Middle East. An interesting place, yes?

Doctors tell us that we should forget about Saddam Hussein; forgetting him will help us relax.

I think that forgetting about doctors will help us relax more. At the beginning of the war, medical advice, particularly psychological tips for handling the problems of children, helped. Even hearing about some of the psychophysical symptoms was interesting; it's nice to know that you are not the only one suffering with problems urinating, etc. But enough is enough. People—doctors particularly—never seem to know when enough is enough. We are tired of hearing about physical symptoms that are the products of anxiety.

Let's talk about something more pleasant! Even Saddam Hussein.

Today, a full-page portrait of General Schwarzkopf in the newspapers; it is a cigarette ad. "Be a man and smoke N——."

SATURDAY, 9 FEBRUARY: ANOTHER ATTACK; WE PREPARE TO REJOICE

Last night, Friday, was our Sabbath. After the Kiddush, the blessing made on drinking wine—we use a sweet red wine that is probably not familiar to those who have never tried it although I remember that it was cherished not only by Jews in my days in the U.S. but also by alcoholics, who called it "Sneaky Pete" even though it was sold as "Old Rabbinical" or "Mogen David"—we had an uneventful and delicious Sabbath meal. We began with the soft bread we call *halla* and then a lemon chicken soup on which delicious dumplings made of chopped turkey breast floated gently. This was followed by slicing a whole turkey and eight of us ate the dark and white meat, according to our preferences, with a casserole of sweet potatoes and pineapple and a large salad. After tea and cake we said grace. Then my oldest son and his wife and two children walked home carrying their three gas masks and an incubator for the two-and-one-half-year-old with them.

The classical music station of the radio, "The Voice of Music," has been my salvation since the war began, providing both a point of stability for me in these terrible times and a source of the familiar and the pleasurable. It is good to know that even in times of concern and distraction there is pleasure to be had in old familiar friends and activities. For the first few days of the attacks on us, this station joined the others as they all broadcast together, usually with popular or rock music only between announcements of attacks and war news. What a change from normal times! From times when four brief news announcements were the only interruptions in eighteen hours of broadcasting a good selection of classic music. After the first week of attacks, "The Voice of Music" was returned to the air in its own right, joining the other stations only at the time of an attack. This was understood as a move to normalcy.

With observant Jews who neither turn on electrical appliances or turn them off on the Sabbath in mind, "The Voice of Music" was sacrificed last night. In normal times, such a decision would have produced a vocal and indignant protest from the antireligious here, who appear to be every bit as religious in their antireligiosity as are the religious in their faith. But these are not normal times and—for the most part—old battles have been put aside, to be fought again once the danger is over. I did think with some compassion of the nonreligious who this night had neither the flavor of the Sabbath meal nor the consolation of good music. At least I had one, the one that I had chosen.

■   The relationship between religion and state in Israel is not simple; the dual nature of Judaism is religious-nationalist and secular-nationalist. Some Jewish reform movements insist that there is a religious form of Judaism that does not involve nationalism. They are talking about a private form of Judaism, not the historical religion. In Judaism, prayers for return to a literal Zion are recited several times a day and more often on the Sabbath and holidays.

The law of the land is not, in general, religious law. In one area, however, religious law is in control: marriage and divorce. For those not acquainted with Jewish law, this situation may appear strange, but these laws really constitute the most important area of religious sensitivity among religious Jews. The problem underlying this special interest in marriage and divorce is the relationship of these laws to the *mamzer*—inappropriately translated as "bastard"—the child of a married woman with a man not her husband. Such people, the *mamzerim*, are excluded by the religion from marriage to Jews, as are their children. It may appear a cruel law, perhaps, but it reflects the importance to Jews of not touching another man's wife. To ensure that no Jew falls into the trap of marrying a mamzer and producing children who automatically become mamzerim themselves, it is necessary to have relatively lenient divorce laws, and the Jews were leaders in that area long before divorce became the fashion.

Religious control of marriage and divorce laws produces some problems in obtaining divorces and getting permission to marry. Some marry out of the country to avoid religious injunctions; such marriages are accepted in the state courts. Divorces, by contrast, remain a serious problem in certain cases, particularly when one of the partners, usually the man, refuses to grant a divorce or disappears.

There are other restrictive laws of marriage, involving male descendants of the priests who are not allowed to marry divorced women, but these are less troublesome. Jews are required to prevent such marriages, but if they do take place, they become retroactively legal.

At the local level, cities or towns decide which, if any, additional religious laws are to be observed. Thus, Haifa, the third largest city, has no public Sabbath observance, while in Tel Aviv and Jerusalem public transportation is shut down for the twenty-five hours of Sabbath.

The Israeli court system is roughly based on that of the British, but some Turkish law and, to a lesser extent, religious law are used in undefined areas. There is no death penalty in Israeli law, except in the case of crimes (that is, murder) against the human race as a whole. The death sentence has been handed down twice, in the Eichmann and Demjanjuk cases, and was actually carried out only in the former case. Demjanjuk's conviction has recently been appealed, of course. Religious law lists many cases in which the death penalty is called for but notes that a court that gives out more than one such sentence every seventy years is called a hanging court.

A number of religious political parties run for office in both local and national elections. In the Knesset, such parties now hold 18 of the 120 seats (15 percent). The religious are estimated to be 13 percent of the population, but as many as 27 percent more consider themselves religiously inclined—and since neither of the two major secular parties holds a majority, the religious parties usually join coalition governments in return for political and financial considerations. Thus their influence greatly exceeds their numbers, but not sufficiently to change the character of life in the country, which remains primarily secular.

"The Voice of Music" was to remain silent all Friday night and Saturday until sundown—unless an alarm was to be given. The station was indeed silent when I went to sleep, rather early—as I usually do on Friday nights. I slept well until I was awakened

Saturday morning at 02:39 by the siren blasting in my ears—it was the radio. Only a minute later was the siren heard outside. We were somewhat confused and slow getting to the sealed room; we were a bit out of practice after five consecutive nights without any alarm. (Later we would remember that this was the third attack on four Friday nights since the war began.)

Five of us (two men, three women) sat in the room, listening to the radio, readjusting our gas masks, asking each other how he or she was. Five is a maximum number for comfort in this room—not that we think of comfort; we have managed with as many as nine without difficulty.

The reports were quite slow in coming, as if the radio services in the time of attack had also gotten slightly rusty; it seems so natural to forget, to want to forget. It took more than ten minutes before Nahman Shai confirmed that there had been an attack, that one missile had been fired (the thirty-first directed at Israel out of fifty-nine Scuds fired), that it had landed and that all Israel was confined to the sealed rooms, in their gas masks. Some five minutes later we were told that it was now safe for all those not living in greater Tel Aviv and the Shomron to remove their masks and leave the sealed rooms. We were included in this partial all-clear and we removed our masks but remained in the sealed room to hear more; we felt the need to know more. Moreover, the radio was still active, broadcasting—for the most part—rather loud and distracting (definitely not classical) music. Sleep would not be easy.

Some five minutes later, an all-clear notice was given for the entire country. The weapon was conventional; no poison gas, no biological warhead. (We do not even allow ourselves to think about nuclear warheads.) No siren was sounded. There is usually a siren that announces the introduction of the Sabbath; this has been canceled since the beginning of the war to prevent confusion and panic. There is also a siren—a continuous blast instead of the rising-falling shriek of the attack warning—that is meant to indicate the all-clear. Following negative experiences with this signal and the multitude of false alarms that result from confusion and wrought nerves, this signal has not been used either for more than a week. The only siren to be heard now is the signal for a real attack.

We no longer hear translations of the announcements—other

than one, directing all listeners who need or want translations to listen to Channel A, the intellectual and mostly talk station, which is now set aside during attacks for translations in the languages commonly heard here.

Sleep does not seem possible until we know more. Nahman Shai reports that there is damage from the missile, but does not say where or how much. And are there wounded? Dead, God forbid? His voice seems to reflect nervousness; I comment on this and others agree. Only my wife thinks that what we hear as nervousness may be nothing more than distortion in the quality of the sound resulting from problems with the portable phone he is clearly using. He is at the scene of the missile landing; in the background we can hear noise of activity and people giving orders and calling to one another. He has never sounded nervous before. It must be pretty bad.

Forty-five minutes go by before we are told that a Scud missile has landed in the center of the country, that there is damage, and that there are wounded. Twenty-five wounded, two fairly seriously, but without danger to their lives; three hundred apartments are damaged, with many rendered homeless.

Eyewitness reports are heard. It appears that two Patriot anti-missile missiles were fired at the Scud and that there was an explosion as one or both of them hit the missile. It seems that fragments of the missile (missiles? How much did the Patriots contribute to all this?) landed in two adjacent streets and on the roofs of houses nearby. One young man who, while bringing his girlfriend home, witnessed the Patriots hitting the Scud, says that the time between the siren and the Patriot hit was less than one minute. If this is true, what has happened to the five-minute warning we were promised?

If we are right in thinking that the missile has landed in greater Tel Aviv, which lies along the Mediterranean coast, and was downed by a Patriot, there is a difficult question that has to be asked. If no Patriots were fired, wouldn't this missile have continued on into the sea, not producing any damage? Are the Patriots that are protecting us the very cause of the damage we are suffering?

At least no dead, only two badly wounded and their lives are not in danger—one we know had a shattered knee and had to undergo an emergency operation. We are somewhat relieved; it could have been much worse. Meanwhile the radio becomes silent; the station has reverted to its pre-attack status.

We go to sleep, more tired than we thought we were.

This morning we go to synagogue for Sabbath prayers. It is the Sabbath before the New Moon, which will be on Thursday and Friday of next week, and we recite the special prayer for the New Moon.

> May it be thy will, Lord our God and God of our fathers, to grant us this new month for happiness and for blessing. O grant us long life, a life of peace and well-being, a life of blessing and sustenance, a life of physical soundness, a life of piety and dread of sin, a life free from shame and disgrace, a life of abundance and honor, a life marked by our love for Torah and our fear of Heaven, a life in which the wishes of our hearts for happiness shall be fulfilled.
> Amen, Selah.

The New Moon will introduce the Jewish lunar month of Adar, which is the sixth or twelfth month of our calendar. (We have more than one way to count the months.) Adar is the month of Purim, the Festival of Lots described in the Book of Esther; this festival takes place on the fourteenth of Adar, three weeks from now. It is the most joyful and abandoned of Jewish holidays—one with-it rabbi even suggested that all Jews should turn on to celebrate the holiday, a suggestion that has not been generally adapted. Purim is a festival of farcical dramas written for the occasion and acted out or read in the *yeshivoth* (the religious equivalent of the university). Games, even forbidden card games, are allowed, and you are commanded to drink until you can know longer tell good from evil, a practice that seems to be followed only by the most religious and the most antireligious.

Jews are commanded to celebrate all the month of Adar—in moderation. And we try to, but it is difficult, these days, to contemplate joy, let alone with abandon. The very religious tell us, "Nonsense! A holiday is a holiday." They have faith; we will try to have as much. We will try to forget that there is much to worry about.

Today I noticed the first blooming of the narcissuses in my garden, an early sign of spring. The rain in the streets dried slowly in the cold sun; the yellow and white blooms appear delicate and virginal, thin and upright in the cold, daring to show their faces.

■   How do I feel about the Iraqis, bombed and frightened out of their wits? Opponents of Saddam Hussein are not friends of mine; the

Iraqis, as Arabs, are united in their hatred of me, as an Israeli, as a Jew. The United States supported Iraq as the enemy of Iran, America's enemy. It is a horrible mistake to allow "my enemy's enemy is my friend" to dictate private judgments and even more dangerous when it forms the basis for international politics and action.

My first reaction is to say, "Let them all be damned." They want my skin; I can hardly afford to sympathize with them. But I am Jewish and it is not so simple a matter for me.

The book of Jonah (which we read every Yom Kippur) tells of Jonah's anger at the sparing of the city of Nineveh—in Iraq, by the way—a city of corruption. God, whose relation to Jonah is highly personal, attempts to convince Jonah that he should feel mercy and care for these people, sinful as they are. Jonah sits in the sun; God has a shade tree grow over Jonah to shade him. But when God sends a worm to attack the tree and the tree withers, Jonah becomes very angry. At this point God says to Jonah, "You pitied the tree, for which you did nothing, nor made it grow; which grew in one night and perished in a night. Should I not spare Nineveh, that great city, with 120,000 inhabitants who cannot tell the difference between their right and left hands, as well as much cattle?" Thus the Book of Jonah ends, and we Jews learn from it that all of God's creatures, and humankind particularly, are to be pitied.

We also have an *aggada* that tells of the angels breaking out in song, singing the *hallel*—the joyful litany of praise of God sung on holy days—when they see Pharaoh and his forces drowning in the Red Sea, foiled in their attempt to destroy the Jewish people. God stops them immediately in anger and says, "How can you sing now when my creatures drown?" Once again the lesson for us is that we do not rejoice at the death of God's creatures, even if they are enemies, even if they seek our lives.

Thus, I cannot wish the death of Iraqis. But this reverence for life does not render me passive. I am commanded to kill those who threaten my life, and I will, but I regret the loss. I draw no joy from the sight of their sufferings or from their deaths. I want them to lose, so that the threat against my family, against me, against my country and fellow citizens, will evaporate. They may have to die in great numbers before they will be willing to surrender; I regret that, but my priorities are clear.

I wonder about their fear; I know what fear is these days. I wonder if the religious Iraqis are comforted by their religion. I do not find religion comforting in the face of death; I am willing to accept that I may have to die, but I do not want to give up a life that is good and rewarding, give up my family, give up my country. Is this the feeling of the Iraqis? Or are they convinced that they will be better off in the next world? And what do their nonreligious feel? I do not know.

We religious Jews believe that there is a reward for pious Jews in the next world. But am I pious enough? How can I know? I do not ■ hasten to find out.

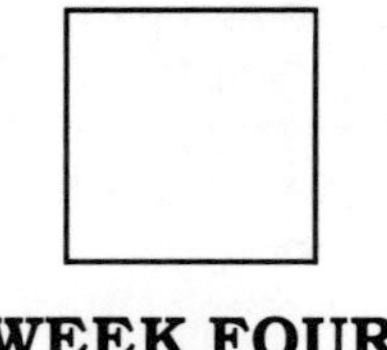

WEEK FOUR

It is a warm, sunny, springlike day; a light sweater is all I need to go out. More than a day has gone by since the last attack—I still think about it.

Even though there are others in the sealed room with you during an attack, and you talk and try to share and at the same time listen to the radio together, you are *quite* alone there. And you feel a heaviness slowly creeping over you—I remember the stories about what it is like to freeze to death in the snow, and it seems very much like that, a sort of dying—you feel the inevitability of the situation, the helplessness. And you remember that, although you are doing what is best for the case of a chemical attack, the huddling in the sealed room is always accompanied by the knowledge that you are not really very safe against a conventional attack.

I speak to a friend from Tel Aviv; he tells me that on Saturday morning (2:45 A.M.) they first heard the Patriot missiles being fired and, only after that, a boom, the noise of the explosion. The Patriots, he tells me, have a mechanical sound to them, like turning on a noisy appliance, while the fall of the Scud has a full sound to it. He tells me there was approximately five minutes from the siren until they heard the noises. He does not really know which to prefer, the two- to three-minute advance warning that they had at the beginning or the long wait of five minutes before hearing the fall of the missile that they now have. He says, "That wait is eternal!" Sitting in the sealed room, huddled on the floor (we have been told not to sit against external walls, so we have started to sit on the floor, sometimes with a blanket on and still feeling perfectly naked!) and waiting for the minutes to pass, endless minutes. (He reports that he jumps when he hears alarms that are not really there and that at such times he finds his heart racing. Strangely, this reaction is absent during real attacks.)

The Mayor of Tel Aviv, retired General Shlomo Lahat, no longer speaks of "deserters" although it is clear that he still disapproves of Tel Avivians who have left the city, which he calls "The Front." This remark has produced many reactions, mostly negative. Some estimates suggest that as many as 40 percent—or even more—of Tel Aviv residents slept out of the city during the first wave of attacks. Today we learn that some of the inhabitants of the area where the last missile fell were not in their houses at the time, perhaps accounting for the fact that there were not more casualties. Who is right?

Lahat has also confessed to being one of the Tel Avivians who run to his roof to see the "fireworks." Nahman Shai last week spoke of those who did so as "crazy." Rooftops have become a major battlefield in this war; there are the Palestinians who cheer the Scuds on and the Jews consumed (thus far only figuratively) by curiosity.

■ The Iraqis appeared to be aiming their Scuds only at civilian population centers without any military targets in mind, both in Israel and in Saudi Arabia. A less likely possibility is that their aim was grossly off, the result of not having enough time in the face of U.S. and coalition bombings or technical failures in the missiles. I think their motives were to strike terror into the hearts of civilians in both countries, thus dragging Israel into the war and undermining coalition support in Saudi Arabia. The intrinsic inaccuracy of the Scud missiles may have at least partially dictated these motiva-
■ tions.

We are curious. Shai tells us over and over again not to come out of our homes to see the "action." The spectators do come, however, and appear to interfere—hopefully not too much—with the rescue operations. In the last attack four people were arrested as looters (store windows were smashed)—apparently on the basis of being strangers. They were all released when they were identified as being guests of residents of the neighborhood struck. Apparently some people are now staying in the dangerous areas in order to be part of the "action." It takes all kinds, someone once said.

We are concerned about looting; it would be a sign of the degeneration of our society, a degeneration that would not be acceptable to our self-image. Thus far there have been only rare cases; one looter who was caught was given a quick and heavy jail sentence.

It is a beautiful day and we walk; we pass a hospital and the reality of the situation we are in again hits me: in preparation for a gas attack, there are rows of showers installed outside the hospital and so many stretchers! The showers remind me of the past, of what we have suffered. Showers once were a disguise for poison gas; they are now meant to treat the effects of poison gas.

I am told that on a Friday night live entertainment television show a group of American soldiers operating the Patriot missiles launchers appeared. They say that they are overwhelmed by the welcome they are getting. The announcer asks, "Who is manning the missiles while you are here?" They reassure the audience, saying that there are other trustworthy soldiers keeping an eye on affairs, in their place.

The soldiers have improvised a song and they sing it. Some excerpts from that song:

> I'm a Scud-buster, baby.
> Saddam, Saddam watch out what you do,
> I'm a Patriot soldier.
> In these times, that will do.

Depression seems to be both a phenomenon that concerns us—it still is not prominent—and is the source of jokes. Thus, apparently there are three types of people these days:

> (1) Those who are depressed because the war is over;
> (2) Those who are depressed because the war is not over;
> (3) Those who are depressed because they do not know if the war is over or not.

Israel has an old account with U.S. TV which does not get better with time. We do not enjoy the treatment we get; we feel that TV treatment of us to be not only unfair but also hostile. Some of it is of such low level as to be ridiculous, but there is much that is invidious and hateful.

■ Television image making, of course, is only one aspect of the media's capacity to influence and even form public opinion. But these days television is the medium with the greatest and most rapid access to its audiences. We are indeed upset at the hostility of U.S. television to us. There is little doubt that our views of country and patriotism are considered old-fashioned and even laughable by many in the United States. We are very sensitive to our image in the world—just as we are the first to laugh at our stupidity when it is benign and to cry at it when it is potentially malignant. We also do not understand how we are not to censor sensitive material when our enemies are so ready to make use of such material against us, not to blacken our names but to harm us physically. Americans feel that it is acceptable to attack everything in sight, both at home and abroad. Despite the seriousness that underlies such criticism, it often has the quality of a game, a sense that nothing really counts. Americans can also afford—for the time being—to pretend that there are no limits to freedom of the press, that there are no sufficient reasons to
■ restrain the press or to insist that the press restrain itself.

For those who believe that there is never any justification for censorship, my words will have no meaning. We, who feel that our lives are on the line, disagree. Too often, the motivation for wanting to publish censored material is not to expose corruption but to get a good story. It does not make any difference, say the "civil libertarians": the chance of exposing dirty dealings is so important that anything is worth it. We differ: we say that the possibility of saving lives takes precedence over every other consideration. And so the argument goes on, neither side happy with the other's views.

We find that those who live most in danger, those who have the most to lose, are not less disgusted than others at corruption or cover-up; but we do have a different order of preferences in our world. Life for the Jew—unlike others who believe that another world awaits them, one that makes up for loss of life—is the prime value. Nothing else takes precedence. This view does not make us cowards, either; our soldiers have shown that time after time. And we are all soldiers here; we all serve. Every soldier is trained in rescue exercises; we all know that if we are wounded we will not be left on the battlefield. That helps; it helps to know that human life is the prime consideration, and I pity the civil libertarian who does not know that. His life is less valuable than it should be, as are the lives of others around him.

When Noam Chomsky, a distinguished linguist, can write an introduction to a vile neo-Nazi book in the name of free speech, I—for one—pity the man. Use of the slogan "free speech" does not justify this action; indeed, it is not only in bad taste but also endangers lives. And as such it must be condemned.

■ Noam Chomsky, distinguished linguist at the Massachusetts Institute of Technology and a Jew, is a persistent critic of Israel and perhaps even a hater of the country. He justifies his position as that of a civil libertarian.

His civil libertarian activities led him to head a petition protesting the firing from the University of Lyons of Robert Faurisson, who contended that there were no Nazi death camps; Faurisson dismissed the evidence of all witnesses to the holocaust as liars because Jews are liars. Chomsky, in his petition, spoke of "intimidation" of Faurisson as a result of making his "findings" public. Chomsky proceeded to write an introduction to Faurisson's book, *Mémoire en défense*, which was published by the neo-Nazi organization La Vieille Taupe.

Chomsky's behavior produced much reaction in 1980. In a *New York Times* interview (5 December 1980), Chomsky was quoted as saying that he "sees no antisemitic implications in denial of the Holocaust." In *Commentary* (September 1980), the late historian of the Holocaust Lucy Dawidowicz wrote, "In a letter to me . . . Chomsky expressed complete agnosticism on the subject of whether or not Faurisson's views were 'horrendous,' saying that he was not ■ sufficiently involved in the issue."

George Orwell pointed out that arguments for free speech have meaning only within a democracy; when dealing with our imperfect world, he pointed out, totalitarian governments use these arguments to further their cause, to kill and to repress.

If war is a special state, one in which lives are more on the line than in other situations—as it indeed is—and if, as we believe, lives are the primary value—doubting that there is democracy either in Heaven or in Hell—then democracy, or at least some of its attributes and characteristics, must take a back seat. For the duration, as we used to say. How much of a back seat? How lenient can we be? As little as possible.

At the beginning of the Lebanese war, TV crews who found themselves free to cover almost everything were frustrated by having to pass their material through the hands of an Israeli Army censor before getting permission to release the material. The censored material—for the most part—was not the result of what most civil libertarians would call attempts at cover-up but was material that was seen by our censors as having security and strategic value that they were not ready to release. There is no doubt that here—as in all cases of censorship—politically motivated decisions were also made and that material that showed screw-ups was usually disallowed.

The American TV producers—clever folks they indeed are—decided on a method to pay Israel back by withholding the coin they felt Israel most wanted. What could be better, when Israel was motivated by a desire for good publicity, than to plaster a label over every frame shown from the Israeli side, announcing that the material is censored? And this they did, as punishment. (How simple-minded clever people can be! Did the journalists not see that there were other motives in Israeli censorship than robbing them of good television footage?)

They never mentioned that their access to news on the other side was limited. This form of censorship does not count; there is no good footage here, there is no footage at all. Here nothing is being withheld from viewers; there is nothing. And so it does not count.

Reporters seemed particularly vicious with Pete Williams and General Kelly in the Pentagon briefings. It was clear that the press entered the briefing room with the stereotype of an unprincipled military firmly fixed in their minds. They acted as if they were confronting a military not to be trusted or believed, paid guard dogs defending a government led by officials who were themselves corrupt and self-seeking.

It is interesting that Israel—one of the most disliked countries in media representation—is actually one of the most open to press coverage. Israel is neither proud of nor indifferent to the wrongs committed here. Nor are we more stupid than other countries are. Israel does believe in a free press—within certain limits, defined by the security of the country. After all, we are a country that is the offspring of a British mandate, and we were influenced by Britain and its Official Secrets Act.

Just as Israel was a lot cleaner than painted by the press, the generals turned out to be much more honest than the reporters were willing to give them credit for—and brighter, too.

Now footage from Israel, from Saudi Arabia, and from Iraq is all treated to the same label, relatively inconspicuous, at the bottom of the screen. And usually with a vocal reminder, at least in the cases of Israel and Iraq, that the material is censored.

Are the situations the same? Not at all. But the treatment is. The cover of *Newsweek* (not television, but the same principle applies) showed a Patriot missile launcher, an impressive photograph, with one of the most identifiable structures in Israel clearly shown in the background. The Israeli censors were greatly disturbed at this and withdrew the credentials of the head of *Newsweek*'s office here. TV footage of Patriot missile launchers in Israel is quite common. Has anyone seen one frame of a Patriot launcher in Saudi Arabia?

Peter Arnett continues to broadcast from Iraq—perhaps I am a bit oversensitive if I think that his record as an Israel basher has made him more acceptable there—and his interview with Ramsey Clark (Is he still alive? And seeing them together! I never realized how short Arnett is.) is interrupted by shots of hospital scenes showing wounded children. Who would allow that in Israel? Every TV producer would refuse to accept that from us. And rightfully so. For this is pure propaganda, cynical manipulation of the TV.

And what is Clark doing in Iraq? And Boston cardiologist Philip Lown before him? They are civil libertarians. That is what they are. What if American lives are on the line?

Here we would call it treason. Vive la difference.

In addition to the genuinely perplexed antiwar people who were caught unprepared by the possibility of a justifiable war (see my entry for 23 January), others, cut from different cloth, engaged in attacking the Gulf War itself. These were more professional—more professional in their commitment to the radical Left, more professional in their hatred of Israel, more professional in their condemnation of war, in any shape or form.

Although they continued to operate, selling the same wares, operating at the same stand they always had, their voices weakened in the face of the overwhelming support that this war enlisted in the American people. They were deserted by most of their following, by those who could see that there was something different in this war. Only the hard-liners remained, and their voices soon became inaudible, drowned out by the voices of those who were proud of their country's endeavors or could at least justify the war as a battle against unbridled aggression that threatened world peace.

But programmatic commitments die slowly, if at all. I suddenly discovered a new source of attack, both against Israel and against the war effort. This time the attack wore the guise of a "scientific" study.

I am not a social scientist, and before the war I knew little more of the field of communications than that it existed as a discipline of study. One of the electronic mail nets—CRTNET, the Communications, Research, and Theory Net—that picked up my diary and disseminated it to its members deals specifically with the problems of communication. I found myself scanning the other material that appeared on that net, particularly submissions that were opposed to my views, at times opposed even to use of the net to publish my views.

I did not feel impelled to respond to those who disagreed with me as I did not view what I had undertaken as polemic or as an invitation to debate. I am not against debate; I simply had no time for it, for I was preoccupied with describing life in Israel in this trying period. In fact, others took up the challenge and defended publication of my views as included in—even as an integral part of— my reports.

A report summarizing a study undertaken by three University of Massachusetts professors (published in the CRTNET on 10 February) did elicit a response from me. I felt that "science" was being misused, turned into a handmaiden of preconceptions; and thus I responded.

Subject: Reaction

I have never understood fully what Communications Research and Theory are, but I have been flattered to have my reports reprinted in the CRTNET.

My pleasure has been tempered by reading the posting "The Gulf War: A Study of the Media, Public Opinion, and Public Knowledge" by Professors Sut Jhally, Justin Lewis, and Michael Morgan.

Under the guise of science, using the blanket of objectivity, they survey the public's acceptance of a series of prejudices and distortions that are held by one sector of the American public to be fact. They present these prejudices as fact and show disappointment in the public's not always sharing them.

The authors seem to be unaware that there are different perceptions of fact than those they present as such. They use loaded words such as *occupation* and *illegal* with reference to the Israeli administration of territory captured from aggressors who themselves captured it in violation of UN decisions. The legality of Israel's position certainly has neither been tested nor proven.

The U.S. vote in the United Nations has indeed made life easier for Israel (though not in the recent past, when appeasement of coalition partners has taken precedence over support for Israel), but to call this support voting against the search for a political settlement to the Palestinian/Israeli conflict—as they do—is itself a political statement, a limited and charged perception of U.S. activity.

Certainly the press cannot be faulted for not trying to convince the U.S. public that Israel is guilty of great and unjustified crimes in its treatment of the Palestinians. Despite this, the U.S. public refuses to buy this picture. Is it just boorish ignorance, as the authors suggest? Or is it the result of native resistance to overkill? I don't know, but the authors are either unaware that the disproportion exists or do not care.

I too am indeed guilty in my reports of one-sided presentation. But I know that I am involved in disputation, that I have a political bias. Are the authors of this study unaware of the politicization of their work? Or are they cynically hiding behind the skirts of mother science?

I seem to have the advantage (naïveté?) of knowing what I am and what I am doing; I do not pass my perceptions off as science. I—as a scientist, myself—have too much respect for science to attempt that.

If this be science even with a small *s*—how the mighty have fallen.

■ Once again, I might have left the work to others. I was hardly alone in attacking this study; others from within the field, particularly one scathing and telling criticism from a man at MIT, did the
■ work better than I could have.

MONDAY, 11 FEBRUARY: IS ISRAEL IN THE WAR?

There was no attack last night. During the day, four or five mobile launchers, three with missiles pointed at Israel, were destroyed by coalition aircraft—a great success for the bombing tactics of the U.S. and its allies. But this very success brings to our attention another source of concern; does this mean that the Iraqis are about to attack us in the daytime? This could be disastrous, with so many more people concentrated in the cities, so many more out on the streets during the day. Can the coalition aircraft keep all of the launchers from firing? We are concerned.

The Russians deny giving any SS-12 missiles to Iraq. Meanwhile, examination of one of the missiles downed in Saudi Arabia indicates that it used solid fuel. The Scud (here pronounced *Scod*, as in *cod* or *rod*; there is no *uh* sound in Hebrew) uses only liquid fuel, while the SS-12 uses solid fuel. This too worries us. The SS-12 is an accurate intermediate-range missile which can deliver twenty times the charge the Scud does, twice as far. It can even carry a nuclear warhead; it can be directed with sufficient accuracy to hit any chosen building.

It is a springlike day, almost sixty degrees Fahrenheit outside, sunny and pleasant, as winter days often are in this part of the world. Jordan TV still calls Jerusalem part of their country, the Western Heights, even though we never were, even though they have announced that they have withdrawn all claim to this country in favor of the PLO. They give the weather report for our area on TV; we do not want to give away that information to the Iraqis, so there is no weather report here. I do not know if Jordan's weather reports are any better than ours used to be. I tend to doubt it.

Jordan has come down on the side of Saddam Hussein. On Friday three terrorists crossed the Jordanian border below the Dead Sea and fired on a military transport, lightly wounding four soldiers (mostly glass from the shattered windows). The three were tracked down and killed by army units. In the past Jordan has kept a tight rein on terrorists, not allowing them to operate directly from Jordanian territory. Has their new alliance with the Saladin of the twentieth century led them to change their position on terrorist operations? Israel has reinforced her positions along the Jordanian border.

We heard Saddam Hussein speaking on the radio last night at 21:00; he promised to capture Al Aksa (a Muslim mosque and shrine in East Jerusalem) and Mecca, the holy city in Saudi Arabia.

We are not sure that we are in the war; the Americans tell us we are not in the war when we ask for financial aid as a participant. Saddam, on the other hand, thinks we are: he says we are his only opponents; the other countries are merely fighting for us. He fires missiles at us as if he really meant it; thus far more Scuds have been fired at us than in the direction of Saudi Arabia and the coalition forces.

We are not sure if we are in the war or not. Or want to be.

The PLO has backed Saddam Hussein. As a result the Kuwaiti government in exile has stopped giving the PLO its yearly contribution—half of what Israel gets in loans and military aid from the U.S. This money was used for terrorist activities and keeping PLO officials comfortable.

Instead, Kuwait is now supporting—to the same tune—a relatively new organization which has become quite strong in the administered territories; it is called Hamas. The local Palestinian support for this new group has grown greatly in the past three years—to such an extent that the PLO offered Hamas 30 percent of the votes in the PNC, the Palestine National Council, as Hamas's representation, in exchange for joining the PNC and following their decisions. Thus far Hamas has declined this offer.

Unlike the PLO, which is for a secular Arab state here, Hamas wants an Islamic state and enjoys strong backing among religious elements in the Arab population. This week Hamas called for violence against the Jews of Israel, called for ascending to rooftops at night to cheer on the missiles on their holy journey to cities where Jews are concentrated.

Now Kuwait supports Hamas instead of the PLO. Kuwait and Iraq are on opposite sides in this war; both want us out of the Middle East. Whose side are we on?

Saudi Arabia was also a major supporter of the PLO; when the PLO supported Saddam Hussein, Saudi Arabia also cut off its grant to them.

Both wealthy Saudi Arabia and economically rather distressed Syria are in the coalition; they both have stated that our destruction is a primary goal of their policies. The Saudis are defending their homeland against invasion. The Syrian soldiers have been—so it is told—instructed not to fire at Iraqi soldiers—fellow Arabs, fellow members of the Ba'ath Party—but to the side.

So it goes in the Middle East.

We are not sure that we are in the war. We do know, however, which side we support, and that is the coalition. We see Saddam Hussein as the greatest threat to us; he has attacked us and we want to pay him back. (We do not believe in turning the other cheek. That is another religion.) And we are against unchecked international aggression—which Saddam Hussein's invasion, annexation, and ravishing of Kuwait is.

The Palestinians have an unenviable record in their support of aggressive dictators. Led by their leader then, the Mufti of Jerusalem, they supported Hitler in World War II; now they side with Saddam Hussein.

Once again there is confusion here as to which is better, a bomb shelter or the sealed room. This has been compounded by an appearance on TV of the head of civil defense, who said that a shelter that can be sealed is best—providing that we can get there within two minutes. As a result, apartment house residents began running down the stairs (the shelters are usually below ground) with stopwatches. I was told that it takes one and one-half minutes to get from the fourth floor to the underground shelter. This is for adults, of course, and provides no help for those who are old, have young children, or live on higher floors. (Most modern apartment houses in Tel Aviv are at least eight stories high.)

Today Nahman Shai reasserted that the threat from chemical attack is so much greater that we are still to use the sealed rooms. Many live in old houses and are obliged to go out of their homes to get to public shelters; these would be at great risk from chemical attacks while in the street.

The effects of Friday night's attack still reverberate here: so many apartments destroyed, so much damage. Many of the residents of destroyed apartments were absent at the time of the attack. Relatively few were hurt. There are many uncanny stories circulating now. One man left his sealed room to fetch his eyeglasses which he had, in his haste to enter the room, forgotten; the room collapsed at that moment. A religious family with small children decided at the last moment—14:00, two and one-half hours before the entry of the Sabbath, hours that usually involve much preparation, since neither work nor cooking is allowed afterwards—to go to sleep a few blocks away; their apartment was badly hit—only an Israeli flag, flown from a balcony, remained intact.

People speak of miracles. The religious find their faith reaffirmed; the antireligious are even more convinced that it is all chance.

Sami Micha'el, one of our more interesting novelists, was a member of the Communist Party in Iraq until 1949, when he came to Israel. No longer a Communist but still associated with the Left, he is interviewed on TV early in the morning.

He speaks both of the Jewish community in Iraq—there were 125,000 Jews in Iraq; now there are about 150, of whom 20 were able to leave just before the war broke out—and the politics of the country. For the past sixty years there has been a conflict between two options for rule, the police state or the army state. The British fostered the police state, which allowed them—through suppression of all dissent—complete rule. Saddam Hussein succeeded in setting up a police state with the cooperation of the army, for the first time ending the rivalry between proponents of the two options. Other possibilities were not possible, never had enough support. One of the first acts of Saddam Hussein's government was the castration of all antigovernment intellectuals who did not flee the country; the resulting condition is considered particularly disgraceful in an Arab country.

Iraq is a country with unlimited water and oil; if it were not involved in wars, it would be sufficient unto itself as few other countries are or can be, certainly not in the Middle East.

"When the Palestinians say they have suffered and were slaughtered and beaten—everybody says that they can understand why the Palestinians have turned to violence. But when the Jews in Israel say that they have suffered and were slaughtered and beaten—everyone says that they must not—under any circumstances—act vigorously or with violence."

The statement was made last week by Amos Oz, another novelist associated with the Left, who favors (favored?) dealing directly with the PLO.

■   Saudi Arabia, through its ambassador to the United States, began making noises that sounded as if the Saudis were willing to make peace with Israel or to change the relationship. I am afraid that these were just words meant to confuse the U.S. public, statesmanship whose purpose was to draw attention away from the facts.

The Saudis, like the other Arab nations—except for Egypt which signed a peace treaty with Israel at Camp David in 1977—are signatories to the Khartoum Agreement which commits all these nations not to recognize Israel. For these nations Israel is a cruel fiction, a nightmare which will eventually go away.

Saudi Arabia was not the only Arab member of the coalition that made noises, for the United States' benefit, hinting that it would change its stance toward Israel. The Kuwaitis also made such claims during the war, and the Syrians have hinted that they would consider dealing with Israel. The other Arab countries in the coalition, Egypt and Morocco, did not join in. Egypt had been ostracized by the other Arab nations for signing a peace treaty with Israel in 1977; only in the past two years has it been let back into the pan-Arab councils. Egypt is not able to speak out for Israel and maintains a low profile in this area of vulnerability. Hassan, king of Morocco, has always maintained friendly relations with Jews who remained in his country and sees Israeli delegations with some regularity, but secretly or at least discreetly. His position is, however, vulnerable. A rally of three hundred thousand pro-Hussein Moroccans in Casablanca during the war, a war in which he sided with the United States, embarrassed him no end. He remained silent on the issue of Israel.

I do not believe that the Arabs have either the courage or the desire to deal with Israel. They have consistently refused to do so from the beginning and have met with Israel only in cease-fire arrangements, when they have been forced to do so to avoid further destruction of their armies. Even on these occasions they have usually managed not to face the Israelis at the meetings but have dealt with third parties. Kuwait, the major beneficiary of the war, was the first to recant on its offer to deal with Israel. Within two weeks after the end of fighting, Kuwait had announced that it would neither recognize nor have any dealings with Israel.

Syria wants the Golan Heights back, but it does not want it enough to recognize Israel. The Syrians still think in terms of armed conflict with Israel, just as in 1948, 1967, and 1973. They think their chances are improving, that they have done better in each attempt. They continue to purchase ground-to-ground missiles from the Chinese and Scuds, too. They, like the Iraqis, have developed chemical warfare. And, as in the case of Iraq, the United States is willing to adopt Syria as a client state, as the enemy of its enemy, as a member of the coalition against Iraq. The United States needed Syria as an important Arab member of the coalition, necessary to give international legitimacy to their war with Iraq, to fight the claim of imperialism. The United States is willing to forgive and forget Syria's long-standing relationship with the Soviets.

The Saudis want nothing of Israel except its disappearance. They remain the major broker of anti-Israel activities. They give grants for attacking Israel, just as other nations give grants to further research into elimination of cancer and other horrible diseases. As a consequence of the action of the United States and its allies, Saudi oil production is intact; the Saudis will continue to earn enough money to do anything that money alone can buy. Unfortunately, that includes financing terrorist attacks against Israel.

It might have been interesting to see if the United States could have forced the Saudis—who have no common border with Israel, who have not directly fought with Israel or lost territory to Israel, who are not threatened by Israel, whose only conflict with Israel is as a Muslim state—to deal with or at least to recognize Israel. Would they have been willing to risk their precious oil or the holy cities of Mecca and Medina, which Saddam Hussein coveted so much?

An illusory ray of hope was offered to an unwary public in the form of the Madrid and Washington "Peace" Conferences. The Saudi ambassador played a visible role as a peacemaker, but he hinted not at peace if Israel was "flexible" but only at possible capital investments. The Syrians—bowing to Washington's pressure—showed up, but they admitted that they are still not ready for peace with Israel, even if Israel were to return the Golan Heights. No one seems to be shocked that the all-too-quickly rehabilitated Jordanians are now making self-righteous noises and blaming Israel for all the troubles in the Middle East. And the Palestinian Arabs are happy to show their muscle, frightened to accept the autonomy they could have had with better terms and greater self-rule ten years ago, frightened that their lives may be at risk at the hands of their more extreme contingents.

Whether the pressure that the American government applied and the promises they gave to Israel and the Arabs were a political ploy or whether they were an honest effort to move toward peace is not yet clear. At this writing, the situation is unchanged: Israel and its Arab neighbors are at loggerheads; the situation on the West Bank remains perilous; and peace seems as elusive as ever.

You cannot make peace if only one side wants it. It is as simple as that, as complicated as that. ■

TUESDAY, 12 FEBRUARY: THREE ALARMS

Yesterday I felt free to speculate on whether we were or were not in the war; today that is not possible any longer, not after the three alarms we had last night. It is surprising but nonetheless quite distinct both in time and thought how what was an abstract problem can suddenly, effortlessly, become an existential one.

The first siren came while I was still at work:

18:58   I hear the alarm on the radio; only a few seconds later it is echoed by the local siren. I gather my mask and the radio and go to the sealed room; a new one—more intimate and also not unpleasant—in my department.

19:02   In the sealed room with mask on, radio working. I look around me; there are ten of us there, five without masks.

I am angry at them, and angry at the Iraqis, at Saddam Hussein, at the Americans. I say nothing; they know every bit as well as I do that they have been foolish. I try to record the progress of the attack as seen here.

19:05   Nahman Shai reports that a missile has landed in Israel and that those in all regions of the country other than Tel Aviv and Shomron (Samaria) are free to remove gas masks and leave the sealed rooms.

19:08   I am already back in my room, at my computer, using IRC to locate Israelis on the net from the struck area. The first I find is in Rehovoth, southeast of Tel Aviv; he tells me that he usually hears the explosions in Tel Aviv, but this time he heard nothing.

19:10   I locate someone in Tel Aviv who tells me he saw the Patriot and then heard a small boom. (What does a small boom mean? That the intercept was far away? That the Patriot struck the tail instead of the head of the Scud? That there was no intercept at all?) On the IRC war report, I hear that CNN has already reported a missile attack directed at "central Israel."

19:17   We are told that those in Tel Aviv and Shomron may remove their masks but are to remain in the poison-gas-proof rooms.

19:22   A general all-clear is announced. The warhead, from a single missile, was conventional. No wounded. (Later we learned that two Russian immigrants in the Tel Aviv region, one thirty-nine, the other forty-six, died of heart attacks while running to or sitting in the sealed rooms. These, too, are casualties. They are listed as unpaid debts. We are showing restraint now, but our memory for this sort of thing, this business of being killed, is very good. We have had enough practice.)

I feel very angry now. It is in the air. American obtuseness to our needs does not help. Certainly not the senator who suggested that the cost of the Patriots be deducted from the aid to be given us this year. We show restraint and we gain some sympathy, sympathy which will disappear when the war is over; the Middle East settlement we neither need nor want is being formulated in remote places, ready for the first moment when it can be rammed down our throats. The U.S. government says we are not participants in the war; do they tell that to the wounded, to the families of the dead, to those who have lost their homes? Do they forget that no Scud was fired on us before the beginning of the coalition bombings? Or do they think that the relationship is coincidental?

The confusion about proper behavior in the time of an attack continues; we act as if we expect a poison gas attack, but we are blasted by conventional weapons. We suffer from Scud attacks, we suffer from the results of Scud and Patriot collisions. American engineers have improved the Patriot performance in Saudi Arabia; is that information being shared with us? Caspar Weinberger refused to share knowledge about Iraqi development of unconventional weapons with us; Jonathan Pollard stole the information and transmitted it to us. He is guarded in the basement cell of a penitentiary, in complete isolation, serving a life sentence for giving that information to us. (Americans who write to me are under the false impression that he transmitted data about American defenses or nuclear information. Nonsense. He passed on information about Arab arms that had been promised us and then withheld.)

Last week, a man convicted of spying for Russia, an enemy of the U.S., was punished with a twenty-year sentence; apparently that sort of spying is more acceptable. After all, the Russians are supposed to spy.

At this time the Americans are sharing information with us. Not everything; not aircraft identification codes, for example. Will this sharing last?

The map of Iraq showing the position of Iraqi factories producing nonconventional weapons that Pollard transmitted to us is now featured on the front pages of newspapers throughout the world. Ironic? Not really. Israel destroyed Iraq's first military nuclear plant in June 1981; we were condemned by the world. We warned the U.S. about the Iraqi threat; we were again ignored. These are the norms. The current war is an exception.

Sharing information is a two-way arrangement, or is meant to be. The U.S. declined to give us the information on Iraqi development of nonconventional weapons. We apparently told the Americans that we had successfully penetrated the George Hawatmi Palestinian terrorist group operating in Syria. We asked that the information be kept secret and provided plans for terrorist attacks against U.S. agencies. When bringing Syria into the coalition, this information was passed on to President Assad, as a gesture of good faith (to him, not to us). As a result, two agents were exposed and executed.

The confusion about what to do when the siren sounds is particularly striking in the Tel Aviv area, the site of most Scud attacks. Despite statements by Army Chief of Staff General Shomron and by Nahman Shai on TV, the controversy about use of the sealed room as opposed to the use of the bomb shelter continues. Shai has even pointed out that bomb shelters have been destroyed by the attacks, but the most compelling argument is that the casualties from a poison gas attack—which we fully expect despite American experts who tell us that gas masks should never have been distributed—will be much greater than from a conventional warhead.

Spontaneously, and without prior discussion, most residents of apartment houses in Tel Aviv decided that the best tactic is to descend to the bomb shelters (if you are not located too high, more than two minutes from the shelter) or to use the stairwells, which have no windows. A Tel Avivian reports to me that this behavior had two components; one, the desire to take matters into their own hands and, two, the need for some kind of extrafamilial human contact. Many waited four minutes and then ran back to their sealed rooms, attempting to get the best of two worlds.

If you can't beat them, join them. This morning the civil defense agreed that a windowless staircase is also a good place to stay during an attack.

Sirens are no longer sounded for the all-clear. In schools bells are no longer rung: nerves are too tense. The children jump in fright. Some firms are distributing small presents to schoolchildren; a secretary reports that her fourteen-year-old daughter received a bag with plastic bottles of shampoo and hair conditioner—to make the girls feel better. Believe it or not, the daughter and her friends did feel better.

21:18   I am at home. Both the radio and TV give out alarm
          warnings, interrupting the programs on the air; soon we

> hear the outside siren as well. We quickly go to our sealed
> room, five of us, all with gas masks.

21:31   All clear; a missile was fired, but not in our direction.
        Presumably, it is directed at Saudi Arabia. Later we hear
        that a Scud missile is downed over Riyadh, with some
        property damage there.

We are a cigarette-smoking country; we smoke far too much, just as we drive too dangerously. Psychologists say it has to do with tension, with living with the sense that life is constantly at risk here—from war, from terrorists. The one cigarette manufacturer was designated an essential industry during the period when most factories were closed as we organized for defense against missiles at the beginning of the war. Cigarettes were produced in quantity to deal with the anticipated increase in use, a phenomenon found in each of our previous wars. Surprisingly, use of cigarettes actually declined, and the manufacturer is stuck with large stocks of unsold cigarettes.

Chocolate seems to have partially replaced cigarette use. Sales have increased markedly, as has the sale of coffee. Sweet and fatty foods seem to lead the list of food items purchased.

Before the second alarm I developed a distressful heartburn which did not respond to antacids. I began to worry that this was a heart attack. (I had not yet heard about the two Russian immigrants who had died.) I thought that this would be a particularly ungraceful way to die, that my timing was poor indeed. (Jerry Phillips reported that he was having his own symptoms at the time. Our exchange of notes about our respective cardiac conditions, as of 1 December 1991, occupy five megabytes of disk space.) I tried to sleep and dozed off at about 1:10, 1:15 in the morning, only to be awakened by a siren. The third alarm this night.

1:27   Awakened by sound of siren on radio, outside. The five of
        us get to the sealed room—I stall, urinate, but get there
        much more quickly than it seems to take—we don
        masks, listen to the radio; I turn on my computer termi-
        nal. The tape sealing the door has gotten worn from re-
        use; my son replaces it with new tape.

1:32   Nahman Shai tells us that this is a real attack. We are all
        to remain in sealed rooms, with gas masks on.

1:37   Once again, we are all released except those in Tel Aviv
        and Shomron.

1:40   I use IRC to find someone in Tel Aviv; there is nobody on
        the line; it is too late at night.

1:42   We are told that there was one missile fired which landed
        in Israel, the thirty-fourth thus far.

1:49   The warhead was conventional; all-clear for the entire
        country.

2:24   The curious are asked not to come to the place. (We are
        never told where; only later—through a grapevine that
        was even more efficient than IRC—did we learn the exact
        site of the landing.) The spectators who are there already
        are asked to leave. They interfere with the rescue opera-
        tions. There is property damage, six wounded, one mod-
        erately; the others suffer only light wounds.
        My heartburn? Oh! Gone.

We are restrained. We are bombed. Our children do not always
handle this too well; some of our adults do not do too well either.
Some die of fright.

Seventy-five hundred apartments have been damaged. Of these,
six hundred were severely damaged, and two hundred of those will
have to be rebuilt completely.

So we are not in the war.

Angry? Yes. Very angry.

An acquaintance returns to Israel. On the phone he tells his wife,
"Save a Scud for me." His plane lands in time for the first alarm. He
spends the waiting period in the sealed plane. The second alarm
catches him in a taxi on the empty road to Jerusalem. They pull
over, put on their gas masks, and wait. He arrives home, falls asleep,
and is awakened by the third alarm. Homecoming.

WEDNESDAY, 13 FEBRUARY: AIRPLANES

There are airplanes above us, all the time. We hear but do not see
them. In peacetime there are almost never any flights over Jerusalem; the contrast now is great. The planes were very busy in the
skies over Jerusalem the first week of the war but not since, not

until this morning. We had a quiet night last night; it helped after the alarms of the previous night. But now the skies are filled with the droning and roar of unseen planes; the sky is quite cloudy.

We hear from American TV and newspapers that the IFF codes which allow planes to be identified as friendly have finally been given to Israel. One source adds that the codes were given with the understanding that no Israel retaliatory action would be undertaken before the beginning of the ground war. The Pentagon denies this news item categorically; our spokesmen refuse to comment. We tend to believe Israeli silence more than the Pentagon denial.

Are the planes we hear related to this new rumor? Are they practicing using the IFF codes? Are they practicing for a retaliation mission? Is this the beginning of such a mission? We do not know.

We are concerned about the tender and loving relationship now being shown us by the United States and by the European nations who only recently condemned us.

Although this special treatment is public and visible to all, we feel the threat that lies behind this massage; we already feel our arm being twisted.

All our requests for aid—other than the Patriots—from the U.S. have been torpedoed in the past few months by the State Department. Even requests that have been approved by the Congress and that should have been delivered months ago are not honored. For example, the $400 million credit for dealing with the new Russian immigration that we have been asking for is pushed aside time after time. Congress approved Israeli industry participation in the competition on defense tenders in Europe—in those very countries which have failed to support the Gulf War with more than token efforts, if at all—for repair and renewal of weapons systems; this possible source of badly needed income for us has been blocked by innumerable State Department barriers, both political and bureaucratic.

The Hetz (Arrow) missile project has also been shelved by the State Department after it was initially encouraged and even funded. The U.S. does not allow us to buy a badly needed supercomputer; repeatedly our requests are blocked even though it sells them to "friendly" nations like India. These projects are not only of importance to our defense posture—and perhaps that of the U.S. as well in the long run—but would provide important sources of badly needed income and employment.

■ There is a feeling among many Americans—a feeling present before the Gulf War—that Israel costs the United States far too much, that the Jewish lobby and political considerations rather than U.S. national self-interest dictate the degree of support that Israel receives from the American people. With financial problems— the rising national debt, recession, the savings and loan scandal— besetting America, aid to Israel, and at such a high level at that, is seen as a luxury that can be explained only as a foible of sentimental or politically hip politicians.

Yet American aid to Israel is far less than it gives to other nations that return much less for the aid dollars. Consider U.S. aid to its NATO allies. Belgian lack of support for the U.S. and coalition effort in the Gulf War was remarkable. German and French vacillation were an everyday topic of news reports. These countries are not opposed to taking U.S. money, in amounts that far exceed what Israel gets, in amounts that have no relation to the defense expenses of the recipient countries or their strategic importance to the NATO alliance.

Recent developments in the now-defunct Soviet Union have not reduced the threat of nuclear attack on the West. The instability following the crumbling of the Soviet Empire has led to progressive dissolution and fragmentation. Soviet nuclear resources will apparently be under the control of a number of different and unpredictable governments of the newly independent republics. The proclamation of the Confederation of Independent States now leaves the issue of nuclear weapons even more in doubt. Who controls the buttons? The situation does not seem the least bit improved. Correctly, NATO support for Europe continues; no move has been made to cut it. Some of this support, however, can still be considered wasted.

Denmark, for example, is a member of NATO that receives no direct U.S. aid. Both the population and area of Denmark are close to those of Israel, suggesting a basis for comparison. Like Israel, a constant ally and the only pro-Western country in the Middle East that the United States can count on, Denmark has a natural strategic importance, controlling as it does the exit to the West through the Baltic Sea, the major path to the west for the Soviets. But unlike Israel, Denmark's identification with U.S. interests is half-hearted. Unlike Israel, whose technological achievements were recognized by the United States in Star Wars contracts, Denmark is not highly developed in technological achievements and was not offered such contracts. Moreover, Denmark was lukewarm at best to U.S. efforts to control Soviet expansionism.

Denmark is one of the richest countries in the world, its GNP being 10 percent per person more than that of the United States and more than twice that of Israel. Should such a rich country be the beneficiary of U.S. aid even if it is a faithful ally? But in the case of a wavering friend at best, is not this aid to be questioned? It is not.

Denmark's contribution to its own self-defense is 1.8 percent of its GNP, not a serious sum. Its army is a joke, as are its navy and air force. Denmark receives—and accepts without anyone there or in the United States putting in a word of protest—about $10 billion a year toward its defense, which comes to more than five times what the Danes themselves pay; in contrast, aid from the United States to Israel is less than 40 percent of what Israel puts out. In fact, Denmark does not receive any direct money from the United States; there is never any congressional debate on giving the money to Denmark. The money is given to that country as part of the yearly NATO appropriation. This support, forty-two years of it, has contributed greatly to the wealth of Denmark.

By contrast, Israel puts up more than 10 percent of its GNP for self-defense; non-Israeli sources say that if all expenses were counted, this figure would come to 25 percent. Nor does this figure take into account the added expenses of war; there have been quite a number of these, six by my count, since Israel's establishment in 1948, and none in Western Europe. Nor does it take into account the loss to its economic productivity in maintaining a standing army—about 11 percent of Israel's GNP against less than 1.5 percent of Denmark's.

What does Israel do for the United States in return for the aid it gets? First of all, Israel supplied information about Russian weapon systems that saved American lives, as well as large sums of money, in the Gulf War. (Different American military estimates reach sums of $50 to $80 billion saved.) Israel tests American weapons developed to counter Soviet weapons on the systems themselves under conditions of war, potentially saving more U.S. lives and dollars by eliminating inappropriate weapons or strategies and revealing errors that can be corrected.

In addition to actually stealing a whole, intact Soviet radar installation, Israel has provided to the United States captured tanks and Soviet planes flown by Arab deserters. The United States has analyzed those weapons and built systems to neutralize their capacities. Israel has tested antimissile systems in its wars against the Arab nations; the success of these systems has provided valuable information to the United States.

In addition, billions of dollars of U.S. weapons are sold each year partly on the basis of their success in Israeli hands. Ironically, Israeli successes with U.S. weapons have driven Arab countries to stop buying Soviet weapons and to buy U.S. weapons instead.

Israel may be an expense to the American taxpayer, but it is a worthwhile one, a cost-effective expense. We provided the United States with assessments based on wartime experience of Arab strengths and weaknesses that could have aided the U.S. effort in the Gulf War. For example, we insisted that Saddam Hussein would not back down when U.S. intelligence sources would not believe that he would invade Kuwait. If the United States had accepted our evaluation, if the U.S. ambassador had been instructed to tell the Iraqis that America would fight if Kuwait were invaded, would that have deterred Hussein? (Hitler was not deterred by a British warning and invaded Poland.) We do not know; but it was worth trying.

We are the only constant U.S. ally in the region—forty-three years without changing sides. There is no one else.

It appears that the State Department is interested in withholding all aid now in order to increase the pressure to be applied to us to accept their policies in the treaties that will be drawn up for this region at the end of the conflict in the Persian Gulf. The joint statement issued by Secretary of State Baker and his Russian counterpart about solution of the Israeli-Palestinian conflict is a hint of what is to come. President Bush shelved this statement—for the time being; this is just not the right time.

Meanwhile the State Department caresses us publicly.

The Persian Gulf War provides a living for the media. All over the world they deliver their merchandise—not literature, not history (not even journalism, I think at times) but merchandise—tens of millions of words, and countless pictures, TV and photographic shots. Hundreds of millions of readers and listeners and viewers pay attention to what is going on in the Persian Gulf twenty-four hours a day. The bitter truth is that neither we nor they have the least idea of what is going on.

There are two types of reporting from the Gulf now. In the first, the reporters of the great newspapers sit quietly, like well-disciplined high school students before the spokesmen of the U.S. and British (occasionally Saudi; rarely French) armies, who feed the reporters what the military wants, and these newsmen quietly take it all down, as if they are schoolroom assignments. If one of them gets a bit smart, he will find himself on the first plane back home. There are no wise guys in Saudi Arabia.

It is paradoxical that I was able to say whatever I liked. There is really no effective way to control information in an electronic age. But I did not depend on official sources of information. Those who do—if they displease those sources once—will find themselves cut off.

The Americans have set the stage by placing heavy censorship on details, limiting movement of reporters to and on the fronts.

The great journalists sit with folded arms in a tent—scene of desert splendor—to listen to a briefing once a day—and then to say, "Thank you." Freedom of the press? The right of the public to know? Forget it. Army people say just what they want and only what they want to. They do not expand and are frugal in their offerings.

The journalists stand on the roofs of Riyadh and say any nonsense that comes to mind. These are the same journalists who screamed against Israeli restrictions on them, spoke of the right to know, freedom of the press. And now they have no problem accepting the oatmeal served them—predigested, no less.

Then there is the other kind of journalist, the one who reports from behind the enemy lines, who allows the most flagrant propaganda to be shown while he is broadcasting. (Did he have a choice? Of course not.)

Some have written me that Peter Arnett of CNN, broadcasting from Baghdad, chooses what to present in his broadcasts. If so, he is simply an evil, destructive man. But this is clearly not the case: he shows what he is told to show, he is a journalist and the show must go on. Oh, is that the theater? Well, this is journalism as theater, entertainment—of a sort.

■ I have heard Arnett's postwar defense of his position. I remain unconvinced. I still see him as a tool of the Iraqis. He worked too
■ hard to put in the details that Saddam Hussein wanted.

Mr. Shalom Rosenfeld, one of our leading senior journalists, has made the interesting comparison of Peter Arnett to Ed Murrow.

Murrow broadcast from London during the blitz in World War II—night after night, bravely, just as does Arnett. But the cause, the cause? asks Mr. Rosenfeld. Every day that Murrow broadcast, he did so not only with bravery but with a sense of mission. Does Peter Arnett have that? Does he have a mission? A cause? What mission? What cause?

■ We have no reason to conclude that Arnett himself believed the Iraqis or favored them in the war. It was, however, incumbent on him to be more than scrupulous about what he agreed to include. When Ezra Pound broadcast from Italy, he was condemned as a traitor. There is a difference. Arnett was treated as a hero, both during and after the war. There were also Tokyo Rose, Axis Sally and Lord Haw-Haw as well. Like them, Arnett was broadcasting from an enemy capital. There is a difference. They believed in what they broadcast and acted as propagandists, while Arnett was only a medium for propaganda. Yes, he wanted to stay alive; none of us question that. And, remember, Arnett did not denounce the allied war effort, as did some of the captured pilots who were interviewed on Iraqi television. They appeared rather battered. Arnett did not.

Arnett persists in interviewing the Americans who visit Iraq, even now. Ramsey Clark returns to the U.S. after his Arnett interview and relates that he saw no evidence of bomb damage to military targets. Where did they take him?

Reflex or knee-jerk liberalism has its positive side and its negative side. Israel seems to suffer from both. The positive is an awareness of the possibility of unfair treatment, a heightened social sensitivity. When a limb is scratched, there is reflex withdrawal. If the danger appears persistent and follows the withdrawal, we may reflexively flee the danger. When pain is felt in response to ischemia, a lack of blood, to the heart muscle, we are warned that treatment is required.

Some of the things that Israel has to do have the appearance of social injustice. There are protests at the use of force by Israeli troops against unarmed youths, the expelling of Palestinians by Israelis, the sealing off or destruction of Palestinian homes by Israeli forces. These all have the earmarks of social injustice, and the liberals have been quick to condemn Israel for these actions.

The negative aspect of knee-jerk liberalism is that all reflexive activity has only limited and short-term survival value, limited as compared to activities impelled by reflection and thought. When scratched by a tiger, neither withdrawal nor running is an effective strategy. To survive, we must develop a different strategy, one using higher, nonreflexive resources.

Another limitation to reflexive action is that it is dangerous if carried too far. When the heart hurts enough from ischemia, shock can result, completely immobilizing the sufferer and preventing him or her from reacting. But even worse, by reducing the blood flow, this reflex action, meant to warn and aid, further reduces the already compromised blood supply to the heart, threatening life.

What is missing in these failures of reflexive activity is the ability to differentiate between phenotypic and genotypic expressions. Is Israel evil in its treatment of the Palestinians, or has it merely been left with choices that are either less or more evil?

In Israel's case, the inability to discern differences has led to further condemnation of our country by the reflex liberals. What looks like social injustice may be the mildest solution available short of national suicide.

We have more deadly weapons than we have used. We have shown great restraint, but the Palestinians are both persistent and highly motivated. They have captured the attention of the world as has no other disenfranchised group; they have captured the attention of the television cameras. They know it and make use of it.

We cannot allow our troops to be urinated on from rooftops or wounded by stones thrown at them. Nor will we allow our cars to be stoned or bombed with molotov cocktails and their passengers injured, even burned to death. We will not allow our citizens to be murdered, to be knifed to death. We will not allow those who incite riots to continue their work unrestrained.

We are weak in some ways; the Palestinians know this and take advantage of it. If one of our soldiers is captured, we will trade five hundred prisoners for that soldier. We have already done that. Do not tell us we have no respect for life. We have never used the death penalty against terrorists, not even those who entered a schoolhouse and in the name of Palestinian liberation slaughtered the schoolchildren.

We will try not to kill or maim, but we will not allow our soldiers or citizens to be killed or maimed. The risk is known to the demonstrators. They continue to demonstrate at their own risk.

We think our cause right; we will not commit national suicide. There are liberals who will not see beyond the social justice on the surface. They even have the temerity to say to us, "If you cannot live without these faults, you do not deserve to live." We do not listen to these people. They spout nonsense; they are irresponsible. We will
■ not commit national suicide.

Responsibility in journalism. It exists; Ted Koppel tells ABC's Tel Aviv correspondent not to point in the direction of the latest Scud impact.

One correspondent writes to tell me about a news report where a soldier was interviewed and stated that he did not know why he was in Saudi Arabia. U.S. soldiers who saw this wondered how many dozens of troops the reporter had to interview to find one that would provide that answer.

Now we learn that Arnett has been allowing Iraqi government officials to use his satellite telephone. CNN quickly claimed that he allows them to use it only to speak to the Iraqi embassy in Jordan to arrange press credentials. This story is contradicted by CBS evidence that the Iraqis have a functioning Telex line to their embassy in Rabbat Ammon.

Fantastic!

An interesting observation is that most people of advanced age—

including my eighty-six-year-old mother—behave surprisingly well during the attacks here. Even those in Tel Aviv. Even those whose homes are damaged. Even those wounded. They seem to have a great calmness that envelops them. They are more worried about their children and grandchildren than they are about themselves. They are not apathetic, they are just grand.

THURSDAY, 14 FEBRUARY: ANNIVERSARY; HODESH TOV

Today is my thirty-seventh wedding anniversary; on 14 February 1954 I was married to Golda, the mother of my four children and the grandmother of my five grandchildren. We were married in New York City and soon moved to southern California; we subsequently lived in New York City, Cambridge, England, the U.S. Midwest, and, since 1967, in Jerusalem, Israel. We believe that there are rules; you make up your mind and live by them. We know that there also are passions and we have had them, and still have them. We have felt strongly about one another, about our children and their spouses and their children, about country, about religion, about ideas, about books, about friends and relatives. But our religion teaches us that there are rules, and the America we grew up in also taught the same thing—that there are rules.

We know that we support values that others disapprove of: religion, nationalism (even patriotism), marriage, ideas, feeling strongly, rules. We have heard each of these condemned both as values and as institutions. Nonetheless we believe in them, live with them and by them. And not infrequently the most important of these values become rules. There are times that, without rules, none of the others is possible. Certainly not marriage.

Even our religion distinguishes between life with and without rules. The greatest holy man, says the Talmud, is a man with the greatest inclination to evil, but by a life of rule manages to overcome this evil inclination. The Talmud relates the parable of the great sinner and the holy man who—after death—present themselves for judgment. The sinner is shown his evil inclination and it is as small as a hair, a very small one, indeed. The sinner says in disappointment with himself, "The drive to evil in me was so very small and yet I could not overcome it." The holy man is then shown his evil inclination and it is as large as a mountain; he is amazed that he was able to defeat so huge and powerful an enemy.

Without rules, our marriage would not have lasted. Could not have lasted. Inertia is no longer a reason to stay married; it is almost easier to obtain a divorce these days than to get married. Rules. Golda and I have common ideas and passions; we enjoy doing things together. But our friends are not the same and we frequently disagree about courses of action and what is right. These days we share preoccupations if not occupations; we are both busy writing. Usually our work involves activities as disparate as it is possible to get in the same culture.

We had a quiet night: the best present for our anniversary that anyone could give us. I remembered the date but bought Golda nothing; she forgot but went to her exercise class early in the morning and returned with a present for me—a canvas bag ($7.50) for carrying my gas mask.

■   How good it is to be able to think of family, the only social anchor that counts in times of adversity. When you are alone, country—as beloved as it may be—and friends—how very wonderful they can be—are not there; they are not whom you lean on. The family, those we take most for granted, those who love us despite what we are— they are the ones who are there for us in these difficult times. And we all know that; this is not privileged information, not the secret of the few. And yet how easy it is to forget family when times are good, when career soars, when personal pleasure is great, when rewards are there for the plucking. Like good health, the family is best loved when threatened or absent.

These were days when the family was very real for us, when career, pleasure, rewards, friends were less important. Even our country, attacked and brutalized as it was, was not threatened; we knew that our country would survive. But not so our families: their lives were on the line.

The very war that made the family so real, immediate, and important also distracted us, did not allow us to love our family enough. Nor to help it enough. Nor to protect it as we knew it should be protected. The bombs fell, they landed unexpectedly, they produced terrible, terrifying damage. And they came from the most
■ unexpected directions.

On Tuesday morning, after the very disturbing night when we had three alarms and two actual Scud attacks, I went out into the garden and saw the messenger from Federal Express with a twenty-four-hour letter. It was for Golda; I signed for it and brought it into the house. Golda opened the envelope. The letter inside was to become our fourth siren, our third attack; she had been fired from her position as coordinator of an overseas program for third-year Indiana University students at Hebrew University.

When the war was about to break out—in early January—almost all of the students in the program wanted to stay. But administrators at the university panicked, called the student's parents (in the case of a fifty-five-year-old student, they even called her son), and told them that the university could no longer be responsible for the students' safety in Israel and then wrote letters to the parents with the same information. Under this barrage, the parents pressured their reluctant—some more than others—children to return home. I recall a phone conversation at this time—the call was from my house—in which one student berated an administrator for not consulting with the student before contacting her parents.

My wife has worked at this job for the past eighteen years; the dismissal was hard for her to take, hard for me to take. It was not completely unexpected; the program had become a financial burden to the university as fewer students were willing or able to come to Israel. There was a recession; the winds of war were already blowing in the summer when the students came.

Nor was the letter unkind or illogical; even some sort of continuation of Golda's work was offered. The reasons were spelled out; the regret was genuine.

The university had its priorities, its concerns; when they coincided with hers everything was fine. When the financial burden grew too great, when the possibility of litigation loomed, as well as accusations of irresponsibility and the attendant bad publicity, the university saw its interests to be different from ours, and acted accordingly. This is natural.

The West, with the U.S. at its head, now favors Israel; its interests coincide with Israel's interests. Israel's actions (inaction, actually) are the very ones that the West needs and wants.

Tomorrow, we fear, the U.S. and its allies will see their interests in a different light than Israel does. At that time, with less explanation than Golda received, with less courtesy and thoughtfulness, the U.S. and its allies will dismiss Israel.

Today is Rosh Hodesh, literally the head of the month, the New Moon, the beginning of the Hebrew lunar month of Adar. Adar is the month of our most abandoned holiday, Purim, the holiday described in the biblical Book of Esther.

Gibbon, in a footnote to *The Decline and Fall of the Roman Empire*, describes first-century C.E. Purim celebrations in which Jews killed 75,000 and 100,000 non-Jews in Cyprus and in Alexandria. The source of this contention is not given and it is not substantiated in any Jewish or Roman sources. We celebrate the holiday now by exchanging presents, especially food, by giving children money and gifts to the poor, by reading the Book of Esther in the synagogue. Some drink, play cards, produce satirical comic dramas.

At the New Moon we say to one another *Hodesh tov*, "Have a good month."

It is clear that the ground phase of the Persian Gulf War is getting closer and closer; the air phase has been very successful and soon significant targets will become rare. Thus far, Saddam Hussein shows no sign of willingness to pull out of Kuwait. One of the armchair generals who writes to me says that Saturday, the sixteenth of February, two days from now, is the day. On that day—or not too much later—the U.S. and its allies will use ground troops to force the Iraqis from Kuwait.

By the logic of the Middle East, Saddam Hussein's first reaction to the advance of coalition troops into Kuwait and Iraq will be to bomb Israel, with missiles and perhaps with aircraft as well. If he is committed to using poison gas, he will use it on Israel first.

Our greatest fear is that Saddam Hussein will indeed try to use poison gas against Israel. There are a number of components to that fear: the horrible photographs and TV clips of soldiers burned by the gases in the Iraqi-Iranian war; the death of all inhabitants of a village of five thousand Kurds killed by the Iraqis using poison gas dropped from airplanes; a fear that signals our lack of experience with poison gas warfare; the memory of the Nazi attempt to wipe out all Jews using the poison gas Zyklon B.

The poison gas motif keeps recurring. We are always reminded of it, as we were in the trials of Eichmann and Demjanjuk. We remember it when we remember the "scientific extermination" in the concentration camps. We remember that two-thirds of the murders

were carried out after the probability of German defeat was apparent. We also note the Allied refusal to bomb Auschwitz or the rail
lines leading to it even though bombing missions passed over the
camp routinely. They claimed that it was not one of their war goals.

Many citizens of Jerusalem are convinced that our city is being
spared Scud attacks because we have been targeted for the first
poison gas attack. Where this rumor started I do not know; there is
no logical or factual basis for it. But this is the Middle East, where
logic and fact are not always the most important elements in decision making.

More and more Israeli Arabs have begun to find their voice. We
hear more statements of identification of these Arabs with our fate,
qualified by obviously sincere concern for their fellow Arabs on the
other side, in the administered territories, and in Jordan. Arabs
have offered to help repair missile-damaged houses, to house Jews
rendered homeless by the missile attacks, especially the elderly.
Israeli Arabs complain that they are always required to reaffirm
their loyalty; that they are committed to a joint fate, living together
with Jews in Israel, and that this fact should be obvious. They say
that traitors in their midst are a marginal phenomenon and no more
prominent than the incidence of traitors among Jews.

Most Israeli Arabs, despite being citizens, identify with Palestinian Arabs, whom they see as brothers. In Israel they would like to
have more voice in government. At the same time, they support a
Palestinian state and back Yasser Arafat and the PLO. Ironically,
most Israeli Arabs who favor the Palestinian state would not leave
Israel to live in it. Quite a few Israeli Arabs, particularly those
associated with fundamentalist religious groups, supported Saddam Hussein during the war; worst of all, a ring of spies, ten Israeli
Arabs spying for Iraq, was uncovered during the war.

Meanwhile, in Jordan, overwhelming support for Saddam Hussein persists and has even grown more audible following King
Hussein's speech last week. Scud missiles compete there with
Saddam Hussein himself for popularity. Scuds are featured on
watches, flags, T-shirts. Even cakes and rolls are now produced in
the shape of a Scud. The Saddam-burger is reported to be the most
popular fast food in Rabbat Ammon; it is a missile-shaped roll filled
with meat. Barbers report that Saddam mustaches are definitely
"in."

Barbers in the U.S. are still not reporting a surge of demand for a Bush hairdo.

I do not know whether the bunker in Baghdad where so many unfortunate civilians were killed was a command post as claimed by the coalition. I tend to believe the coalition, mostly because the Iraqi record of reporting has been so completely filled with fantasy and lies. One comment: the boy shown with burns reportedly from the bombing of the bunker could not possibly have gotten them there: the burns are old; any physician can tell you.

We will not go out to a movie or restaurant this evening to celebrate. We do not feel too safe away from our home after 19:00 these days. We are not in too much of a mood for celebration, either.

FRIDAY, 15 FEBRUARY: A PEACE PROPOSAL

We did not celebrate our anniversary in any special way. We enjoyed the quiet of another alarm-free night; we spoke with our son, back from the Far East, who is to go to his reserve army unit today. We read with pleasure the many warm letters of congratulation that we received from electronic mail correspondents, some unknown to us, some from old friends, some from new friends made during the past month, some from people who have disappeared from our lives. A former student of Golda's writes to say that he has been following my reports and wondered if I were related to a woman named Werman in Jerusalem whom he knew. The warmth is pleasant; we become quite indulgent and allow ourselves to bask in it.

The start of the ground war in the Persian Gulf is in the air; we expect it and expect that as soon as it does begin Saddam Hussein will attempt to strike heavily at Israel. If he can deliver a poison gas warhead or bomb at this distance, he will attempt it now—this is our strong feeling. Here, in Jerusalem, we do not believe that he has spared us because of our Arab population. We think that he is not concerned with Arab lives any more than Jewish ones; we see how he surrounds and fills military targets with innocent civilians in order to inhibit coalition bombing, while making use of every casualty for propaganda purposes. He also uses a number of actors; for example, the woman who appeared at the bombed shelter yesterday, screaming at the West, calling them "Bastards"—we know her as an official of the Iraqi Foreign Office who has already participated in a number of such performances.

We in Jerusalem expect to be attacked. We know that the attack will come here; don't ask me how we know, I cannot answer. It is in the air, it is knowledge purchased by living here, it is part of the strangeness of this place. When life was simpler, years ago, I walked in the hills east of Jerusalem. It was quite safe then; now, no one in his right mind would try, certainly not alone, certainly not without being heavily armed: it is no longer safe and is certainly not recommended. These are brown hills with sparse vegetation; in the spring, after the winter rains, there is a fine grass cover, something like a fine beard, two days' growth, which looks better from a distance than when you walk on it. I walked alone at that time on these brown, flat hills and heard nothing, until, later, I felt more than heard the thin, high-pitched voice of a shepherd's pipe. I knew then that I was not completely alone, that there was someone out of sight leading the customary flock of goats. I watched the rocks change colors as the angle of the sun's rays striking them became more shallow, colors that turned from red to rust to brown and finally to gray. I remember feeling an epiphany envelop me then; I understood how three major religions could be born or nourished while still quite young and fragile here. Here, in the hills around Jerusalem.

We do not believe that Saddam Hussein will hesitate to attack Jerusalem; indeed, we expect him to do just that when the ground campaign begins. We do not know what his remaining capability is. Does he still have functional Scud missiles and launchers? Does he have chemical—a euphemism used here for poison gas—warheads for these missiles? Can he get an airplane through our defenses? We do not know. We have our gas masks and our sealed rooms. The Arabs who make up 20 percent of the population of Jerusalem share our fate; they, too, have gas masks.

Our chance to retaliate for the attacks on us is slipping away—if it is not already gone. We have been relegated to the sidelines, but we are not in the stalls or in the balcony; we are still actors in this war— by virtue of the thirty-two Scuds fired at us—two more than fired at Saudi Arabia, the location of the real threat to Iraq. Every day we become more accustomed to attack; every day we are told that the Iraqi capacity to attack us diminishes. Yet we still are anxious.

We have good reasons to retaliate. Ever since the Holocaust—yes, Professor Chomsky, there was a Holocaust—we Jews no longer feel that it is proper or even possible to leave our fate in the hands of others. We also know that in the language of Middle East politics not retaliating will be interpreted as weakness on our part—there is no turning the other cheek here, in this part of the world—and will be an invitation for more aggression against us.

But we show restraint, partly out of the growing conviction that retaliation might bring down on our heads political damage in its wake far greater than any benefits that might accrue.

The other reason we do not retaliate is the fear that we do not have an adequate solution to the problem Saddam Hussein has set us. In the past we have been impelled by a view of response to threat that has three components: a fast response; a strong response; an elegant response. There is no longer any possibility of a speedy response; too much time has gone by. We could possibly respond strongly, even with nonconventional weapons, some claim. But such a response is clearly not elegant and is even out of proportion in any scale of values: it is true that our security has been threatened by Iraq, but not our existence. Undoubtedly we could respond elegantly, but because of the long distances involved it is unlikely to be a strong response—unless we were to kill Saddam Hussein, which itself raises a whole new set of problems.

Our willingness to show restraint, to renounce retaliation, means that we have ceded our right to protect ourselves. It means that we are willing to let others do the defending of Israel. *Others*, it should be understood, means the U.S. The U.S. is our friend. The U.S. even likes us. The U.S. is our friend and likes us—today.

While I was writing this report, Radio Baghdad announced what at first seemed to be a surrender. I was filled with conflicting thoughts. My first feeling was relief and then a flood of joy overtook me. No more killing, no more wounded, no more homeless. But what is happening? Saddam Hussein is not only intact and alive, but he may remain in power. Two-thirds to three-quarters of his tanks and motorized divisions remain intact—almost all of his air force, too. His hatred for us is unabated; his vision of himself as the leader of a pan-Arab force expelling us from here is—if anything—fortified. I was saddened by this; and angry as well.

Was I disappointed? Strangely enough, no. I am surprised at my reaction, my lack of reaction. But there is more than anger and the desire for revenge in me. The end of war is most important for me. I try to reconcile the apparent contradictions I find in my response. I hope, I say to myself, I would like to believe the things I tell myself—such as, Time does not always work for the tyrant. Perhaps we could find some other way out of this trapped state.

Joy was still in me.

Later it became clear that the surrender was accompanied by at least four conditions that made it completely unacceptable. Saddam Hussein insisted that the ruling family of Kuwait not be returned to power; he insisted that the coalition pay for all damage done to Iraq; he insisted that Israel withdraw from the Administered Territories; he insisted on coalition withdrawal from the Arab subcontinent.

The UN declaration calls for unconditional retreat from Kuwait. Not this porridge. It is not all over.

Still later, Radio Baghdad further reduces the sense of it all being over; they announce that this was only a working statement toward a settlement.

Israel is still in the picture; we will be dragged in, over and over again. We must expect that and be prepared, know what has to be done—and do it.

It is Friday afternoon; the Sabbath approaches. A day of rest, from sundown to sundown on Saturday. There have been four Friday nights since the beginning of the war; on three of them we have been attacked. We prepare for the Sabbath; is there nothing more that we can do to prepare for attacks?

SATURDAY, 16 FEBRUARY: DINING IS CIVILIZED

We had fourteen for dinner last night. The major addition to our table was my daughter, her husband, and their three daughters, eight, five and a half, and one and a half. They live in Omer, a suburb of Beer Sheva, nearly two hours from here by car. I have not seen them since the war began but Golda visited them once, traveling by bus.

Friday night is always our time for entertaining; until now our commitments were varied and many, and it was difficult to arrange other evenings during the week when we both were free. (I am in no shape on Saturday nights to be patient and civil. My civility and patience are necessary for a successful dinner, according to Golda.) We believe that socialization is meaningful only at dinner, and we try not to have too many people; we both are frustrated at the thought of missing part of the conversation. Perhaps that is why neither of us enjoys cocktail parties. The table must not be too long; everybody has to be within earshot.

This is an ordinary Shabbat (Sabbath) dinner, which we try to make a bit extraordinary with good food, good wine, and good conversation—our recipe for making memorable evenings out of the ordinary. Golda is a fine cook; she once loved working at it but no longer has the patience needed for great cooking. She remembers enough, however, to manage a very good meal most Friday nights. I always keep at hand a full case of a white wine with a pale pink tint from the Golan Heights that I like; I am enough of a boor and enough of a man of conviction to use this wine with everything. I have found this most palatable wine, and it is kosher, and it is delicious with fowl, fish, and meat. The good conversation? We expect our guests to work in exchange for this purple treatment. Wine, food, and expectation do wonders for encouraging people to talk.

■ The summer Sabbath differs from the winter Sabbath. The short Friday, until sundown, in winter is very hectic, with so many preparations and so little time. In summer everything is more leisurely as it gets dark late—the same holy day, but so very different in quality. In the summer there is time to take long walks, to visit friends. The Sabbath is too short in the winter; you eat dinner on Friday night, after returning from synagogue, soon after dark, which is good for little children. But our day of rest ends all too soon the next day. It is interesting that the sense of length of day—even in a Jewish day, which is from nightfall to nightfall—is independent of the number of hours in the day itself; instead, it is determined by the time from getting up until dark. In the summer we come back from the synagogue late, often too late for little children. For that reason some start their Sabbath early in the summer—early prayers, early dinner.

Formerly you almost never saw a car on the Sabbath in Jerusalem, but those days are gone forever. Now there is only one day a year without cars, Yom Kippur. I am told that youngsters use the highways and major thoroughfares in Tel Aviv on Yom Kippur to ride their bikes and skateboards freely, but I have never seen that. I have never spent Yom Kippur in Israel outside Jerusalem.

Some neighborhoods—including one adjacent to my house—are closed to traffic on the Sabbath and holidays. Barriers are placed across the streets even in the middle of the city. On the Sabbath the area next to my house, more than twelve square city blocks called *Sha'arei Hesed* (the Gates of Righteousness), resembles a Polish village of the early nineteenth century more than part of a modern city. Girls wear long-sleeved dresses and stockings even in summer and jump rope, calling out the play in Yiddish while boys do the same in more violent games, wearing black caps formerly seen only in prewar Poland. The women wear dressing gowns in the street, the men black silk coats and fur hats called *streimels*, which are made of twelve fox tails. Just as the children are filled with energy, all movement, the grown-ups stroll slowly, with ponderous steps.

Our Friday dinner is always festive. We begin by blessing the wine and the soft bread, *halla*, then going on to soup, meat, vegetables and salad, tea and cake. We usually have guests: children, grandchildren, friends, visitors, these days a Russian family. The conversations always buzz and go on, at times everyone participating, at times breaking into smaller groups. Good food and good conversation mark the meal. Often we talk about the weekly *Parasha* (reading from the Torah, or five books of Moses; we go through them all once every year). And there is gossip, too. "Did you see the lovely girl that J——is going with?" And news. And new ideas, too. We are kings and queens, our food is unlimited (dangerous!), our conversation is unlimited (exciting).

I want the Sabbath to last as long as possible—except for the cigar I give up for at least twenty-five hours. I go to prayers early in the morning, at seven, and finish by nine. In addition to reading the Parasha, we pray. Some of the prayers we say on the Sabbath are different, special. Unlike most synagogues, we do not sing our prayers, or not recognizably sing. There seems to be a rule excluding anyone with a good voice (with a few exceptions) from *daven*ing (praying) in my synagogue. Afternoon prayers are said any time between noon and twilight; next week's Parasha is sampled.

After morning prayers there is *Kiddush*, a sanctification performed over wine and a light and tasty meal, served cold in my house. We have our regular lesson in Psalms with Yoshua and Ruti, our friends who live across the street. He is a professor of French literature, she a musician who sells real estate. They are not religious but do have a great respect for the material; they love the language of the Psalms and—together with us—try to understand the meaning of these frequently difficult poems. After four and a half years we have finished only 68 of the 150; we have much yet to do.

We have a large lunch at 13:00; since we cannot cook on the Sabbath, the food has been placed in an oven or on a hot plate before the Sabbath and heated for almost twenty-four hours. Only certain foods will take this treatment—beans, potatoes, carrots, whole eggs, dumplings made of flour, oil and water, as well as chicken or meat. The result, called *hamin* (Hebrew) or *cholent* (Yiddish) is a wonderful—if indigestible—treat. The aroma is enchanting, inducing Pavlovian responses in all. We often have guests for lunch; we are still kings. We sing at the Sabbath meals, in our case badly; we hope for guests who carry a tune.

Afternoons are for visiting or receiving. We see old friends, find out what is happening to them, tell what is happening to us. We tell about a new insight we have had in religious studies or in understanding the Parasha. We talk about the news. Why is our government always so stupid, so unresponsive, so late in implementing solutions? Have you read this marvelous new book?

The Sabbath ends all too early, with evening prayers and *Havdallah*, the separation of the holy from the profane, said over wine (we are still kings), spices (to take away some of the flavor of the Sabbath into the week that follows), and a candle, which we are not allowed to light on the Sabbath. We look at the reflection of the candlelight on our fingernails; the week, with its work and other intrusions on the life of a would-be king or queen, is upon us.

Fourteen people for dinner, with five children, is not the way to have civilized conversation. But these are our children and our grandchildren; this is a family dinner. It has its own dynamics and rules; no wine other than the sweet Kiddush wine we bless to introduce the meal after I tell everybody that my wife is a rich and desirable woman (Proverbs 31; the King James version translates it "a woman of virtue"; Jewish translators prefer "a woman of valor"). Many conversations go on at once; there are children's demands and parents' coaxing and even screaming. Completely random activity seems to underlie the progress of the meal; nonetheless, the meal moves from course to course, children leave, fall asleep, and when we reach the traditional tea and cake that seal the meal, we are happy, full, and have a sense of accomplishment and the glow of seeing one another, of experiencing feelings of love which are ordinarily shelved in the helter-skelter of our daily activities.

Families are therapeutic; everybody treats everyone else. We are comfortable and enjoy. We can even be quiet together. And smile. We deflate swollen egos and support fallen ones. We are a family. We marvel at how the children of my son and those of my daughter get along so well even though they see each other so little.

This dining is not civilized, but it is good and we need it.

But this is in normal times. And these are not normal times. I worry. My daughter has come from what seems to be the safest region of the country. And then there is my penchant for finding patterns; three out of four previous Friday nights were marked by missile attacks. My daughter and her family will stay with us tomorrow as well, and I worry that the ground war in the Persian Gulf will begin on Saturday, a phase of the war that I expect to be marked by more attacks on Israel. Even a poison gas attack on Jerusalem.

These are not civilized times.

We are fourteen and we have never had more than nine in our sealed room, nine who filled the room nicely. Now we have two incubators to put in the sealed room, accounting for an appreciable part of the room.

Dinner went well, no attacks, everyone ate well, and we were happy to be together again. Golda added some spice to the meal by mentioning that she had invited another three people to lunch tomorrow. "How could you!"

And the lunch goes well, too. One of the guests is a new Russian immigrant, a widow—her husband killed by Stalin—of about sixty-five who told us that she played violin in the orchestra in Moscow but sustained an injury and had to give up her career for teaching in the Conservatory of Music in Moscow. She is a large woman, of grand proportions, who surprises us by telling us that she has recently taken off 22 kilograms (48 pounds); she had weighed 100 kilograms (220 pounds) and now weighs only 78 (172 pounds). All this in a mixture of Yiddish, which she speaks slightly, and Russian, which only one of our other guests understands slightly. The other guests are a young couple who have recently moved into a tiny house down the street. They are fresh and handsome and make good company, even with the children blasting into the room at irregular intervals, asking for justice.

Life goes on—even in war. And death goes on, normal death—even in war. Not everybody who dies in wartime dies from the war itself. In the afternoon I went to a friend's for services. Her father had died after a long illness. I stayed until dark, praying as part of the obligatory *minyan* (ten adult Jewish males).

I return after *Havdallah*, the prayer that separates the Sabbath from the prosaic, from the rest of the week. It has begun to rain hard; dressed in a light sweater, I rush home. There my daughter tells me that they are not staying the night; they want to return, they have a party to go to. We attempt to dissuade them: the thought of being on the roads at these times unsettles us. But they insist and drive away.

20:15   The radio program I was listening to begins to broadcast the alarm for an attack, without the sisma that used to precede the sirens. The local siren joins in after a few seconds. I call my wife to join me in the sealed room. Only the two of us are left in the house. Peeing, putting on the mask, sealing the door—now a complete routine; no problems. But why does there seem to be a space between the rubber of the mask and my face? We are very worried about my daughter, son-in-law, and the three girls, Adi, Anat, and No'a. They should still be on the road.

20:18   We are told it is a true attack.

20:22   Nahman Shai tells us that two missiles have been fired at Israel from Iraq.

20:24   I attempt to hook up to other computers in Israel to find out what is happening; but IRC is down. Later, using Decnet, I locate some people on the computers in Tel Aviv; they do not respond to my VAX/VMS phone calls.

20:28   Nahman Shai tells us that both missiles have landed in Israel. He says that those who have heard nothing can now be reassured that they are safe. But we are still to remain masked in the sealed rooms until they determine the nature of the warheads.

20:38   The missiles have landed in two different places.

20:42   All-clear for all areas of the country other than the south. But the south has never been attacked before! And this is where our daughter is now traveling! We take off our masks and call our daughter's number; we get the automatic secretary and leave a message telling of our concern.

20:51   No wounded! What a relief! We are very quiet, my wife and I—very concerned. My mouth is very dry. Those in the south are freed from masks but must remain in sealed rooms.

20:53   General all-clear; the weapons were conventional.

21:15   We may leave houses.

21:18   Our daughter calls; they are all safe. She relates that they saw or heard nothing; when the alarm sounded they continued driving, knowing that the south, where they already were, was never attacked. When, at 20:42, they understood that the south was indeed attacked, they stopped the car until the all-clear for the south was sounded.

23:00   One of the missiles was seen by Bedouins in the Negev Desert, where it landed without producing damage.

This is what we know. It is late. I must finish, go to sleep. I am tired. I do not feel civilized. Just safe—for the moment—safe, tired, and alive. And thankful that my family is all alive and well.

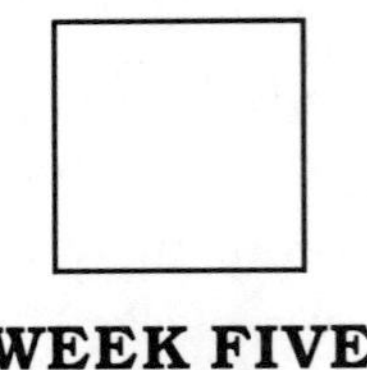

WEEK FIVE

Things are getting back to normal. The few days—and even weeks—when all the good guys were wearing white cowboy suits and working together against the bandits in black may be slipping away from us. The originally reluctant members of the coalition once again appear reluctant; the theme that was initially common to the activist members of the coalition as well as to the minimalists—stopping Saddam Hussein—no longer appears to be a sufficient bond to unite all members of the coalition. There are those, like Russia and some of the Arab members of the coalition, who see Saddam Hussein's conditional agreement to withdraw from Kuwait, announced on Friday, as real and providing a basis for negotiation.

France—relatively uncommitted even at the beginning—is again wavering. After initial reluctance to participate actively, France joined in the bombings with some appetite, but now, who knows? And France is not alone.

Some of the allies think that Saddam Hussein's humiliating terms for withdrawal (including reparations for damage done to Iraq; withdrawal of foreign troops from the Persian Gulf; and forcing Israel to withdraw from the Administered Territories) should be accepted; others reject them for what they are—a cheap trick, with publicity as its aim, attempting to create a picture of Iraqi willingness to negotiate as opposed to the intransigence of the U.S. and its allies.

Amazing to me is that there is one area of agreement that still binds the allies together, a desire to get Israel to enfranchise a Palestinian state. Even more amazing to me is that this purpose is shared by the other side, by Iraq. And by the PLO, hero of this new drama whose staging is actively being prepared backstage, the new production slated to follow the Persian Gulf War. The same producer, the U.S., is hoping to have one success follow another. The PLO, the accepted voice of the Palestinians in the world, in the UN (where Yasser Arafat is allowed to hold forth, gun in hand), in the Vatican (which accepts the PLO but does not yet recognize Israel), is to be rewarded for its support of Saddam Hussein by getting the leading role. Israel, for its restraint, praised by all, will be the villain again—a matter of typecasting.

Hollywood, Hollywood. A wonderful town.

■   Will we be able to judge the image of Israel in the United States by that usually faithful barometer, Hollywood? It has been a long time since Israel was last the subject of a Hollywood film; it has been a long time since Israel has been popular. Presumably, the two facts are correlated. Except for a brief, unconvincing, post-Entebbe flirt, not since the Six Day War has Hollywood made films in which Israel was the subject. Hollywood will certainly take this war and run with it as long and as far as it can, influenced by the decisiveness of the victory and the unpopularity of the enemy. Will Israel share in this coverage?

If Israel returns to the screen, it may be the best indicator of its popularity. I imagine that Sean Connery could play a credible
■ Israeli.

But while there seems to be some confusion as to whether or not the Iraqis are responsible for the bombings and casualties that country has suffered, there is little doubt in anyone's mind that Israel is guilty of some great crime and must be punished.

The U.S. State Department has shown great irritability in response to Israeli complaints that the State Department has blocked Israeli bidding for defense contracts that Congress has approved, for ignoring the promise given to provide guarantees for an Israeli loan to deal with the problems of absorbing the great Russian immigration that has already arrived here and continues to stream in our direction, for asking why noncoalition countries are given licenses to purchase a supercomputer while Israel is denied that right.

Irritability, yes. Denial, no. Correction, no. These requests of Israel will not be honored—unless. For showing restraint at the specific request of the State Department, Israel a friendly nation or even ally, a fellow sufferer in the war, is to be bent at the rack. Every bit of ammunition available will be used to force Israel to enfranchise a Palestinian state in its midst. No, none of Israel's requests is enough. So let us use them all together to force the Palestinian state down Israel's throat after the Persian Gulf War is over.

The streets of Moscow are filmed with a large procession of Russians carrying placards inscribed in red and black paint denouncing the Jews in general and Israel in particular. No Jews in the government, say the signs. What Jews? It makes no difference that there are no Jews; perhaps Gorbachev is thinking of converting. No fighting a Jewish war, read the posters. What Jewish war? Presumably this proclamation is responsive to Saddam Hussein's claim that Israel is Iraq's real opponent in the Persian Gulf War and that the coalition is merely doing Israel's fighting for her. And the conservative and military elements in the Soviet Union are applying pressure to get out of the Persian Gulf. The government is eager to accept Saddam Hussein's conditions as a basis for negotiation—if he would only relax them a bit. They need to end their participation in the war to thwart the antiperestroika forces.

The Muslim states in the USSR are interested in gaining their independence. They fight the central government on any issue possible; given their religious identity, it is only natural for them, too, to support the new Saladin, the hope of Muslim regeneration. And they do.

In the face of this backlash, in the face of growing and outspoken anti-Semitism in the USSR, it is also no surprise that Russian Jews continue to flow into missile-attacked Israel. The economics—where the coin is life itself—of the move are simple. It is safer for a Jew to be in Israel now than in today's Russia.

The foreign minister of the USSR and the U.S. secretary of

state—at their very first meeting after the onset of hostilities in the Persian Gulf—rush to announce jointly the importance of settling the Palestinian problem immediately after the Persian Gulf crisis is resolved. There is nothing more important on their agendas. The first order of business—on the very day the war ends, I presume—will be to punish Israel for cooperating with the U.S. and its coalition allies and reward the Palestinians for their unflinching support of . . . of whom? Of Saddam Hussein.

Syrian and Moroccan troops in Saudi Arabia, members of the coalition in good standing, break out in hurrahs of joy and triumph and fire automatic weapons into the air on hearing that Iraqi Scuds land in Israeli cities. A celebration is a celebration—and cannons are also fired. Finally a Saudi force has to be sent to calm them down. More than one hundred Syrian officers have been arrested following their outspoken criticism of Syrian involvement on the U.S. side in the Gulf War. They demand to be returned to Syria. They, too, know that Israel is the real enemy.

■ The forces that drove Arab countries to join the coalition were different, but all Arab states would have preferred a solution in which the United States and its Western allies were not physically present in the Gulf. The Arab countries perceived the United States and its European allies as imperialistic nations whose only interest in the Arabs and the Arabian subcontinent is exploitation and control of their resources, particularly oil.

Arabs have no difficulty fighting among themselves: witness Lebanon, where internal civil war, aided and abetted by Palestinian and Syrian forces, has continued now for more than fifteen years.

Why, then, did the various Arab countries join the coalition? The cases of Kuwait and Saudi Arabia are easiest to understand. Kuwait disappeared as a nation with Saddam Hussein's invasion and annexation of that country. Saudi Arabia had good reason to believe that it was next on Iraq's list. Both knew that there was no Arab army or combination of armies strong enough to halt the Iraqi conquest. They had no other choice but to enlist U.S. and coalition aid.

Egypt joined because President Mubarak was deeply angered by Saddam Hussein's perfidy and betrayal of the Arab cause. Mubarak had attempted to keep the West out of the Gulf crisis by attempting an all-Arab solution. Saddam Hussein agreed to a peaceful solution to be brokered by Mubarak. Included in this agreement was Saddam Hussein's word to forego conflict until an Arab solution to the problem could be found. Such a solution would not only have enhanced Mubarak's status but would also have proved that the

Arab nations are mature enough to handle their own disputes without outside interference.

Like Iraq, Syria is ruled by a Ba'ath Party leader and a Sunni Arab elite that is a minority in the country; likewise, both Iraq and Syria depend on the Soviets for arms. Thus, Syria would seem to be the last country in the world to oppose Iraq. The motivation for Syria's participation in the coalition can be found in the long-standing mutual personal antipathy between Syria's Assad and Iraq's Saddam Hussein; this mutual repugnance led Assad to join the coalition. Syria hoped to win U.S. favor to replace declining Soviet foreign aid.

The last of the countries to join the opposition was Morocco, a strange case. Morocco, located in North Africa, remote from the Gulf, joined the coalition as a Western power. The ambition of its French-educated absolute monarch and king, Hassan, is to be considered a Western power, a potential broker in peace treaties between Israel and the Arabs, a moderate force among intemperate and extreme Arab nations.

There is also the Arab Jihad, an interesting organization with a strong Palestinian element, headed by Sheikh Assad Tamini, a former resident of the Hebron region in Israel. He was expelled a good number of years ago for fomenting riot and revolution and now lives in Jordan. It is frightening to listen to him on TV; he is an avuncular and sweet-looking man who speaks softly; no histrionics for him. And in a soft voice he enunciates legions of hate. He now threatens to assassinate President Mubarak of Egypt, "just as we killed Sadat." "Hussani Mubarak," he continues, "has sold his soul to the Americans and he too will die." He threatens all members of the coalition with acts of terrorism. But the chief object of his animosity is Israel and the Jews. "We must kill all the Jews," Tamini says. "They have always been the source of mankind's troubles. Hitler saw us as firm allies against Zionism. We would like the unified Germany to help us now."

Clearly, as all nations (almost all?) are agreed, Israel is guilty of crimes against humankind. Or at least against the Palestinians. And must pay.

What is this great crime that Israel is guilty of? I have neither the time nor space to tell it all here; but in brief, the recent history (one can go back to the Crucifixion or earlier, too, but . . .) of our "crime" began in November 1947, when the UN decided to divide the British Mandate in Palestine into two countries, one Arab, one Jewish. Led from within by the Palestinian leader and former ally of Hitler, the Mufti of Jerusalem, and from without by five Arab states, five Arab armies invaded the new Israel with the explicit purpose of destroying her. Arab leaders told Palestinians to leave their homes for a short time to clear the field for the invading armies, and a great number did, creating the refugee problem which still exists. Badly outnumbered and outgunned, the Israelis managed to stave off the attack, but not before Jordan seized the West Bank and East Jerusalem and Egypt seized Gaza.

In 1967, Egypt and Syria once again decided to eliminate Israel from the map of the Middle East. (CNN has done the work for the Arabs; the name *Israel* does not appear on the CNN map of the Middle East.) Israel, arming for the struggle, warned Jordan to stay out of the conflict. Jordan did not accept the warning, and when the dust of battle cleared, Israel had captured East Jerusalem and the West Bank from the Jordanians, the Golan Heights from Syria, and Gaza and the Sinai Peninsula from Egypt. Israel hoped to return some of these territories in exchange for peace. Only Egypt has agreed to deal with Israel and, following the Camp David agreements, received Sinai. (Egypt refused to take back Gaza, a constant source of trouble.)

Other than Egypt, which maintains correct but not friendly relations with Israel and exchanges ambassadors with us, none of the Arab nations recognizes the existence of Israel or is willing to sign a peace treaty with her. That is—in a nutshell—Israel's crime.

The Palestinians have been the great losers throughout, not without their own fault. But the Arab nations which have absorbed them have hardly been outstanding in helping them, leaving many in refugee camps without work for years—in Jordan, Egypt, and Lebanon. The reasons for this include both indifference to Palestinian suffering and use of their poverty as a political football to arouse the sympathy of the world. The Palestinians (like Sheikh Tamini, one of them) want Israel out of the Middle East; they (sometimes) say that they are willing to live in peace with us—but the organizational charter of their most representative political body includes a paragraph on the necessity for exterminating Israel.

Forgive us for our opacity and what seems like cruelty. But we are not willing to allow armed enemies bent on our destruction to live in our midst; we are worried about the short distance to our cities, we are worried about the ability of countries like a still-armed Iraq to march to within ten miles of our coast, where they could cut the country in half.

Do not forgive us if it is not in your heart to. But we will not commit suicide. That is not our style.

Meanwhile, under the threat of the Scuds, under the threat of a poison gas attack, we stand mostly united, hoping for the best and expecting the very worst.

MONDAY, 18 FEBRUARY: REPORTING THE GULF WAR

I would like to talk about the other reporting, the reporting of the professionals, on TV, on radio, in newspapers, and in news magazines. There appears to be strong feeling in the U.S. in support of these reporters. A great deal has to do—I think—with the fear of tyranny, of cover-up. A free press provides an important—perhaps the most important—check on these crimes. As such, a free press is a necessity and must be forgiven all mistakes.

■   A contact in America suggests that I may have been wrong on this matter. According to him, the general perception is that the press came out of the Gulf War looking very bad while the military looked very good to all. Peter Arnett and Betsy Aron, broadcasting from Baghdad, were almost universally perceived as villains. Forgive me ■ for underestimating the American viewer.

I would suggest—as a spectator—that this freedom and the extreme degree of latitude given the reporter in the name of freedom of the press obligates him or her to a degree of seriousness and dedication to principle. I have failed to see these qualities in those who report the Persian Gulf War. I see more of the entertainer than the investigator. The reporters have not returned the great credit extended them; they have failed to be as serious and concerned as their mandate requires of them.

The word *mandate* brings to mind the problem of election. We neither elect nor select our reporters; they are selected for us by unnamed others. I am not sure that purely commercial considerations are not the only criterion in this selection. I am sure that so serious a function requires a more rounded set of criteria.

From the very beginning the war reporting has failed the viewer. It is easy to blame censorship for impeding reporters' progress, but censorship does not explain the lack of seriousness—I do not mean in describing technical aspects of the war—and the lack of morality that has characterized most of what we have seen.

The reporting of the war is often very abstract, as if describing a spectacle in which people do not take part. The role of technology increases from war to war, and in this war we are treated to the technology of advanced camera techniques applied to advanced weapon systems. It is easy to spend hours watching smart bombs spotting the target, locking in, and finally striking and blowing up the building, bridge or tank. But we learn little about the people under fire, about the soldiers and civilians bombed, wounded, killed, miraculously saved.

Never do the correspondents relate reasons for the war. This makes the war an abstraction instead of a purposeful effort on the part of some countries to control what they see as unprovoked aggression on the part of another country. This plucking of their reports from the conceptual anchor in which the war takes place adds to the sense of spectacle.

Is it because they do not know the reasons for the war that the reporters do not relate them? If it is true that they are ignorant of the conceptual basis for the war, this is indeed a sad comment on the nature of their endeavor. Have they become technicians of the visual, nothing more than the special effects artists of the movies—admirable but not central?

Is it because they do not accept the validity of the reasons put forward for engaging in war? Is this the reason for their not putting their reports in the context of the reasons? But why do they not share their views with us? Is it a reflection of their disdain of the audience? Are we not intelligent enough to understand? Or will it be more effective to instruct us in an indirect way, suggesting, showing examples, rather than explaining? In other words, is this reporting or propaganda?

Is it because they want to be "fair" to both sides that the correspondents do not give the reasons for the war? But both sides are convinced that they are in the right, and being fair to both sides is certainly not being fair; it is favoring the side with the most unpopular position. And why is that side deserving of special attention? By the very virtue of its unpopularity?

Or is it that the reporters and their producers do not feel that it is their concern to deal with reasons—as reasons, for them, simply do not fit into the category of news. What then is news? Is news material only for perceptual but not for conceptual consumption? Is news geared only for the senses and the heart, liver, and kidneys? Not for the brain at all?

If the head is left out, we are left with entertainment alone. Certainly entertainers have an important place in society. But we do not usually look for entertainers to give us reliable pictures of the world. (Are these war correspondents all embryonic Woody Allens? Allen is, by the way, no favorite of mine.) Entertainers favor the grotesque, the exceptional, the amusing. Is this what we are being served in reports of the war? And only this?

If reasons for the war are not to be discussed, if the events we see and hear about are not related to the reasons for the war, we have a strange situation indeed. If we are not shown the relation of events to the underlying reasons of the war, there is a strange, lifeless quality to the most horrifying happenings, to the wounded, to the dead, to the homeless, to the starving and sick.

If we are not allowed to see the relationship of events to the underlying reasons for the war, the implications of events become fuzzy and undefined. What does all this technology mean, all this destruction and death? Can it have any meaning other than in context with the underlying reasons for the war?

Are we to understand the reluctance of the reporters to relate events to the reasons for the war as a philosophical statement, such as "War is hell"? That the reasons can never be sufficient to justify or explain any war? That there is no such thing as a guilty party in a war? This is a possibility; but I doubt it.

By avoiding relating the events of the war to the underlying reasons, reporters and newscasts have failed us. They have renounced their right to be taken seriously.

The tone for reporting the war was already set on the first night, when correspondents spoke only of the lights bursting in the sky in the bombardment—as if describing a Fourth of July fireworks display. They added an air of authority by adding a name, calling a bomb not just a bomb but a smart bomb, just as the sports announcer tells us that what we have seen is a triple half-nelson. And that is the tone that persists. Just as sports announcers are much better when reporting canned film than reporting live, the war correspondents do much better with canned film. Just as sports announcers never admit making a mistake, so, too, the war reporter never makes a mistake. They both assume that the mistake will be forgotten or that what they say is just not that important.

Is it in the framework of entertainment or sport that we must forgive Peter Arnett for allowing the Iraqis to use world TV as a platform for undisguised, often crude anti-U.S., anticoalition propaganda?

In retrospect, I can see that sports offers a much better analogy than entertainment does. Sports is a form of media endeavor that has come to include more commentary than viewing the play. You would think that fast, active sports such as track and basketball might be different, more difficult to comment on; but they are not. Both my oldest son and I turn off the sound when we watch basketball; we are greatly annoyed at the level of nonsense the announcers dish out. We both know too much about the game to need it.

Football turns out to have an added similarity to war; the use of heavy machinery, frequent changes in personnel, and complex tactics are shared by football and war. In fact, much of the explanation of the military strategy in the Pentagon and Saudi Arabia briefings was in the language of football strategy. ("Making an end run" and "dropping a pass behind the enemy front line" are two examples that come to mind.) Schwarzkopf looked like nothing if not a former football player, and he used the language of football in his briefings. His wife, though, spoke of him as a lover of ballet and opera—not a contradiction.

Their disdain for the audience is something that can never be forgiven the war reporters. Even boorishness is more acceptable. For many, this war is much more than entertainment. There are those who are directly involved or whose relatives or friends are directly involved in the war; this is no light matter for them. There are those whose country is directly involved; this is no light matter for them. There are those in the audience who want to know what is going on so they may make an informed evaluation; are they, too, to be treated to disdain? Or should they change channels? Where to?

Without presenting the context in which they occur, events are nothing more than pornography, meant to stimulate, titillate, excite. Such events lack reality. I suppose that pornography has a place in some countries, at some times. But war, to our sorrow, is much more than titillation; war is dangerous to man, animal, and property. Very dangerous.

A few words about the appearances of experts on various phases of the war in the media and about those who interview them.

I have, after hour on hour of watching the experts, never heard one confess that he had been wrong. Almost all of them have, in my experience, been wrong a number of times and even consistently wrong. (I have never seen one consistently correct in his analysis; some have not been tested by time or by me.) They are not abashed by their performance, by their failures. As if their past record means nothing, they continue to radiate confidence and the air of expertise.

The producers who continue to invite them are also undisturbed by the failures of the experts. The interviewers never remind them of their failures.

I too would like to be an expert. But I do not think I have the chutzpah.

■　　But of course I *was* being the expert. In the midst of the war I did not see that I, too, was filling the role of expert, offering my opinions as fact, as the basis for others to understand the situation—but it is quite clear to me now. I hope that I have not made all the mistakes that I have laid at the feet of the experts; I hope that the readers will
■　take me, too, with a grain of salt . . . and forgive me my chutzpah.

One expert [General Michael J. Dugan] who was consistent in refusing to speculate in the area of his expertise—apparently out of concern for revealing information of military value—was fired by the network for which he worked.

Responsibility is not one of the desired qualities of an expert.

The interviewers of the experts are another matter. Many do not seem to listen to the answers given; they have an agenda, expect certain answers, and proceed as if the answer anticipated has indeed been given. Sometimes they feel the necessity to restate what the expert tells them, at which point they get it all wrong. At other times, they seem to get hung up on a word, or on a technical term, to the exclusion of the intended meaning, and beat the word or term to an ignominious death.

If it makes others happy, Israeli interviewers do exactly the same thing.

I have been told that I exaggerated in stating that the CNN map of the Middle East did not show the name of Israel. I looked once again and confess that I was wrong. The name *Israel* can indeed be found on the CNN map—not over the country's shape, as is true for all her neighbors with their large areas, but in the Mediterranean Sea.

Israel: this is the country, too small to put a legible name on it, that they want to cut up into two countries.

The only other small country in the Middle East is Lebanon. This unfortunate state has been a battlefield for more than fifteen years, since the Christian Arabs ceased to be perceived by their Muslim Arab countrymen to be a majority. Long before Israel's unfortunate invasion of Lebanon in 1982—to put an end to ceaseless attacks from that country on the northern settlements of Israel—internal strife claimed, and since Israel's withdrawal continues to claim, the lives of hundreds of citizens each year. This country is torn apart by unresolvable strife between different Arab groups, with the main divisions being between Muslim and Christian Arabs.

Israel is the country that they want to cut up into two, one part Jewish, one Muslim. Israel is the country that they want to fashion into the same anarchy that is Lebanon's.

TUESDAY, 19 FEBRUARY: GREENS ARE GOOD FOR YOU

Two quiet nights in a row. We wait. What is next? We look at the sky. The moon is in its first quarter now, a thin crescent of brilliant white from four to eight o'clock. The rest of the moon can be faintly seen, pale and very large, resting on the sky that hovers over Jerusalem. The pale image of the moon is—I am told—the reflection of the moon's light back from the earth, a phenomenon visible only in the clearest of cloudless and dust-free skies. The rains have washed away the dust. We have the clearest of skies.

We enjoy very good weather. The sky is absolutely cloudless, by day as by night. During the day, the smoke trails of barely discerned jets make lovely patterns across the sky, long parallel white lines, gently curving in the sun-splashed pale blue sky. The two lines change; first they are thin, penciled in the sky. Later the white tracks thicken, become soft and feathery, edges fuzzy as definition begins to blur.

I feel a great silence about me in the streets of Jerusalem. Everything is quieter than usual; not that Jerusalem is ever a noisy city—there is no heavy industry allowed here. But it is noticeably quieter now. Even the automobiles make less noise, fight less with one another. I imagine it is because everybody shares my feeling of waiting. Either waiting for the cease-fire that rumor tells us is less than twenty-four hours away, or for the ground war in the Gulf to begin. Both hold uncertainty for us.

The Russian peace offensive is seen here as an attempt to regain prominence on the world stage and to put an obstacle in the path of the U.S. Rumors about frightening—to us—terms of settlement for Iraq abound. Even ones that make no sense at all. For example, that the Soviets have promised to rearm Iraq after the Iraqis withdraw from Kuwait—an unlikely event in the face of Russian financial problems. But other possibilities are more reasonable and not one bit less frightening.

■ Soviet motives in attempting to thwart a complete U.S. and coalition victory were complex. At this time coalition victory in Kuwait was already a foregone conclusion. Meanwhile, nationalist movements and poor economic conditions were threatening to tear apart the Soviet empire. Even anti-Semitism, officially banned since the 1917 revolution but practiced more or less secretly by Stalin and others in power, was now both rife and public.

If Gorbachev could broker a peace that left Saddam Hussein and Iraq relatively intact, he could satisfy his critics and gain a customer for Russian arms who could pay in cold cash. A postwar Iraq would need to be rearmed. Would they not approach the nation that had bailed them out of threatened destruction for these arms? And Iraqi oil wells were, unlike the Kuwaiti ones the Iraqis had set to torch, intact, ready to produce and earn the dollars to pay for the arms.

Although Gorbachev's immediate attempts were not rewarded, they undoubtedly played a role in President Bush's decision to stop the land battle after only one hundred hours, while Saddam Hussein still remained in control and a working component of his army remained with sufficient means at hand to quell revolts among Iraqi ■ Shiite and Kurdish rebels.

Allowing Saddam Hussein to remain in power is clearly one of the components of the Soviet-Iraqi deal in the making. Saddam

Hussein is hated here, seen as a force for evil, as someone who will try and try again to destroy us, with whatever means he has. He is responsible for the terror that has swept through the country, for the fear of poison gas, for the fear of the next missile attack. He is responsible for putting one and a half million children into gas masks. We see Saddam Hussein as being impelled and driven by the ambition to be one of the great—even classic—Arab heroes. Since the destruction of Israel is the only objective that all Arabs can agree on now, there is no other way for him to achieve his ambition than to deal a mortal or at least extremely damaging blow to Israel.

We love life and peace, too. And the thought that the bloodshed in the Arab subcontinent might end is a welcome one to us. We are not single-minded, not even in our hate. (Yes, we hate.) And we feel guilty for wanting to see the war go on—at least long enough to depose Saddam Hussein, who threatens us, at least long enough to destroy the Iraqi war machine, which threatens us.

The onset of the ground war also worries us. We feel sure that Saddam Hussein's reaction will be to throw everything he can at us. That is the logic of the Middle East.

Hospitals are ready in every city for a massive poison gas attack. Outside the hospitals long rows of showers have been installed to wash the victims; stretchers stand at the ready. Medical teams are at full alert. Antidotes are stocked and available. We wait.

We wait; an announcement from Radio Baghdad is promised in one more hour.

We can now summarize the human damage done by the Scuds: 35 of the 67 Scuds fired landed in Israel, 8 in greater Tel Aviv, 3 in Haifa, 24 elsewhere; 1,035 wounded as a result of the Scuds arrived at hospitals. About half of them—539—were victims of hysteria and overwhelming anxiety; these were all treated in emergency rooms and released. Of the rest, 226—almost all in the first two weeks—injected themselves with atropine, fearing that they had developed symptoms of gas poisoning.

Of the 230 physically wounded, only 60 were hospitalized. At present only 2 patients remain in hospital.

Of the 230 wounded by blast, flying glass, structural elements, and shrapnel, 220 were considered to be lightly wounded, nine to be moderately wounded (serious but not life threatening), and one critically wounded.

Thirteen deaths can be directly attributed to the Scud attacks. Of these, four died from heart attacks. (Dozens of others, not included in this list, did not die.) Seven died of gas-mask accidents, choking to death, usually as a result of not removing the air plug from the filters. Two died as a direct result of wounds incurred from the missiles.

It could have been much worse. The average death rate in Iran from Scud attacks was eight for every Scud. At that rate we would have had 280 deaths here. We are better prepared.

It might still get worse. There is tension in the air, but no signs of panic.

We are up in arms at the intended visit of a delegation of the Greens here. This German political party, which seems to see environmental reform as an end in itself, even taking priority over human lives, is not popular here at this time.

Their political platform is grotesquely anti-Israel. They—together with Saddam Hussein—see us as responsible for the Persian Gulf War. They are against supplying Israel with Patriot antimissile missiles but agree that we should be given gas masks. I presume they see the defensive Patriots as an environmental threat. Or is it Israel that they see as the environmental threat?

The stated purpose of their visit is twofold: (1) to determine our guilt; (2) to see why the Shalom Achshav (Peace Now) Party here has been prevented from demonstrating.

I will not relate to their first purpose. As to the second, the Peace Now people haven't got the heart to demonstrate these days. Who is going to demonstrate now for making peace with the PLO, ardent supporters of Saddam Hussein? They might get a few dozen hardliners to come; that would be an embarrassing show.

We are still not comfortable with the Germans; we still remember that this was a nation whose main purpose not so very long ago was to exterminate us, who undermined their own war effort to further killing us faster, more efficiently. And now these fellows want to come here to determine our guilt.

It does not go down well. I think I will not eat cucumbers this week.

WEDNESDAY, 20 FEBRUARY: THE WAR DIARY; BEGINNINGS

The weather continues very good; good for me, less good for the country. We need water badly; the major source of our water, the Kinneret (Lake Tiberius or the Sea of Galilee), is very low. Bad for us, good for archaeologists.

Two longboats from Roman times were found preserved in the mud bed of the receding lake a few years ago. Now a marina is discovered near Kfar Nahum (Capernaum).

Is there a rule here? Is one man's adversity always another's fortune? Is there someone who actually benefits from the death and maiming of the many victims of war and tyranny?

Rumors abound; they surround us. We listen to the news on the hour, on the half-hour; some leave the radio on all the time. I think people are not really working; I have the feeling that they are merely going through the motions.

We hear that the Russians are preparing a way for Saddam Hussein to stay in power, with a substantial amount of his military strength intact. We hear that the Americans will start the invasion of Kuwait and even Iraq momentarily. We listen and believe everything. We listen and believe nothing. We continue to listen.

And then we have another attack.

19:49   We hear the siren. There are only three of us in the house; I had come back from work only twenty minutes earlier. My wife is out; my son and his friend join me in the sealed, poison-gas-proof room; we don our gas masks, listen to the radio.

19:53   Nahman Shai tells us that one missile has been fired at us, but has not yet landed.

20:02   Shai tells us that the missile has landed, but no further details. We understand that since we have not heard an explosion we are likely not to be in the area of the landing.

20:05   All areas of the country other than greater Tel Aviv and Shomron are clear; we can remove gas masks and leave the sealed room.

20:08   Tel Aviv is also released from masks and the sealed room.

20:22   We are told that there are no wounded. A sigh of relief.

20:28 A general all-clear is announced, now including Shomron as well; the weapon apparently carried a conventional warhead.

23:00 We are told that two Patriots were fired at the missile; some shrapnel fell in built-up regions, but without producing any serious damage. It seems that the performance of the Patriots is being upgraded from day to day; these two hit the warhead of the Scud and exploded it remote from its target.

We know that Saddam Hussein will attack us with all he has left to throw at us as soon as the land war starts. We wait.

Readers have asked me how my reports began. I will try to reconstruct the history and the motives that impelled me to write these reports.

Once I began—I can testify without doubt—I was impelled to persevere, to write daily reports. These reports, it became apparent to me, without planning, began to include more and more of me (far too much, some claim), of what was happening to me and those around me and to include my personal views.

I then began to think of the reports as a diary. And as a diary they must be read and judged, it seems to me. My reports are not journalism, for I am not a journalist—not by training, not by virtue of talent, not with special sources of information. Nor are these reports analysis, for I am not an expert—not in war, not in siege, not in missiles, not in civil defense.

So I began to think of the reports as my war diary. I wrote daily entries that served a need for me and met—I soon learned—a need in others. How did it begin? Where were its sources? These, it seems to me, are questions that can only be answered in the framework of biography, personal and cultural.

The Beginnings

My diary began in the sealed room, sealed against poison gases, in this safe and yet unsafe shelter that is also a mausoleum, with its window obliterated by metal shutters on the outside and by thick black plastic—actually from a roll purchased in 1969 from Sears, Roebuck, when I sold my house in Bloomington, Indiana, and shipped its contents to Israel, plastic never before used—shielding the inner surface of the window. More precisely, shielding us from fragments of the taped window glass when blasted, from the poison gas on the outside.

There, in that sealed room, I felt the need; there the diary was born. What need? Or needs? After two consecutive days of attacks, the first on Israel, I wrote my first hesitant report.

I was struck by the ultimate loneliness of the sealed room, the sense that other people, even family, there did not counteract loneliness. We attempted to cheer one another, to comfort, to empathize. But we were alone, I was alone—alone while with others, alone in the face of fearful, uncontrollable elements rained on us from a distance. We were threatened by missiles that came to us after passing through the skies of three different countries. Did Thor's hammer, Zeus's bolts ever travel such distances?

I did not know if I was to survive this loneliness, but I felt I had to share my knowledge if I could. I did not feel the sense of purpose that directed Emmanuel Ringelblum in the writing of the *Warsaw Ghetto Diaries*; how could I? This was not extermination; mine was not the last voice. The closest analogy I could find was the tales told by those who died or almost died and were brought back to life.

We are terribly frightened by the thought of dying, some of us by fear of pain, many more by the ultimate uncertainty of how death is perceived by the one who dies. We wonder if there is any life—certainly not "life" but consciousness, continuation—after death.

Strangely enough, I myself am one of those who have "died" and come back to life. In January 1977, also on a Saturday night, I became terribly ill and asked my wife to call a friend, a cardiologist. He came, spoke to me, asked me to lie down, and did an electrocardiogram, an ECG, on me. While this was going on, I lost consciousness. Later, my wife, who was present, told me what happened at that time.

My eyes suddenly rolled up and I became blue; the cardiologist discerned that I had developed ventricular fibrillation, a condition of uncontrolled beating of the heart incompatible with life. He pounded my chest and began to perform artificial resuscitation on me. (Later I discovered he had broken three ribs, a small price for me to pay to be resuscitated successfully.) He asked my wife to call an emergency cardiac ambulance while he continued with the resuscitation for the twenty minutes until the ambulance arrived.

I awoke a few minutes later, sat up in bed, and vomited. I had been treated with two electric shocks, one to stop my heart gone wild, the second to reinitiate its action, this time with a normal rhythm. Two round burn marks, one on the front of my chest, the second on the left side, each about three inches in diameter, would slowly fade over the next six months—reminders of my ordeal, of my remarkable salvation.

I was carried down the stairs—it was the middle of the night—sitting in a chair. At the door, I saw my son and daughter, looking concerned. I smiled (tried to smile?) and was taken to the hospital in the ambulance.

■   Looking back, I ruminate on the meaning of this long digression about my heart attack so very close to my hospitalization for cardiac symptomatology. Actually this was the day my symptoms became so patent that I could no longer deny them, the day that I called my cardiologist, Shlomo Stern, asking for an appointment; we agreed that I would see him on the morrow. Did I call him before writing the piece? I do not think so. Nor do I remember if I had symptoms while writing this piece, or before. Was it after? I cannot remember.

I think that psychologists would agree that my concentration on cardiac symptoms paved the way for my hospitalization. Recalling the traumatic first heart attack may well have produced stress and taxed my heart. At the very least these thoughts were responsible, in their eyes, for lowering my resistance to the symptoms. Concentrating on your own heart disease can only hasten the expression of the process.

I see things differently. I see the body registering the cardiac symptoms that I was too busy—too much of a denier of illness—to admit. I see the body's knowledge fighting for expression through a reluctant consciousness, finding a way, unsatisfactory as it might be, relying on the mechanisms of sublimation, of upwards displacement: writing about a cardiac event, writing about it in terms of the past. The past is never as threatening as the present can be. (Sometimes the body will not accept compromises; heart pain, meant to be a warning that something should be done, can become uncontrollable, even producing shock, further adding to the heart's distress.) I see my writing about heart disease not as a cause of the heart disease or an inciting factor but the expression of a subconscious knowledge that my heart was not in order.

There is the possibility that both views are right: that the writing was an expression of internal heterostasis, or imbalance—a warning that the heart was ill and needed treatment—and, at the same time, that writing about the heart made things worse. I had exacerbated my cardiac condition by not having treatment, by focusing on the heart the wrong way.

Three explanations. You judge.

Forty years ago I worked on denial of illness with Edwin Weinstein, a pioneer in the field. He focused on the psychotic expression of a normal personality trait, denial of illness, in the acutely brain damaged. The patients who, when normal, would never admit being ill, who would go to work with a fever would—when brain damaged—show striking and often morbidly humorous expressions of the now greatly exaggerated trait. In addition to saying that they were not ill and not in a hospital, such patients spoke of multiple heads, good and bad. Some believed that they had up to eight heads and would give elaborate descriptions of each. They spoke of not being paralyzed; when they were shown their paralyzed limbs they would deny ownership. They spoke of different hospitals with the same name, the good one where they were hospitalized and the bad one where they were not. They gave names to the hospital that reflected underlying thoughts, so that Mount Sinai Hospital became "Saint Sinai," "Hotel Sinai," or "Mount Cyanide."

I always thought the investigators to be every bit as crazy as the patients. To elicit the strange responses, it was usually necessary to ask pointed and, to me, insane questions. (But not always. How would the researchers have discovered the phenomenon if psychotic denial and replication were not sometimes quite open and spontaneous?) "How many heads do you have?" "Where are they?" "What do they each do?" "How many Mount Sinais are there?"

So I, too, was a member of that select group, those who had been to the other side and somehow come back. I was one of those who spoke of seeing a tunnel with a brilliant light at the end, or of being in a brilliantly illuminated room, of feeling an indescribable peace and other unusual experiences and sensations. I was one of them—and yet not one of them, for I remembered nothing. I think, at times, that I remember black, complete black. A world in which there was only black. Was I in hell? Is hell all blackness? And were the others in heaven? I am not sure. I am not sure that I remember anything.

Perhaps this experience made me conscious of my impelling need to report, to bear witness. Perhaps not, but there was no escaping the drive to report, the need to report. That was there.

And so the diary began, Saturday night, the nineteenth of January, with a brief report of the aftermaths of two Scud attacks (and two false alarms). I reported on personal feelings, on the general situation in the country, on the damage produced by the missiles, and on morale in the country. I even ended with an attack on the peace rallies. All the elements of my later reports were already present. As if a spring had been coiled within me, ready to leap forward.

THURSDAY, 21 FEBRUARY: THE CALMER

A small booklet called *Margion Kis* ("Pocket Book about Being Calm," or "The Calmer") has been distributed to the soldiers here. This booklet provides tips to our soldiers on how to deal with stress situations: for example, by concentrating with all your might on a very good moment from the past or imagining something very pleasant. It appears that not only are the civilians under tension, but the soldiers are, too. But theirs must be a very different kind of tension than ours. We are struck by the reversal of roles, by the civilians now being at the front in this form of warfare, while the soldiers are now on the home front, in the background. There is a joke going the rounds here, emphasizing the reversal of roles: soldiers have been asked to write letters of support to children at the front. Of course, our soldiers are just as exposed as we are to the threats of missile and nonconventional weapon attack.

We civilians should get the booklet, too, it seems.

I have been enjoined to relax by correspondents both abroad and in Israel. "It is not as bad as you describe it," they tell me. I hope they are right. (Here I thought that I sounded patriotic, calm and brave. See how wrong you can be?)

■ And was this tension, too, a sign of my impending hospitalization? Whether coincidence or contagion, at about this time both Jerry Phillips, my associate on this project, and Kenney Withers, ■ director of SIU Press, began to experience serious heart problems.

Perhaps I am concentrating on the worst-case scenario more than I should. But is that scenario, bad as it is, so remote, so unlikely? I do not think so, nor do army spokesmen here who continue to warn us over and over again that the chemical threat is still there. If I am a Cassandra, are the generals here Cassandras as well? If so, they have changed. If so, they have learned to sing in a new key.

Everybody is giving grades to the civilian population these days.

The prime minister says that we should be given medals, and the mayor of Tel Aviv, Shlomo "Chich" Lahat (who earlier accused those who left Tel Aviv during the worst phase of the bombings of being deserters), says that the civilian population is behaving fantastically well. They tell us that the *oref* ("rear," "home front") is holding out in an exemplary fashion under the circumstances. More role reversal.

But we are sitting here, really doing nothing, showing restraint. And how do you distinguish restraint from impotence? A hell of a lot more is said than done.

The details, the mechanics of our lives these days are difficult to accept—when you think about it. There is something degrading in the situation in which we find ourselves. Yes, it is reassuring to have a routine to deal with the attacks, we know exactly what to do, and we do it. Heroes do it and cowards do it. Only the fools ignore the instructions. But is there not an element of black magic in what we are doing? Are we not warding off the evil spirits by entering the plastic- and tape-sealed rooms, putting on our masks, adjusting the tapes that provide the last element of the seal, turning on the radio, following instructions? I have that impression after almost twenty—including several false alarms—of these entombments in the sealed rooms.

Then there is the problem of banality. It seems that the "heroic" part of our war is over. We Jews are experts in the banal, in the banality of persecution, in the banality of death. Even the Holocaust, the 6 million Jews slaughtered by the Nazis, no longer says that much to the world.

How much have you died for us lately?

Hannah Arendt, Jewish disciple of Nazi philosopher Heidegger, accused us of partial responsibility for the Holocaust by our failure to resist; she spoke of Eichmann's role as banal—the "banality of evil," she called it. I do not find evil banal; am I in the minority? Am I in the wrong? Has mass murder become banal? And war?

■ The mundane, the banal. Where do these two words—both meaning "commonplace"—come from? *Mundane* is clearly from *mundanus*, or "worldly," while *banal* originally referred to the common and therefore trivial duties owed to the feudal lord.

Both words have roots in church history. We know the proclamation of banns in anticipation of marriage, as we recognize *mundane* as meaning belonging to the world as distinct from the church. This idea of the church, as powerful but separate from the world, as a separate entity from God, is unknown to Judaism. The Jews—if English were their first language—would understand *quotidian* (Latin, "daily"), another word signifying "commonplace," better than either of these words. This word has not had the misfortune to acquire the shady, even pejorative associations of *mundane* or *banal*.

Is it possible to do something daily and not reduce it to the trivial? Although dentists may argue with my position, brushing your teeth is trivial in terms of its importance to life. Many of our daily activities—perhaps most, sometimes all—are trivial, mundane, banal. They may fill our life with activity, but they do not fill it with purpose or meaning.

For traditional Jews, their religion—based on the study of Torah, three formal prayers every day, and love of and a yearning to return to Zion—is both quotidian and essential. Just so is the family essential to Jews and central to their religion. But the family is also mundane, banal.

I imagine that some first find the value of their families in the time of illness; in fact, I have seen the phenomenon while lying in the hospital. How important the ill find a touch of home, the sight of familiar faces; even familiar voices are comforting. A letter? Marvelous. Sneaking in some home-cooked food? Clearly lifesaving. We have a word for it in Yiddish, *heimish*, something like the word *homely*, in its old, positive sense.

Where does work fit in this constellation? Work, according to traditional Jewish thought, is a necessary evil. Rabbis all had trades with which they supported themselves; the paid, community-supported rabbi is a relatively new idea, probably the result of the crusades that wiped out all rabbis in Western Europe; since these men were considered necessary to arbitrate questions of religion, settle disputes among Jews, and pass on the tradition to the young, rabbis were imported from the East, and—in order to attract them—paid. But work was a means to support yourself and your family; it was never a goal in itself. The rabbis of old would not understand people who live for their work, who take their work home with them by choice rather than necessity. They would not easily suffer those for whom career is all. Work was a means to an end. The immediate end was support of the family; the highest end was always freedom to study, the ultimate form of religious observance in their eyes. A city was defined as a place with at least 120 male adult citizens—large enough to support 10 men whose only and full-time occupation was the study of Torah. Such a frame of reference, where quiet and concentration are clearly defined ideals, sets the tone for a society in which the quotidian is, indeed, central.

The banal has its macabre side, too. *Eichmann in Jerusalem: A*

Report on the Banality of Evil is the title of a book written in 1963 in response to the Eichmann trial by Hannah Arendt, Jewish student and admirer of Martin Heidegger, the German existentialist philosopher and supporter of the Nazi Party. Arendt's thesis was that the Jews were in some ways responsible for their own slaughter by their failure to resist the Nazis; Eichmann's role in organizing the transports to the death camps she saw as merely formal, banal. Charming word, *banal*, used in this context.

What is the role of death? Of war? Can we see the killing of people as banal? Is this the result of increased news coverage, exposing death and disaster, natural and artificial, throughout the world, bringing pictures of the horror—in full color—almost immediately and directly to our armchair view? Is it really true that we can no longer sympathize with the misfortune of many; that only individual suffering is meaningful to us? Has there been a banalization of mass death? Sometimes it seems that way. We must be aware of it and its danger to us. We must fight it: loss of pity and loss of the capacity to anger and indignation are bad both for the heart and for international stability. Indifference sets the stage for aggression.

Mundane, in its original meaning, implied the existence of two earthly worlds, the world of the church, dealing with matters holy and high, and the lower level of the ordinary, the secular. But there is no church in the Jewish religion, and the destruction of the Second Temple in 70 C.E. ended all central worship, all functional priestly activity, among the Jews. The rabbis who attempted to preserve the Jews as a nation—or as a religion, if you prefer—centered their attention on the synagogue, a form of local worship based on the minyan. But they also centered the religion on the family, and there it remains, more than nineteen hundred years later. Sabbath and holiday dinners, for example, are sanctified by the equivalent of a libation, a blessing on wine. All meals are finished with a grace that is the equivalent of the thanksgiving offering in the temple. And the dining table itself becomes the equivalent of the temple altar, where sacrifices were once made. This is the *Jewish* sanctification of the mundane, of the family and its meeting place, the table.

Certainly the Scud attacks on Israel have become banal; we are no longer of interest to the media. The Scuds have become a daily event, no more than a nuisance to some. When none of our blood is spilled, we cease to be news. It is better not to be interesting in that sense.

Who in the West can digest that we—a civilized, developed, and modern country—have gone back to the Stone Age? Or at least the Merovingian period. We crouch in terror in caves.

We, just as other Westerners, have enjoyed deluding ourselves that when unpleasant things happen, they will not happen to us. But now we suddenly find ourselves—once again; how very easy it is to forget—very close to the center of the terrible things going on: we are actually one of the targets.

I first sent my reports to a few friends whom I thought might be interested; I also posted them to a few computer nets that deal with the politics of the Middle East and Jewish culture. I began to receive electronic mail in surprising numbers; other nets asked to copy my material, some took it without asking. I received more than one hundred letters a day by the second week of the war; this flow has since slowed to more than fifty letters a day.

Just as I sometimes say something without knowing how I feel about it, I find myself sometimes writing things without knowing how I relate to that subject. Just as the sound of the words—once spoken—can be tested, tried on for size just by hearing them, by asking, Does that sound right? So, too, words written can also take on that exploratory character.

But usually I am ready to write. I frequently amaze myself by having so many opinions that I had never before articulated, so many positions that I had never supported before, ready to express. It is good to know that I was not asleep all these years. I imagine I must feel something like the catatonic after he comes out of his prolonged trance.

And the responses I received were amazing to me, showing clearly that the reports offered something that the media did not or could not give. Some tried to verbalize the quality or qualities that they were attracted to; they spoke mostly of the personal element, or of the emotional content of the reports making the war more real for them.

I have also had negative responses, mostly disagreement with political positions that I expressed. Some were disappointed or even angry at me for what they saw as my presenting stereotypes in discussing groups that I opposed. (As a member of one of the most universally stereotyped groups, the Jews, I should be especially sensitive to this problem.) Others complained that I did not stick to a factual report but instead injected my own self. (One man's wine may be another's poison.)

Many wrote long letters, either confessional or argumentative. I tried to deal with these, but it became apparent to me that I could engage either in debate or counseling on the one hand or in reporting, but not both. I opted to report, to continue to write and distribute my daily reports for the same reasons that impelled me at the onset, but now substantially reinforced by the knowledge that I was supplying a need, even meeting a demand.

There is a final group of writers who know much more than I do about something I have written. I like to think that I am particularly attentive to these writers, that I listen carefully and learn from them. I sometimes use material that I get from them.

I have been frequently asked if I am a professional writer and I answer that I am not. I am certainly not a journalist; I certainly have no specialized knowledge of politics or war. I have written technical and scientific material related to my work. Even more remote are the two books of verse that I have published in Hebrew.

What then are my qualifications? I am a scientist and as such I have devoted my life to science and truth. I am also deeply committed to Israel, the ancient and present homeland of the Jewish people. I am also a religious Jew. These qualifications may be inadequate for the work I have undertaken.

FRIDAY, 22 FEBRUARY: RETREAT

The skies have clouded; rain is approaching. We can tell from the quiet. Quiet has degrees in Jerusalem. There is a special quiet for the hours before the rain here. And that quiet is additive with the old quiet that is Jerusalem's and with the new quiet that has descended on us lately, the quiet of anticipation. None of the various forms of quiet detracts from any of the others. It is not strange that noises add; why then should it be strange that quiet can add to quiet?

It is still quite warm, after another night without a Scud, a night shattered by the news from Russia.

The Iraqis have agreed to withdraw from Kuwait; they have a number of conditions which will be difficult for the U.S. to accept, conditions which keep Saddam Hussein in power and preserve the Iraqi war machine. Linkage is not mentioned; undoubtedly the Iraqis have made a secret agreement with the Russians in which the Soviets have promised to push vigorously for a Middle East conference immediately after the withdrawal from Kuwait.

Saddam Hussein is now the great Arab hero he aspired to be. What a frightening thought. But he lost, you say. Not by the logic of the Middle East; Saddam Hussein took on the whole world and emerged intact: this is a great victory for the Arabs; they will fill their chests with pride.

(Not only in the Middle East. I remember being given visiting cards in India that proudly displayed, after the name of the person, "Cambridge; B.Sc., 19——, failed.")

We do not know if it makes sense to accept Iraq's proposal (Russia's proposal?) and stop all the bloodshed, to open up the Pandora's box of Saddam Hussein as a hero with an almost intact military machine, or at least one that can easily be rebuilt. This option is clearly an invitation to disaster, not only for Israel but for the West. But the cost of a ground war in lives and maimed is a terrible thought.

A part of me says that the coalition should accept the withdrawal and hope that things will work out. But is not this type of wishful thinking just the sort of naïveté that invites tragedy and even disaster? Although they do reappear time after time, the three monkeys, See Nothing, Hear Nothing, and Say Nothing, have—in evolutionary terms—a low potential survival level. And it is survival that we are talking about, Israel's in the short run, the West's in the long run.

It may sound overly dramatic on my part saying that the West's fate is in the balance. Dramatic? Yes. Foolish? I do not think so. There are forces in the Arab world—fed not only by passion but also by hunger and poverty and lack of work—that are simmering and ready to boil. These forces are to a large extent reactionary and fundamentalist, frustrated and living on dreams of past glory and dreams of a not-so-distant golden future.

The Iraqis have not hesitated to use poison gas against the armed Iranians as well against the unarmed Kurds. Given nuclear weapons—and they were apparently not far from that—what will they do? Or rather, what will they not hesitate to do?

It is highly likely that we can expect violent nationalistic reactions in the Islamic world no matter what the outcome of the war.

Initially these will be directed internally, but they are impelled by a *vis à tergo*, a force from behind, that may push them outside the limits of the Islamic world. Even without that, we must expect an unsettling of the rulers in many of the countries in the area and a disruption of the balances that allow cooperation and free trade with the West.

The violence will be directed both externally, against the U.S. and—to a lesser extent—its coalition allies, and internally, against those rulers that sided with the West—Egypt, Saudi Arabia, Kuwait, Morocco, and Syria. None of these countries is embarrassed to use force to suppress antigovernmental foment, but there are limits to their abilities to stifle criticism. If there is a major rallying of the population against the rulers, the dissatisfied citizens will succeed in unseating them. Let a popular revolution based on fundamentalist Islam succeed in one country in the Arab world and it will spread through these countries like wildfire. Revolutionary spirits have been kindled which will not be contained with ease.

We can expect that the leaders of the Arab partners in the coalition will make efforts to demonstrate their allegiance to the ambitions of the Arab world. The obvious and easiest way open to them to prove their allegiance to the Arab dream is to force a solution to the Palestinian problem. Motivated by the need to defuse internal dissent, they will press the U.S. and other countries to call for an international conference on the Middle East with authority to impose on Israel a solution that includes realization of Palestinian national ambitions.

Israel continues to have a (the?) negative role in this Arab outlook: Israel is the only non-Muslim nation (Christian-Muslim Lebanon is now a fiction) in the subcontinent; Israel has stolen the Palestinians' land from them and now suppresses them with cruelty.

Saddam's identification of Israel as the cause of the Persian Gulf War is proven in the eyes of the fundamentalists by his firing Scud missiles at Israel. By this reasoning, why else would he waste his missiles on Israel if they were not guilty as charged by Saddam Hussein?

There is evidence that large elements of the populace of the Arab countries that have cooperated with the U.S. in what they perceive as the attack on Iraq, first of all, but on Saddam Hussein—still seen as a potential Saladin—in particular, are already in ferment, almost at a boil, ready to break out in anger. These groups see the battle of Iraq with the U.S. and its allies as a fight of the Arab nation against an attack by the historical enemy of the Arab/Muslim world, Western imperialism. Saudi Arabia is particularly vulnerable to this criticism, which sees that nation as allowing, even inviting—and thus perverting a fundamental unwritten law of the Arabs—an armed and hated enemy, the West, to physically reenter the Arab subcontinent. The implicit agenda of the West, according to these groups, is to take over the Arab oil resources.

These nationalistic elements, apparently growing in strength from day to day, view the U.S. and its allies as crusaders engaged in a battle to the death with their hero, the modern Saladin, Saddam Hussein. A victory of the West will be seen as wiping the face of the Arabs in the mud; the intractable U.S. and British demands for unconditional surrender are seen as particularly threatening. The apparent unwillingness of these two Western powers—perceived by the Arabs as the classic Western imperialists—to compromise indicates that it is these countries that want to strip Arabs of their resources (oil), strength, and pride.

The other side of the coin: any compromise for less than the maximal demands of the UN decisions will be interpreted by these nationalistic and fundamentalist elements as a great victory for the Arab nation.

It is interesting to note the French and German haste to support the Russian-Iraqi agreement. Why do I have the feeling that it is not concern for the blood that might be spilled that motivates their action? Why do I have the feeling that they are more interested in resuming business—as usual—with Iraq; business that includes rearming Saddam Hussein, supplying him with the technology needed to become an aggressor once more?

A good business partner is hard to find.

Japan has announced that in her plan to help repair the war damage in the area she will not be able to help the bombed-out victims in Israel. Israel, says Japan, is well off, and thus Japan's aid will be directed to Jordan and Egypt, who need it more. That these countries have not suffered direct war damage apparently does not factor into this equation. Just as the fact that Israel has, does not.

Our army intelligence is now convinced that Iraq has ground-to-ground missiles with chemical warheads. These, according to our sources, can reach Israel.

We wait.

Tonight is Sabbath here; this will be the sixth Sabbath since the war began. I hope it will be a quiet one. It is our day of rest. Recently a scholar of international repute and even fame (John Strugnell) said that the invention of the Sabbath is proof that the Jews are lazy. This is actually an old accusation—recorded in ancient Roman sources.

The only good thing anyone is willing to say about us these days is that we have, "in spite of all temptation," shown restraint.

Who was it who said, "'Tis not restraint or liberty that makes men prisoners or free"? Another kind of restraint, perhaps, but somewhat appropriate.

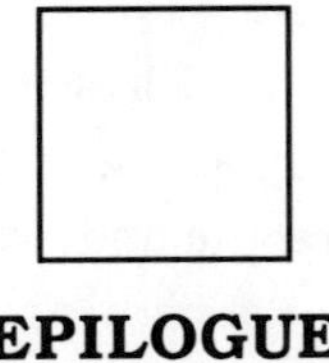

EPILOGUE

I was hospitalized in May 1990 for cardiac discomfort. The pain disappeared after catheterization and release from hospital, but it returned during the Gulf War and peaked during the third week in February 1991. As recorded above, on Wednesday, 20 February, I called my cardiologist, Shlomo Stern; on Thursday he gave me nitroglycerin pills. On the evening of 22 February, less than two hours after sending out my last diary entry and just before I was to go to synagogue to welcome the Sabbath, the pains in my chest became frightening. I telephoned my cardiologist, who told me to go to the emergency ward of his hospital. My youngest son drove me there, and thus began a two-week hospitalization that included a cardiac catheterization, a more or less complete rest, and an end to writing the diary.

My hospitalization coincided closely with the end of the Gulf War. The United States and its allies began the ground war with simultaneous invasions of Kuwait and southwestern Iraq in the early morning hours of 24 February. The war ended one hundred hours later with the Iraqi Army routed and the oilfields of Kuwait in flames—Iraqi's spiteful vengeance on its adversaries.

Kuwait was not the only victim of Iraq's spite; Israel, too, continued to suffer. I experienced the last three Scud firings—the last on

25 February—on Israel while in the hospital—one on one night and two on another. The cardiac intensive care ward where I was hospitalized had been turned into a large sealed room. The windows were taped and sealed; we were given instructions and calmed. Both my roommate and I had our masks in our night tables; we took them out and put them on, remaining in bed. I was still connected to two infusions. The nurses were all wearing their gas masks; one of the younger physicians did not deign to put on a mask. I found his indifference confusing; it is hard to remember that doctors are like other people, running the range from bright to silly. I remembered the physician's motto: "Do as I say, not as I do."

For the first time, I experienced the whole attack sequence with a television—each room had a set—rather than a radio. My preference for the radio was reinforced. Reports were more frequent from the radio, the irrelevant singing less annoying.

All missiles were now directed at the south; none of them hit any useful targets. The firing of missiles at us, useless in the war effort against the invading coalition armies, was what we expected, an example of Middle East logic. Radio Baghdad claimed that the missiles were fired at Dimona—where my son-in-law works—the site of an alleged Israeli nuclear arms center.

On the night of 25 February, twenty-nine American soldiers were killed by a Scud missile that fell in Saudi Arabia; dozens more were seriously injured. Once again we were convinced that we had seen miracles with our own eyes; in all the attacks on our cities, only one death resulted directly from a Scud.

So I was to finish the war as a patient, struck down not by a missile but by a traitor, my heart. My diary would end inappropriately, before the war had ended. I would see the windows and doors stripped of protective sealing tape and opened freely to the spring that was coming upon us. I would hear birds in the streets near the hospital. I would know that there was no war, that my children and grandchildren were safe.

At least they were for the time being. Saddam Hussein was still in power, even if his control was challenged and unstable. His air force was intact, too. Later we would discover that his army had not been destroyed completely; he could still fight the Shiite and Kurdish rebels who threatened his rule in the south and the north of Iraq.

His oil fields were intact and would once again pay for . . . what? For rehabilitation of his country? For the damage done to Kuwait? To Israel? Or would the oil wells pay to rearm Iraq?

The diplomatic pressures on Israel would begin again. The Palestinians would not be forgotten; they would be forgiven their support of Saddam Hussein. Just as we would not be forgiven our restraint, praised though it was during the war.

We were associated with the winning side. But did we win? We suffered losses in lives, in limbs, in property, in work, in our gathering in of the Russian and Ethiopian immigrants. The situation did not look too bright, but it could have been much worse.

The weather was very good; it was good to be alive.